Beyond Singing

Blueprint for the Exceptional Choral Program

STAN McGILL

& ELIZABETH VOLK

*Sometimes, not often enough, we reflect upon the
good things and those thoughts always center around
those we love... and I think about those people who mean
so much to me and for so many years have made me so
very happy... and I count the times I have forgotten to say
'thank you' and just how much I love them...*

—Felice Mancini, daughter of composer Henry Mancini

Copyright © 2007 by Hal Leonard Corporation

Published by Hal Leonard Corporation
7777 W. Bluemound Road
P.O. Box 13819
Milwaukee, WI 53213

Library of Congress Cataloging-in-Publication Data

McGill, Stan.
  Beyond singing : blueprint for the exceptional choral program / by Stan McGill and Elizabeth Volk ;
foreword by Paul Salamunovich. -- 1st ed.
      p. cm.
  Includes index.
  ISBN-13: 978-1-4234-2043-9
  ISBN-10: 1-4234-2043-8
  1. Choral singing--Instruction and study--Juvenile. 2. School music--Instruction and study. I. Volk,
Elizabeth. II. Title.
  MT930.M53 2007
  782.5071'2--dc22

                            2007023363

Printed in the U.S.A.
First Edition

HAL•LEONARD®

Visit Hal Leonard Online at www.halleonard.com

Dedication

This book is dedicated to Gordon Beaver, my high school choir director in Sikeston, MO who taught me the work ethic and passion needed to be successful in my profession; to Dr. Wes Forbis and Dr. Don Brown, my college choir directors at William Jewell College, Liberty, MO who taught me the beauty in the choral art; and to Carroll Barnes, my mentor and friend in Garland, TX who taught me how to teach.

—Stan McGill

Gratefully dedicated to my parents, for their unconditional love and support; to my sister and brother, for sharing the joy of singing and offering both encouragement and wit; to Jane Marshall, professor extraordinare, and the late Dr. Lloyd Pfautsch, my mentor and friend; and to all the students whose love of music, beautiful hearts, and humor have enriched my life beyond measure.

—Elizabeth Volk

Contents

Foreword

The choral profession is a complex world that requires conductors to be highly talented in a host of areas. They must not only be skillful in reading scores and interpreting them artistically but must also be able to communicate their vision to the singers so they can replicate those visions. The list of tasks is endless and each is important to the creation of a masterful work.

There are also non-musical components of the position that must be done equally well. It is a daunting profession so it is easy to see why the job of a choral director can sometimes seem overwhelming. For newer and less experienced directors, there can be substantial discouragement as they view the looming mountain of tasks that must be done, and done well, in order for their work to be successful. For the more experienced conductor, it can become easy to focus on a single group of skills or areas, excluding the all-important area of communication between conductors and their singers, which leads to the ultimate success in rehearsal and performances.

As I consider this book, I am astonished at the minute detail with which its authors have addressed all these areas one by one. It would clearly take many years for a director to learn these things on their own and they may still miss many important places where they could do so much better. Stan and Elizabeth have found a way to address the problems of a conductor even before they occur. This book is both entertaining and enlightening, including all the things they don't teach you in our colleges and universities that are vital to being a successful conductor. It will take new directors "from A to Z" and teach them what they need to know (and don't even *know* they need to know)!

Beyond Singing's section on rehearsal techniques is superb and addresses the many other vital concerns of all choral conductors. It is a thorough insight into the trials and tribulations of the choral profession and I commend it to your use. Both of its authors have stellar careers in the field and they speak from experience. Best regards as you go "beyond singing" to new heights as a choral director.

—Paul Salamunovich

Acknowledgments

Stacie Wheelock Adams

Shelly Bhushan

Kristine Bialik

Sara Hatchett Cogburn

Emily Crocker

The Dallas Morning News

Dallas Symphony Orchestra

Merrilyn Eder

Marcia Haugarth

Dan Hood

Barbara Volk Ibbotson

Matthew Irish

Jane Johnson

Randy Jordan

Sharon Kraus

Alan McClung

Mike Morton

Peggy O'Neill

Linda and David Pennington

Paul Salamunovich

John Salantien

Kenneth and Diane Steele

Melody Vestal

Chris Wilson

David Woo

Preamble

Consider this picture: The music for the year is mapped out. All of your singers are happy, perhaps minus a few sopranos and a tenor or two. The last time a parent called was to ask your advice on universities for a diva-in-training and commend the choir's last concert. Your principal had to call you to the office recently. Apparently, through no fault of your own, you have neglected to spend the overabundance of funds in the choir activity account this year. He reminded you that schools are non-profit institutions with the IRS, and asked that you spend, spend, SPEND! With all tuxes, gowns, and robes carefully catalogued and your music library computerized, your daily focus is on effective rehearsals and upcoming concerts. You can't remember the last time you had a headache. At the end of the day, you find yourself resorting to dinner with your family or, now imagine this: going to a movie ON A SCHOOL NIGHT!

If this picture describes you and your work, please put this book down immediately and enjoy the rest of your anxiety-free day. You have already evolved into a higher life form or hold the secrets of the universe in the palm of your hand. If, however, one or more areas of work in the choral world frustrate you or could use improvement, please keep reading. Whether you're a new teacher ready to take the world of music education by storm, or an experienced choral director, we want to make your life easier. Let us offer you some specific tools, tips, and techniques (with real world examples) that you can use in your classrooms today. You will find that these tricks and resources also work with your church choir, community choir, or any musical group.

A wise man once said, "If the horse is dead, dismount." While at first hearing this could be thought humorous, it is also profoundly true. How many times do we stick with a particular way of doing things, or a rehearsal technique that just does NOT work well, but keep doing it anyway? Someone once said, "If you keep on doing what you've always done, you will keep on getting what you've always got." How true is this! Change does not come easily to most of us. Whether training singers or buying groceries, most of us would rather cling to how and what we already do because it is safe and known to us. It is more comfortable to sit in the ditch rather than risk failure (or embarrassment) in experimenting with a new way to dig out.

If you are willing to consider alternate ways of doing a few things and new solutions for old problems, you have the real opportunity to improve your choral program enormously and, at the same time, make your own life happier and easier. We hope to provide you with concrete solutions to real problems we as music educators have also faced, and a host of proven tricks-of-the-trade to increase your happiness and excellence in the classroom, providing you with a solid plan for success for your choral program. Working smart, not long, will save you time and set your singers free from endless extra rehearsals

Excellence is not something stumbled upon by accident. You won't achieve great things while flailing about in paperwork nor partake of true musical artistry by folly. Success requires a concrete plan of action: a big-picture plan followed by all the little details that, together, create a complex mosaic that forms a beautiful and intricate picture of choral excellence. The fact is that nearly all components of your choral program can improve. In fact, they will improve if you will take on a determined attitude, work hard, and plan for success. You can do it!

Excellence is not contracted like a virus. Choirs reach the highest performance levels, both musical and organizational, because of hard work and meticulous planning. The alternative is leading a choral program that will limp along with mediocrity and some degree of anemia until the final nail is driven into its organizational coffin. Consider the words of these distinguished individuals:

We are what we repeatedly do.
Excellence, then, is not an act, but a habit.
—Aristotle

If you are going to achieve excellence in big things,
you develop the habit in little matters.
Excellence is not an exception, it is a prevailing attitude.
—Colin Powell

It is a wretched taste to be gratified with
mediocrity when the excellent lies before us.
—Isaac Disraeli

It is time for us to stand and cheer for the doer, the achiever,
the one who recognizes the challenge and does something about it.
—Vince Lombardi

I do the very best I know how – the very best I can;
and I mean to keep on doing so until the end.
—Abraham Lincoln

Outstanding people have one thing in common:
an absolute sense of mission.
—Zig Ziglar

Excellence is the gradual result of always striving to do better.
—Pat Riley

So, whether you're a novice who wants to start out like a pro or an experienced professional who is looking for a better way, we offer these resources and strategies with confidence because they have worked for us.

Get Ready...

➤ **The Calendar for the Year**

➤ **The Choir Handbook**

➤ The Calendar for the Year

How to plan a year in advance when you can't even remember what you had this morning for breakfast...

Preparing a complete calendar of choir events for the year is a daunting task. This preparation becomes all the more interesting when it has to be done the spring before the school year that will follow, requiring tremendous time and thought on your part. Invariably, you will add smaller shows for the pop group as you go along, and a last minute invitation to provide the National Anthem for a televised sporting event may come your way. Yes, you'll accept, but before you do you will need to consult your choir to insure that there are enough students available who are free to firmly commit to the performance before you sign on the dotted line. For the most part, however, dates *can* be planned a year in advance.

Your calendar can take the form of a list, or be laid out as a traditional calendar a month at a time, using calendar creation software. See appendix 1a and 1b for sample calendar formats. Appendix 1a and 1b are found on the accompanying CD. Your goal is to provide such an expanse of advance notice that students will have few, if any, conflicts with choir dates you have planned. Suitable excuses are few when one has six months in which to plan for a scheduled rehearsal, concert, or show. By providing the calendar for the year in advance you also equip parents to plan family vacations, orthodontist appointments, and SAT prep classes with an eye toward the commitments that come with membership in school choirs. You will want to give as much information as possible to your singers for each date so most questions can be anticipated and answered. List starting time, approximate ending time, date, place, dress (uniform or other), location, and choirs involved. Make major all-choir events stand out visually.

Some Examples of Choir Events to Include
- Beginning of the year picnic or party
- Informal "preview concert" at the beginning of the school as your Booster Club's kickoff for membership and volunteer sign-ups
- Uniform fittings
- Rehearsals outside the traditional school day (plan ahead for the crunch that will precede contests and festivals)
- All concerts for the year that can be planned in advance (Fall, Winter, Spring concerts, etc.)
- Solo and Ensemble contest

- District, Region, Area, and All-State auditions
- District, Region, Area, and All-State clinic/performance dates (pending selection)
- School Musical auditions
- Fund-raising events
- Choir trip
- Choir banquet
- Commencement and Baccalaureate

Some Examples of Non-Choir Dates to Include
- Beginning and ending of all grading periods
- Exam dates and times
- AP testing dates
- SAT/ACT testing dates
- Prom
- Holidays, staff development days, early release dates

Consult your school's master calendar and mark all major events into your personal planner. This will help you see the big picture so you can avoid scheduling the choir garage sale for the morning after Senior Prom. There may even be community or large church event calendars to consider if many of your students are involved in a particular group or activity that they sponsor. Don't schedule concerts against other major events, even if the stage is available and the weather is great. This puts students on the spot, and places you in a negotiation mode while sorting out all the conflicts. It divides a potential audience between locations and breeds ill will with parents who cannot be in two places at once. Meet with your feeder school

Never assume that others will (or should) change to accomodate you. Teamwork and mutual respect demonstrate your appreciation and regard for others.

choral directors to coordinate major concert dates so no two schools are having concerts on the same nights within the community. All schools will be involved in similar planning between March and May for the following year, so you will need to work in advance on proposed dates. Even with this level of communication and planning, be prepared to cell phone your middle school colleagues immediately as changes are made to your school's calendar. Together, you and your colleagues can decide who can change a date more easily, usually in light of venue availability. Never assume that others will (or should) change to accommodate you. Teamwork and mutual respect demonstrate your appreciation and regard for others.

When a student has a conflict stay cool, and don't personalize the conflict. *It's not about you.* The problem is very simple: there are two places a student is supposed to appear simultaneously. Despite the singer's talented and gifted status, he can still only be in one place at a time, so don't question a student's loyalty to choir. Communicate calmly and be approachable when a singer notifies you of a conflict. Your singers should understand at the beginning of the year that conflicts will be rare but if one should occur, you want to talk to the student at the earliest possible moment to work things out well in advance. Approaching you the day before contest with a conflict that has been on the calendar for months isn't playing fair. Never place a student in the position of a stalemate in schedule between directors and coaches. The adults must be prepared to sort out conflicts without penalizing the young people involved or cause them undue anxiety. Remember, it's not about you! It is our duty as professionals to model effective conflict resolution and creative problem solving. It is far easier to plan in advance, creating as few conflicts as possible, than to ski black slopes of schedule conflict moguls daily. Bear in mind that despite your best efforts, there will still be conflicts: Your football team will have a final practice which runs dangerously close to your winter concert, the volleyball girls won't make it back from the state championship game in time for a concert, and a singer will still be conflicted over having the big solo in her church's Singing Christmas Tree the same night as the school choir performs. Plan ahead, keep your cool, and play fair.

When considering which of two activities a student should attend, we have found it useful to consider this question: who needs the student more? You may want to try this approach in an effort to fairly and reasonably painlessly resolve such conflicts. We have included examples of ways to apply this approach to various situations.

The relative importance of two events:
> Choir has a scheduled weekly night rehearsal. Baseball has a game.
> Practice versus game? Game wins.

The numbers of students involved in each group:
> The men's choir has eighty members scheduled to perform.
> The golf team has six competitors for the district tournament.
> Where will this student be missed more? Golf tournament wins.

The status of the conflict, curricular versus extracurricular:
> Choir has a scheduled, major concert from which a test grade will be generated. It is an important element in the curriculum. The drill team has its spring banquet.
>
> Curricular event versus social activity? The choir concert wins.

The potential significance of the individual student to the activity involved:
> Zeus has a pleasant voice in the a cappella choir and loves to sing. He also doubles as the starting pitcher for the school varsity baseball team, scheduled for a district game. He loves both activities equally. The loss to the baseball team is probably far greater than the loss to the choir. Attend concert or game? Baseball game wins.

The future implications, if any, of doing one or the other in the future:
> Dorothy has enjoyed four years in choir with you and will always continue to sing in her church choir. Dorothy also happens to be one of the top ten soccer players in a five-state area. She is being recruited nationally by five major universities who are currently in a bidding war with scholarship money to attract her to their campus. The recruiters are attending all matches.
>
> Avocation and enjoyment versus significant scholarship money in her chosen field of endeavor in the future? Soccer wins.

➤ The Choir Handbook

Tell 'em what you're going to tell 'em. Tell 'em.
Then tell 'em what you told 'em.

It would be hard to overestimate the importance of an inclusive, well-constructed document given out the first day of school that thoroughly covers your expectations. By explaining your procedures, rules, grading policy and other essential topics, you provide your students a clear overview of the year and what you expect of them. By committing this to written form, you are documenting policies and procedures for subjects that may benefit from clarification throughout the entire year. It is wise to inform students and parents in advance about what they may expect during the choir year for their information, clarification, and planning.

What a gift to yourself as well: a document that answers the questions that can (and will) come up throughout the year repeatedly. Though a thorough choir handbook takes time to write (and will likely evolve over a period of years of refinement, finding your own loopholes and changing ways of doing things), it is more than worth the investment of time and energy in the long run. When the same question comes up in class for the third time, you can refer students to their handbook. Instead of writing instructions for each student who needs assignments during a period of illness or hospitalization, you can direct them to the pages on make-up work. You can review the handbook with your choirs over a period of time, highlighting certain areas daily, without having to drone on and on about rules. Wouldn't you rather be singing? They would! Be firm, but let the beginning of school be more about singing than a slow elucidation of the rules. You will not only save time, you will also avoid arguments, misunderstandings, lame excuses, and may avert plucking yourself bald-headed for yet another year!

The downside of a choir handbook is that you are committing to doing things a particular way for one calendar year, so you must make wise choices about what you write. Review district and school policies in advance to ensure that you are not promoting a policy which will not be in compliance or defensible by your principal and the district administration, should "push come to shove." Ask a friend or colleague to read over your document for tone, content, grammar, and clarity. This document should be available to your evaluator so he can appreciate your ability to plan long-term and communicate your rules and expectations effectively. Send a copy to your fine arts supervisor and principal. Make it a document of which you can be proud and which will serve you well throughout the year.

Hold your students accountable for reading and being familiar with the contents of your handbook. Most importantly, know it backward and forward yourself so you will be consistent with your written and spoken word throughout the year. If you work with an assistant, voice teachers, or volunteer helpers, make sure that they commit to knowing and abiding by the handbook.

Several choir handbooks are included in appendix 1c, 1d, and 1e on the accompanying CD. Read over them carefully, if only to remind yourself of critical topics you may want to include in your own work. Feel free to use these as a guide, the names and places have been changed to protect the innocent and doubly protect the guilty.

He who every morning plans the transaction of the day
and follows out that plan, carries a thread that will guide
him through the maze of the most busy life. But where no plan is
laid, where the disposal of time is surrendered merely to the
chance of incidence, chaos will soon reign.
—Victor Hugo

Get Set...

- ➤ Preparing for Class

- ➤ Rehearsal Structure and Techniques

- ➤ Selecting Literature

- ➤ Blueprint for Teaching Choral Literature

- ➤ Effective Classroom Management

➤ **Preparing for Class**

"Prep" is more than khakis and a pastel shirt...

The fact is that while most plans work to some extent, some plans are just better. On a good day they can even be foolproof. Thorough, effective plans produce faster, better results because they place the odds of success firmly in our favor. Investing time in long-range planning reaps benefits of untold proportion! Time spent planning is ultimately time saved, while lack of planning can ruin the best of days and undermine your work, not to mention your mood and blood pressure.

Lesson plans

There are two basic types of lesson plans, formal, required by your school district, and informal, the ones you actually use to structure and pace your rehearsals. Formal lesson plans, turned in to your Dean of Instruction, department chairperson, or other person designated by your principal, are generally due weekly and document your intended lessons. These will also be the plans you present to your evaluator, to assist in illuminating the many skills and educational reasons for each component of your rehearsal during an observation. In most school districts, your teaching is considered substandard if formal lesson plans are not completed and turned in by stated deadlines.

If your district or local building expects or recommends that you use a particular lesson plan format or form, do so. If you are free to fashion your own format, construct a detailed professional looking form in an elegant font. Include a complete listing of all possible curricular elements, standardized testing expectations, and specific instructional goals. Whether chart-style or in detailed outline format, more is better. The more writing on your fixed form, the less you will need to add or change throughout the year to offer an impressive document. Spend whatever time is necessary, hours or days, to develop this document so it will be a lasting time-saver.

The informal lesson plan is for your own use in daily rehearsals. It may be short, without additional background, explanatory information, or formality. It will simply be the daily battle plan, providing you with clear goals and procedures for each rehearsal in the week. Remember that time spent planning is time well used, so construct a basic format that works for you, including components such as warm-up, sight-reading, and literature. Duplicate the form and have it ready for use. You may find it convenient to jot down important announcements on the back for easy and consistent updates to all choirs. List specific warm-ups and goals and materials for sight-reading for each choir. If your plan already lists your literature, number the titles in the order you wish to rehearse them, and identify which measures or issues you plan to drill, polish, or address for each. Vary the order of your rehearsal components to keep them fresh. The world will not come to a grinding halt if you begin a rehearsal with sight-reading rather than warm-ups. Appendix 2a and 2b include sample formal and informal lesson plans.

Your choral hall

Your room sets the tone for your choral department and personal style as a teacher. A dark or drab room will work against your efforts to spread enthusiasm and energy among your choirs. Let the environment fit your aspirations!

Place folder cabinets and sight-reading materials well into the room to draw traffic away from the entrance door and place a clock on the back wall of the room so you can see it but students cannot. This will keep you paced and help hold student concentration. A vertical file labeled and within easy access to your singers can be useful for storing extra calendars, choir hand-books, choir scholarship application forms, medical release forms, make-up work materials, scratch paper, and anything else students may need that you

Consider creating a message center in your room.

don't want to have scattered about. Near it, a small container could hold band-aids, tape, paper clips, tissue, and other small items for singers' use before and after class.

Consider adding one or more live plants to your rehearsal room to increase oxygen levels. Well-fueled brain cells can absorb your gems and pearls of wisdom all the more. Find a copy of the highly readable book *Brain-Based Learning*, by Eric P. Jensen for the rationale about this and numerous other modifications that positively affect student learning. Ask your maintenance staff to use the brightest possible light bulbs available for all light fixtures, and ask that all fixtures be cleaned inside every couple of years. You won't believe the difference this can make, transforming a dingy cave into a bright room again.

Use one central location for sign-up sheets, announcements, and a choir lost and found, and if wall space is available outside your rehearsal hall, create a colorful display of college audition posters, conservatory and university music department advertising, and flyers for upcoming concerts at neighboring schools and city venues.

Consider creating a message center in your room. One director designated the metal frame under the outside base of the office window as a message center where students could tape small notes for the music librarians, choir officers, or each other. This could also be as easy as taping things to the chalk rail of your blackboard. Music librarians can use the message center to communicate with students about lost or damaged music. You can jot down a note when it's convenient for you and tape it up for later pickup. Used in this way, a message center can be a time saving convenience. Some directors swear by having an answering machine if there is a telephone in the choir room. Use a professional message, perhaps with choral music in the background as a positive first contact for incoming calls. If students answer the phone for you, have them do so in a uniform way, leaving written messages in one designated place so they are not lost. How your phone is answered is yet another indicator of your expectations in the choir hall and positive public perceptions reap big rewards. Do not interrupt rehearsal to answer the phone personally unless it is an emergency.

Creating effective riser arrangements

Standing on risers during rehearsal has countless advantages over allowing singers to rehearse seated. Student focus and energy are improved and there is a mental alertness far more difficult to achieve in a seated position. For these reasons, we strongly recommend that your singers stand for all, or most of each rehearsal. As the bell begins to ring, singers should already be on the risers, in place silently, with all materials. Aim to have the choir already warming up with you as the bell finishes ringing. This eliminates that last-minute scramble to vault onto the risers. (For safety purposes, students should get on and off the risers from the front only.) It also sets a pattern of starting and ending rehearsal promptly. It is conjectured that some highly successful directors may not be any smarter or more talented, but use their time more effectively. There is no doubt that a well-paced beginning and ending to your daily work can help squeeze every moment out of each rehearsal period.

The effectiveness of your various standing arrangements can impact choir blend and balance as well as singer self-discipline and learning pace. (See appendix 2c and 2d.) There are many ways to configure your singers, each having different purposes and strengths. You may wish to identify your weakest section and place it in the middle. Both authors prefer the S-T-B-A placement across the risers and used it with solid success. Consider blocking weaker singers together, even if you otherwise intermingle voices of different parts. As well as keeping your weakest sections together, you will want to diffuse your strong singers by spreading them out. In the end, the goal is for your choir to have its best sound. In a soprano-heavy choir, this could take the form of placing all sopranos across the back row of risers. In addition, performance practice and historic relevance will provide opportunities for variety in your riser formations. These may include both antiphonal and aleatoric choral works that require specialized singer placement.

Keep your strongest singers in the middle of your mid-to-top rows. ("Strongest" in this case refers to the most accurate and best-tuned voices you've got, not the loudest or necessarily those with the most beautiful tone.) In front of them, place the singers most likely to benefit from the help these stronger singers will provide. Put your weakest singers on the ends of each row of the section. Avoid putting loud or inaccurate singers on your top row unless you want their choices of notes and rhythms to affect the rest of the section. When placing individual singers on the risers, you may want to consider partnering newer and returning members, heavier and lighter voices, and various other combinations, giving your students an opportunity to maximize their mastery while working beside a variety of other singers.

Establish a professional demeanor from the start

Many experienced teachers will tell you that it is essential to begin each year with your strictest face forward. You can always lighten up later but it is tough to rein in a choir run amuck over a period of time. It is wise to establish a sense of professionalism and demeanor that will work for you and fit your personal style. In some instances, new teachers may be working with students in a similar age bracket to theirs. In all cases however, "professional distance" requires that we put up an immovable and appropriate "wall of separation" that makes the student-teacher relationship clear to students. While we all want to be accessible to our students, it is tough to be a "pal" and have strong leadership as the authority figure. Be yourself, but be your BEST self! Your goal is musical excellence, not personal popularity. If you are a fine teacher, working with fairness and respect for the benefit of your students, you will enjoy popularity as a mentor, teacher, role model and advocate in a lasting way.

Dress for success, just as you rehearse for success. Sloppy dress makes a poor impression. The dowdy teacher would need an electrifying personality to create the same dynamic with a group as the one more neatly dressed.

Consider initially calling your students by their last names, preceded by "Miss" or "Mister." The bonus in this is learning student names faster, as well as having a unique style in calling roll those first few days. It may also be the first time many middle school or high school students have ever been addressed with this extra measure of respect, fostering a sense of personal dignity and empowerment. Students respond to this with boundless affection and dedication. It is altogether humorous to hear middle school kids calling each other "Miss Sarmiento" and "Mr. Wilson" as they mimic the director, but they love being called those names nevertheless. Whatever your style, call your singers by name.

No man ever reached to excellence in any one art or profession without having passed through the slow and painful process of study and preparation.
—Horace

➤ Rehearsal Structure and Techniques

Barnum & Bailey have nothing over a choral director in action...

The art of pacing a rehearsal is just that, an art. It's actually easy, as long as you can teach with variety while maintaining a routine, have the ability to organize a rehearsal knowing instinctively how long to work on each piece, and know and understand the limitations and abilities of your choir while thinking quickly on your feet. And, if you can identify and solve problems instantly as they occur, including intonation, balance, blend, phrasing and more basic skills like correct pitch and rhythm...okay, so maybe it's not that easy after all! But, it is an art you can master with some experience and understanding of what works, and what works well.

Always prepare for a rehearsal. Identify exactly what you plan to accomplish and how you're going to get it done. Your students will recognize and appreciate your planning. "Winging it" inevitably leads to a less productive rehearsal that drags. A rehearsal that "drags" is no fun. A rule of thumb when pacing rehearsals is to use as much time on a task as your choir is able to remain intently focused. Thoroughness in rehearsal is far more productive than a "quick fix" that could become a "quick broke" five minutes later. Recognize the importance of the "big picture" as you pace each rehearsal relating to upcoming performance and festival dates.

Isolate target spots in each piece of music that need attention and fashion a concrete plan for improvement. ("Search and destroy" all musical defects you can hear.) A musical selection is better off left unattended than rehearsed in a nonproductive "run-through." Repetitions of mistakes reinforce them, making mistakes all the more difficult (if not impossible) to eradicate later. Drill correct repetitions over multiple rehearsals for the material to become completely mastered by the choir.

The Basic Rehearsal

Greetings
Warm-ups: Physical, mental, and vocal
Sight-reading
Rehearsal of piece #1
Rehearsal of piece #2
Rehearsal of piece #3
Closure

15

Necessary business that you will need to include in your plan includes taking attendance, announcements, passing music in and out, placing students in new riser formations, fund-raising activities and positive non-music group time including birthday celebrations, and other special congratulations. Music literacy skills, rhythm drills and historical context of composer and musical works can be effectively presented during transitions, or slipped in during the rehearsal without the loss of momentum. This is affectionately known as "sneaky" teaching. Examples of short history lessons to attract student attention to the background of a particular piece or period in music history could include the circumstances under which "Silent Night" was written, the inspiration and composition of Handel's oratorio, "The Messiah," or the circumstances under which the composer Lully died.*

*On January 8, 1687, Lully was conducting a "Te Deum." He was conducting by banging a long staff (a precursor to the baton) against the floor, as was the common practice at the time, when he struck his toe. An abscess formed on the toe, turning gangrenous. Lully refused to have his toe amputated and the gangrene spread, resulting in his death on the 22nd of March.

Annoying interruptions that can't be planned for, but must be attended to include discipline issues and behavioral "moments," fire drills, and the arrival of office or counselors' call slips for individual students. Shortened or lost class time for assemblies, pep rallies, early release days, or standardized testing, voice lesson interruptions, field trips and other school or non-school related absentees will also impact your rehearsal plan.

When planning rehearsals, bear in mind it is best to work smart, not long. Use every minute of every class period, working from bell to bell. Begin rehearsal with music instead of announcements or talking. Avoid uncontrolled free time for students like the plague, especially at the end of a period. If you have too much time left over in rehearsal, you are either

When planning rehearsals, bear in mind it is best to work smart, not long.

under-programming or under-teaching. The master teacher can always find more to do in any given piece of literature or teaching concept.

Controlled free time can be a welcome respite for students, a few moments to get to know one another better. You might try saving two or three minutes at the end of a rehearsal during which you ask various students questions. The choir members should be expected to listen courteously to all responses. Try a variety of current topics, including last weekend's football game, the Academy Awards®, an upcoming debate tournament, or other non-choir interests of the singers. This demonstrates your interest in the students as people, not merely as voices in your choir, and makes for good rapport between students and students and teacher. Begin and end all rehearsals on time, showing respect for your singers' time and using it wisely for rehearsal purposes only. It goes without saying that extra rehearsals should never be used as a punishment.

Have a student take roll for you, if this is allowed in your school. One quick way to do this is for your section leaders to report attendance in their sections to your choir secretary to record for you. Provide a notebook near your podium with riser assignments and instructions on where you want the list of absentees placed. You can later transfer this information into your grade book or district's attendance software. This leaves the ultimate document of record, your grade book, solely in your hands while facilitating your beginning warm-ups as the bell sounds, if not before. Calling names or running down a chart is a terminally boring way to begin class. Potential momentum will fizzle before it begins!

Know the attention span of your choir and plan accordingly. You can expound with great wisdom if you like, but if no one is listening, you might as well go home and tell it all to your dog. Structuring rehearsals with variety keeps them fresh, while having familiar components keeps them comfortable. Encourage singers to postpone judgment on new literature until after they've mastered its basics. Most of their lasting favorites will not involve love at first sight.

Commit to sight-reading during every rehearsal, every day without fail. The time you dedicate to sight-reading may vary from day to day but if it ever becomes an "if we have time" part of your rehearsal, you are doomed. Your singers will never reach the heights of musical accomplishment they could otherwise achieve if you do not make this commitment.

It is important to be aware of the difference between tenacity in mastering details and getting bogged down. Problems must be fixed; however, if you see that this will not happen in a reasonable period of time during a particular rehearsal, cut your losses and revisit those measures another day. Do not ignore mistakes. *A sloppy rehearsal is worse than no rehearsal at all.* Incorrect repetitions produce lasting errors, carved in cement. Calling attention to mistakes is important, even if they are not readily fixed. It may be hard to learn; it *will* be harder to re-learn. This is an incredibly powerful truth that you need to accept.

More than sixty percent of what a musician will ever learn about a piece is learned upon first exposure. This is a sobering fact that makes your timing of any introduction of new literature incredibly important. With this in mind, don't start new material on Fridays, pep rally days, ends of tough rehearsals, or days when groups of singers will be absent. Make sure that when you present a new section of rhythms or pitches your singers are fresh and focused. Their first impression must be strong, positive, and accurate. There is no truth to the adage, "practice makes perfect." It just doesn't. Perfect practice makes perfect, and you can take that to the bank!

Avoid running through numbers without a purpose. Repetition without a specific agenda only implants a lackluster concept of the music deeper into the singers' understanding of the piece. Music never stays the same. It either gets better, or it gets worse! Consider this at every juncture of every rehearsal. Why are you singing through a particular song? Is the work improving? If not, leave it alone. If it's not improving, it is losing its luster and your singers will know the difference. This is one reason superior directors don't "run through" entire songs in a contest warm-up room. What's the point? Repetition for repetition sake will weaken, not inspire, a great performance. Such "choral regurgitation" tires singers and numbs their minds to the true beauties and vigor in the music. It's easy to rationalize that "running a piece" keeps it fresh. However, this is just not true.

During the rehearsal, maintain eye contact with the choir. This magnifies the communication between choir and director. Strive to include all singers in your focus as your eyes move around the group. This is a pre-emptive strike against loss of attention and behavioral distractions. The choir director should maintain control of the rehearsal at all times. If the choir is talking on the risers, it is because you (as the director) are allowing them to do so. Anticipate what is going to occur in rehearsal prior to its happening, musical or otherwise. In this way you can, "play offense, not defense." Move freely around the room as appropriate while you rehearse the group. Physical proximity to the singers brings variety to the rehearsal, increases awareness and accountability for individual voices, and diminishes any spatial barrier between the podium and the risers.

Expect students to be aware of their own mistakes, attempting to correct errors themselves before you need to intercede. Occasionally, try having students lift their arm or hand in the air (or slap their wrist with their own hand) each time they identify an error in their own singing. Try multitasking to maximize time usage. You might ask tenors to tap their difficult rhythm while the sopranos sing their tough melodic phrase, work to dovetail one vocal section's work into that of another by overlapping tasks, or have section two take up where section one leaves off in a piece, all ways to better keep students' minds engaged during the rehearsal.

Never miss a chance to do some "sneaky teaching" in which you slip pearls of wisdom into rehearsal without formal introduction or closure. Students often remember these historical mini-lessons or musical "tidbits" better than the most complex, tightly planned information you might present.

Finally, try to end rehearsals with an infectious, rousing sound on a solid piece so singers want to leave the room still singing. This promotes enthusiasm, excitement about your program, and increased (if occasionally distracting) visibility in the halls.

Should I sing with my students?

There are definitely pros and cons to singing with your students. On the pro side, it's easier and faster to show something by demonstration than to use many words in an attempt to describe it. Students can mirror demonstrated correctness in pitch and rhythm and hear and imitate a particular vocal sound after it is sung for them. However, the teacher's voice can become a crutch to a section if singing with them becomes a habit. This can cause an abrupt loss of confidence if the teacher's voice stops singing close to a performance. The teacher cannot hear as effectively or realistically when singing, and if the teacher's musical strengths do not include a vocal timbre he or she wants a group to mirror, imitation may not produce the desired result.

There are a few other considerations when singing with students. Female teachers should not sing "down the octave" for the tenor and bass parts. Male singers must learn to hear their part in various ranges. Repeated singing in the octave of a middle school tenor part is a sure fire way to ruin a female director's own voice. An appropriate vocal timbre will not have been demonstrated, and young male singers, already sensitive about their changing voices, sometimes find their own vocal parts "more manly" if they are too low for the female singer. Male teachers can demonstrate upper voice parts for sopranos and altos as it bolsters conception of falsetto and does not tend to confuse female singers' understanding of correct vocal timbre. An additional bonus is increased understanding of the "British" sound found in boys' choirs for which that timbre is preferred.

To use or not to use the piano in rehearsal, that is the question

Using the piano in rehearsal has both advantages and disadvantages. Directors who are keyboard proficient can easily play for themselves during rehearsal, and in some ways pace things more quickly. However, the use of piano to drill and teach parts can quickly change from tool to crutch, robbing a choir of the opportunity to rehearse a cappella. This means that those of you who do not sport gilded fingers and regularly bemoan your lack of piano skills are not necessarily at a disadvantage over those who play with ease.

Tuning, blend, and balance all improve more effectively without use of the piano. Director and singers can truly hear what is going on with their parts if the piano is not covering the choral sound or giving singers a false sense of mastery. A strong sense of relative pitch can be taught by picking pitches from the air, only referring to the keyboard for confirmation as necessary. Pitch memory affords students a good sense of how a particular note "feels" in their voices. If you ask them to hum or sing a particular note, singers will become increasingly accurate in doing so. Imagine the benefits of this in sight-reading; singers' knowing approximately how all the pitches feel and sound in their voices without first hearing them! There are many ways to develop this skill, and it can become a fun ten to twenty second game, reaping wonderful tuning results.

When they are not singing

There must be no such thing as wasted time in rehearsal. We can't afford it if we want a top-notch choir. Time is our most finite commodity and must be treasured and used wisely. There's also little doubt that being bored to death is a "bad way to go." There are profitable ways basses can use their time while the altos drill a tough phrase, and sopranos need not strike up a conversation while your men are working a particular section. (As if sopranos have a natural predilection for conversation…) You can promote effective time management by offering positive activities to students when they are not singing. Interested, engaged students will consistently learn more with less disruption.

Ways to make every (non-singing) moment count:

- Number all measures of the music in pencil.
- Write solfege lightly in pencil above all pitches in the students' voice part.
- Mentally sing along with the part being rehearsed, thinking the solfege symbols
- Think (or silently mouth) their voice part.
- Hum voice parts while another section sings on text or solfege (the humming will be almost unnoticed, volume-wise).
- Listen to the passage being sung preparing to critique the perform-ance aloud when the singers finish.
- Ask one section to keep the beat quietly (index finger of one hand tapping into the palm of the other) to notice how various rhythmic issues relate to the beat.

If extended time is needed for sections to work in detail, arrange for other sections to move to practice rooms to work on their parts as well. For multiple repetitions for the same phrase which may become boring despite being necessary, ask students to repeat once more, "facing the clock," one more time "for good luck," once again so the football team will win on Friday, an extra repetition with eyes closed, etc. For some reason, this nulli-fies most of the feeling of boredom and keeps students on their toes, and more willing to drill. Apart from the song at hand, which is your best focus during moments of non-singing "down time," singers might also work on theory sheets kept in the folder for just such times, or provide such oppor-tunities as working ahead on an octavo from the make-up work file for an absence in the future.

The arts must be considered an essential element of education. They are tools for living life reflectively, joyfully, and with the ability to shape the future.
—Shirley Trusty Corey

➤ Selecting Literature

You can please some of the people some of the time,
and you can please all of the people...occasionally!

Selecting literature for your choir is not unlike buying a painting. You want to find something you truly love and "fits" you, yet is varied enough that your walls aren't all covered with the same watercolor theme and variations on trees. The frame must be appropriate to the painting, bringing out the best in the artwork without distracting from it. So it is with the literature that must "fit" your choir, bringing out the best in your singers without all the literature sounding the same.

The more styles with which you are comfortable, the more varied literature you can bring to your choir. This includes presenting a variety of languages, including Latin, the standard European languages, and non-Western texts. Give preference to performing in the original language rather than using a translation or approximation of meaning. The composer's original intent will usually be vastly superior in syllabic stress, with phrases and breath marks falling into place in the natural way, an outgrowth of the original text.

Choose works that reflect varying nationalities and ethnicities, particularly those reflected in your choir and school's student body. Explore different keys, modes, and tempi, and include traditional and non-traditional forms, music composed by both men and women, serious and light-hearted. You'll want to introduce your singers to both polyphonic and homophonic works as well as literature of sacred and secular origin. Expose your choirs to works accompanied by various instruments and works sung *a cappella*. Delve into texts that represent a multiplicity of world languages.

Some directors have concerns about performing sacred works in a public forum; some schools and districts have devised formal policies on this matter. Your commitment to excellent literature on behalf of your choirs obligates you to choose the best possible works from all historical styles and performance practices. Necessarily, these will come from both sacred and secular arenas, often according to historic employment opportunities for the composers of a particular era. Quality literature is your goal, your charge to enable students to understand what the poet was trying to express through the text, not necessarily agree with it.

Helping your choir embrace diversity and respect differences is key to many good things. It is important to address any concern that singers (or their parents) may have about the singing of sacred music in a public school.

During the first week of school it is wise to communicate that you will be asking your singers to know and understand what the poet is trying to express through the lyrics, not necessarily to agree with the message. Historically, great choral literature reflects both sacred and secular realms and the finest choral instruction and performance will include the best literature of both types. As an actor understands and presents a character on the stage, so the singer expresses the feelings and message of the composer and poet through song. Just as the drama teacher does not expect a student playing the part of Lady Macbeth to commit murder after the play closes, so we choral directors do not ask our students to worship in any particular fashion, or to worship at all. We only ask that singers view the text as an expression of its writer's intent and communicate that to the listener. During any given year, you may be asking singers to portray love and hate, war and peace, and sacred texts from various faith traditions.

It is advisable to provide an option for any student or group of students whose beliefs would be compromised by speaking or singing certain words or about certain themes. Know your students and be responsive to those who cannot sing patriotic songs, the word "Santa," or songs about any particular faith or deity. You may suggest that a singer could sing on solfege any word or topic that would offend their beliefs or those of their parents. This is a simple modification to provide for students and parents, and in the long run, will deflect and neutralize their fears and concerns, benefiting all. Be sure that you assure the student and parent that singing the solfege instead of singing the written text will in no way affect your grading of the student in class. The student will still be learning the music and choral art while you are accommodating personal religious practices, and your community will appreciate your concern. As word gets around that you welcome all kinds of singers and nurture a religiously tolerant program, youth directors and ministers alike may send their young people to join choir at your school more readily. This can have powerful, positive impact on the size and support of your choral program! Your principal will appreciate your sensitivity as well.

In December, you may want to use the title "Winter" (or Holiday or Seasonal) Concert. This program may include every manner of snow songs, Santa ditties, and songs reflecting Christmas, Hanukkah, Kwanzaa, and the winter solstice. By calling it a "winter" concert, attitudes seem to soften about sacred content. Exercise care so that your quest to expose singers to the very best of all types of music will be received with ease. This can be a sticky area and there are no easy answers except to be sensitive to the needs of your students and community. With an attitude and atmosphere of acceptance in the choir room, most singers and their families will be comfortable with a wide variety of music without complaint. For more information supporting and delineating the legal inclusion of sacred music in the schools, visit the MENC web site on this important topic: http://www.menc.org/publication/books/relig0.html

As you select choral literature always choose literature of significant musical value. There is too much music available to choose cheesy, low-quality music unless it serves a unique purpose in the program. Don't box yourself into one style because you're best and most comfortable in that style as a director. Just as you might enjoy wearing a black shirt and pants on a particular day, you wouldn't want to wear the same colors every day for every occasion. Try on new colors and learn new styles. Literature lists may be found in various books and on countless web sites. One good resource is choralnet.com, which not only posts various literature lists but also solicits international responses if you have a question you'd like to put forth to a wide range of colleagues across the globe.

Be aware of the text in each and every song you choose. If there is questionable language or thematic material that does not conform to your community values or family-friendly content, don't buy the tune. Plan carefully to program within your group's capabilities. Know their strengths and weaknesses and "dress them" accordingly. Reach for the stars with a dose of reality when programming. Never fear showing a sense of humor. This could include a P.D.Q. Bach tune, a roller-skating snowflake, or your head coach dressed up as Santa; your singers like to laugh and your audiences will appreciate something light for the "dessert" in your program from time to time.

It is sometimes tempting to repeatedly sing the same songs from year to year, living in a certain "comfort zone" under the guise of tradition. Programming new music helps a director stay fresh and excited about the literature. Be open to new challenges and new pieces. Be an eager explorer of new composers and styles. (However, when invited to conduct an All-Region or All-State Choir, select pieces well known to you. This is no time for experimentation!) Have some fun! Diversify!

It is also important to remember that some great music just won't "fit" you or your choir in a given year. Put it aside for another time, another group. Just as your feet would suffer if their size eight-and-a-half length were forced into size seven shoes, so your choir will be doomed from the start if you choose poorly for their specific strengths, weaknesses, and needs. Just as we know that one size does not fit all, so there is no one "perfect" piece.

In concert programming, consider length as it relates to your audience's attention span. It is best to leave people wanting more than to keep them from returning to a future performance because you over-programmed at the fall concert. Less is more! Concerts stretching beyond an hour are tiresome to most people. You will want to decide how many choirs you will feature on a given concert and program accordingly. Start and end with ear-catching numbers, and for variety, consider an occasional theme concert. Topics might include love, the seasons, songs of childhood, or Americana. Use your creativity!

In selecting contest music, there is ordinarily a three-piece formula. Some options for programming might be:

Option 1
"Jubilate Deo" (big opener, either a cappella or accompanied)
"My Love is Like a Red, Red Rose" (sustained, lush, musical middle piece)
"Ride On, King Jesus" (upbeat, powerful, strong, maybe light)

Option 2
(Chronological programming, not necessarily recommended)
"O Magnum Mysterium"
"Liebeslieder Waltzes"
"Ching A Ring Chaw"

Overriding other considerations and planning, as a festival approaches you will want to consider this highly recommended format:

Your strongest number
Your weakest number (if any)
Your 2nd best number

First impressions are important. It is best to make a strong significant statement with your opener. Your second number will not disappear, but this is the least damaging place to program it. Final impressions are important and come directly before a summary judgment about ratings or winners is made. Leave the stage on a good note. Never end a program with a predictable bad last chord, no matter what!

Extra tips in choosing literature:

- When your music budget could use a stretch, carefully search out octavos that are in the public domain. A work that is in the public domain (sometimes referred to as PD) is a creative work that for various reasons is not protected by copyright law. It may be reproduced and used freely without restriction. Lists of public domain music can be found on-line, including on choralnet.com.

- For some age groups there are words that just aren't going to work, no matter what you do. You'll know what those words are the first time you hand out a piece of music containing them, even if they don't appear until page seventy-two. Students have radar which draws them magnetically to "robin red *breast*" or "the ox and *ass* before Him bow," you get the picture. Can singers overcome the initial giggles? Usually so. Are some songs just begging for trouble eternally? Yes. This is yet another aspect of literature to consider as you choose your music for the year.

- Ask yourself if a selection is worth both the time it will take to master, and be able to hold the attention of the singers while doing so. If the answer is no, pass on the piece.

- Choose your literature as one would choose a specially-fitted garment such as a wedding dress; plan far ahead but save the final "fitting" of choir-to-song until closer to the time of the contest or performance. This gives you the opportunity to reassess your choir's "shape" as it relates to the music at that point.

- If a work is permanently out of print (sometimes marked POP), you must find who currently holds the copyright and contact that person or company to request permission to make duplicated copies for your choir. Turn-around for this type of request can be lengthy, so plan ahead. A fee per copy for permission granted might be expected. If the work is no longer protected by copyright, it may be considered public domain, but it is your responsibility to determine the copyright status of the particular work you are considering.

A postscript, when it's time to purchase the music you have selected: It may be tempting to compare the price of octavos in virtual music stores on the Internet with the prices at the local brick-and-mortar store in your community. Without the overhead of a traditional store and staff, Internet store discounts can help stretch your music budget. On the other hand, where did you find that title you're seeking? At a professional convention, reading session, or music retailer? It is in the best interest of the profession to support our music retailers. They underwrite our conventions, provide the packets of free music for our reading sessions, and serve the profession in countless ways. For the many benefits we receive directly (and indirectly), from traditional music stores, the few cents difference in price per copy is a bargain compared to the potential loss of local music retailers in our towns.

I can't listen to that much Wagner.
I start getting the urge to conquer Poland.
—Woody Allen

➤ Blueprint for Teaching Choral Literature

Developing a choral work, day one through performance

How many times have we heard a colleague complaining about an adjudicator's critique? "We had great dynamic contrast. Did the judge not appreciate the work that went into that phrasing? We were great! I can't believe we didn't do better than we did," and so the festival's outcome continues to be rehashed. The fact is the tenor part came and went throughout the piece. The rhythmic variations in subsequent repetitions of the melody were consistently performed as they appeared in the first section of the song. These are aspects of a performance that had to have shown themselves throughout rehearsals. How did the director miss them? So busy, wanting to shape the phrase contours artistically that they jumped over several pages of rhythm drills the singers needed? Did the director assume the tenor part would magically appear one day or would not be missed by listeners?

Just like building a house, constructing a song depends on building a flawless foundation on which all subsequent development rests. Everything you do is dependent on that solid foundation for which there is no substitute. From there, the sky's the limit on just how luxurious your "house of musical art" can become. Plan your rehearsal time so you can adorn the music with as much finery as possible while systematically passing from level to level of complexity and mastery. Multi-tasking will be a real plus to your work as you prioritize goals for each rehearsal, building brick upon choral brick as the literature develops. Beware the temptation to skip ahead or seek shortcuts. There are no shortcuts.

Level One: The Core Level
Foundation: correct pitches
Walls and roof: correct rhythms

Without these core basics, no choral structure of merit can stand. Don't start picking out drapes or selecting crown moldings until these key elements are cemented in place with your singers. Once mastered, these basics must be monitored consistently so that no flaws resurface. Remember, ignoring a mistake is allowing the error to be reinforced. "If it's not getting better, it's getting worse."

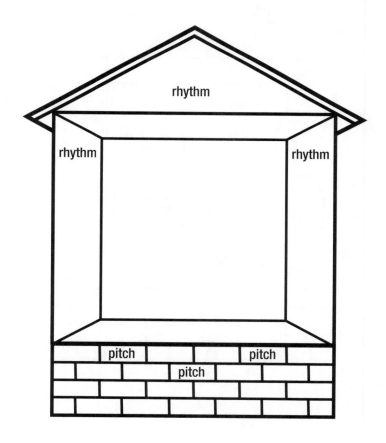

Level Two: Expectations No Builder Would Miss
Doors and windows: tone
Plumbing: intonation
Electricity: diction

Will the house stand without level two in place? Yes. Would you want to live in a structure without them? No. These are basic choral elements.

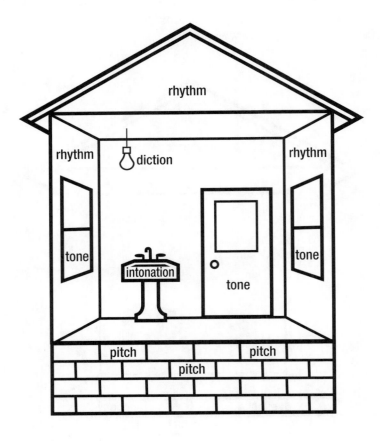

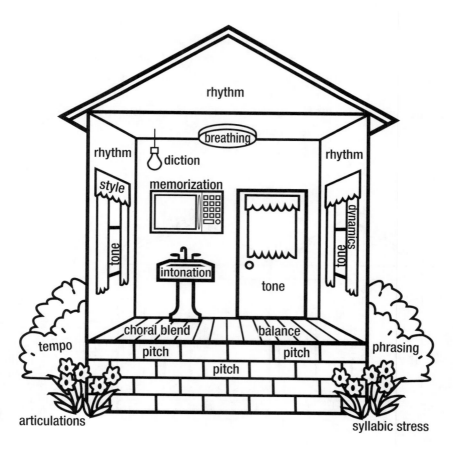

Level Three: Common Comforts We Expect

Flooring: choral blend and balance, within and between sections
Appliances: memorization
Light Fixtures: breathing

Window treatments: style, dynamics
Landscaping: tempo, phrasing
Flower beds: articulations, syllabic stress

Carefully maintain all previous levels of work while crafting these areas. Remember that the loveliest drapery will look foolish hanging from exposed pipes in rooms covered by an unfinished roof. In the same way, the most beautiful music will sound poorly crafted if all the elements are not present in the performance.

Level Four: The Dream Home
Wine cellar and multiple fireplaces:
communication of musical understanding
Hot tub, sauna, and indoor swimming pool:
singer's feeling of artistic fulfillment
Home gym and tennis courts: physical involvement
Tiffany chandeliers and media room: stage presence

Once you've owned a private heated pool, lap swimming at the YMCA will forever lose its allure. In the same way, once you have achieved this distinctive level of achievement in choral performance, you will accept nothing less. It is a level of accomplishment your singers will embrace and expect from their director, themselves, and their peers. The musical capabilities of your choir may sometimes limit the luxury you can attain with a finished choral work of art. You must press on, aspiring to the highest aesthetic level to which each choir may rise.

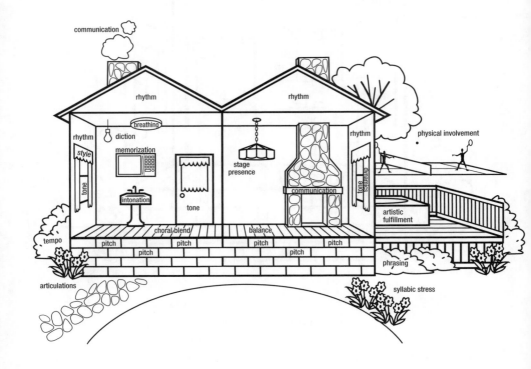

Level Five: The Castle in the Clouds

Sometimes, even when we least expect it, a moment of intense meaning and unity will occur for a choir as it sings. It may happen in performance, or perhaps in rehearsal, transcending words or description. For lack of a more scholarly term, some people call these "goose bump moments." These times represent a heightened sense of meaning and artistic expression that all singers can unmistakably feel, and during which some of our richest memories are made. As we reflect on our work we can recall that moment, or if we are truly lucky, those moments, with specific choirs. We remember where we were, what we were singing, and how terribly wonderful it felt. Aim for the best possible performance, the "dream home," and enter with wonder this realm of aesthetic meaning and artistic expression, knowing how truly blessed you are.

So postpone buying your draperies until the foundation is complete and fully cured. Do not call the movers to deliver your lavish furnishings until the front door is in place, secured with a quality deadbolt lock. You don't want to be the director who is oblivious to acquiring all building permits prior to any construction when the building inspector comes to call for his final inspection!

There isn't a person anywhere that isn't capable of
doing more than he thinks he can.
—Henry Ford

➤ Effective Classroom Management

Let there be peace on earth...especially in my classroom.

The essential goal of classroom management is to maintain a healthy learning environment in which all students may learn without interruption. Classroom discipline is not meant to punish, but rather to re-channel negative behaviors into positive ones. Master teachers nurture positive work and deportment by the individual and group rather than focusing on the negative. Remember, the best form of discipline is self-discipline, and this can be nurtured on your risers so that undesirable behavior is all but eradicated.

State your expectations clearly from the start, always including both students and parents in the communication loop. Widen the informational loop professionally on a need-to-know basis with school guidance counselors, educational psychologists, and special education coordinators.

Your first step in dealing with negative student behavior should be a parent or guardian contact, by phone or in person. Initiate a "same side of the fence, both of us wanting to help your student be successful" rapport with the parent at the first sign of trouble. The teacher's interest and concern for the individual student is demonstrated and the parent will appreciate your taking time to keep them informed. It is common for a parent to become defensive when presented with the notion that their child has erred in any way behaviorally. It is more difficult for a parent to take an oppositional stance when a teacher begins with, "I'd like to talk to you about how we might work together to help your child become even more successful in my class."

Some teachers find that a regular update to parents on a positive basis via e-mail or periodic phone call heads off a certain amount of misbehavior before it begins. When a teacher and parent form a positive partnership, they become a mighty force against which few students can reckon. Conversely, if you allow an adversarial relationship to develop between you and a parent, you give up any support from home for what you are doing in the classroom. Remember, too often the parent hears only their child's side of a situation and perceives it to be exactly as their child recounted it. The wise teacher has already spoken to the parent before the student has arrived home. Build a united front.

Find what works with each student. Fairness doesn't have to mean sameness. Use variety, but be consistent. Try to be creative and flexible, because anything repetitive gets old. If what you're doing isn't working, change what you're doing! "If the horse is dead, dismount." Look for ways to make good behavior the norm so it becomes self-enforcing.

Involve school discipline resources (vice-principals, counselors, detention office, etc.) only when it's an absolute necessity. Take care of your own dirty laundry! This is harder work for you in the short run but professionally best in the long run as you maintain your own classroom discipline. Don't be the teacher who sends a steady stream of transgressors to the office; administrators notice which teachers have a pattern of classroom chaos and which do not. When you do send someone to the office, administrators will be firmer and more supportive since it's not just "one more run-in with the same teacher" over and over again.

Do not let things build up to the point of explosion. Put out small fires one by one as they occur rather than let a raging forest fire develop. Never threaten students with anything you are unprepared to carry out. Idle threats create muted student ears and consciences. Never go outside school and district policy with discipline (i.e. length of detentions, advance notice given to parents, etc.).

Never punish a group for an individual issue. Never punish a group, period. Beware berating individual students in front of the group. While an example is set for others, this can also be an area of concern for parents whose student has been corrected in front of their friends. An additional negative outcome is potential "taking up offenses." This occurs when other students see things from their friend's perspective instead of yours. Their best friend, current girlfriend, and three other students leave the room, all mad at you. The buzz spreads to the hall like bad ripples in a dirty pond. The frustrating part about taking up offenses is that when you mend the fence between you and the original individual who was corrected, these other people (and anyone with whom they have communicated about "what happened in class today with Ms. Jones") will not be in the restoration loop and will continue to carry the leftover emotional residue from the occurrence. This becomes scattered dirt in places you won't know, much less be able to clean up.

Never yell. Never curse. You must model effective anger management and problem solving for your students, even when frustrated. Do not discipline in anger. Catch yourself if you get caught up in the moment and calm down before saying or doing anything you may later regret. You can never take back the spoken word! An outburst taints the positive energy in a room, and it's hard to clean up after a stink bomb of words or feelings. Consider offering disciplinary options when appropriate. "Would you rather serve detention on Friday afternoon or take this opportunity to apologize to the class for your outburst?" is one example of this. Your primary goal is to find ways to make good behavior the norm so it becomes self-enforcing.

When necessary, utilize school and district resources. These may include an office referral to the discipline vice-principal or counselor, detention, or a parent-student-teacher conference. Keep forms for these handy so you don't lose half a rehearsal finding one. What you write on these forms should be something that you can live with if read by principal, parent, parole office, or lawyer, so choose your words carefully while painting an accurate picture of what actually transpired to warrant the referral. Use direct quotes when possible rather than generalities, even if it means spelling out offensive words.

More ideas to promote positive behavior

- Threaten to tell dumb jokes to the class if they don't stop talking during rehearsal, a la drill sergeant. See appendix 2e for examples of real "groaners."
- Give a sermon.
- Contact a coach.
- Write a behavioral contract for a student. This can provide daily feedback to parents, including them in the positive-reinforcement loop while necessitating only your checkmark or a one-word notation on the form you make.
- Have a student (or group) stand up (until further notice) while other students are seated.
- Give a student the opportunity to learn choral work from a book, giving chapter assignments and written work for a period of time. Their educational opportunity is fulfilled while removing them from the risers and their peers. This usually results in a resounding, "I want to sing. Please, Mr. Brady, let me SING!"
- The Walk Out: In an after-school rehearsal (or during school, if an assistant can take over for you with prior notice) a teacher may consider leaving rehearsal for a period of minutes. This can jolt a group into cooperation. This can be done only as a considered choice on your part, not AWOL in anger. It is effective only once, so play this card with care. Never leave a class unattended.
- Do not accept age as an excuse. If a student offers, "but I am only fourteen," remind them of what Mozart had already accomplished at the same age. An introduction to humility can solve many attitude problems.
- Remove a student from the group geographically (to the music library, practice room, behind the risers where you can see them but

their peers cannot, etc.) Do not put a student in the hall; this has major backfire potential.

- Tell a student that you will not talk when they are talking. You might even suggest that you'd be glad to sing on the risers if they feel that THEY should be teaching the class. Being thrust into the director's position for five minutes can silence the most hardened offender on the risers and give them a new appreciation for how tough your job really is.

- Let the punishment fit the crime, and never make extra rehearsal be a punishment for an individual or a group. Rehearsals should be a planned, positive, constructive educational time, not punishment.

Minimizing the madness when you are absent

Leave legible seating or riser charts, and unless you are sure there will be a music sub, tailor your plans for a generalist without choral experience. Create a special folder of information just for substitutes. If the absence is one for which you were able to plan, such as attending a professional convention, you will be able to provide specific lesson plans. Include other, more generic lesson plans you construct which can be used throughout the year at any time for unplanned absences. With all plans be sure to include the number of class periods required to complete the assignment (one class period, two day assignment, etc.), resource materials required (particular textbooks in your classroom, videotape in the classroom or to be acquired from school media center, rhythm worksheets, listening sheets to accompany recordings or films that you develop, etc.), and the specific location of the resource materials (on the rolling book cart, check out from media center before school, etc.). Provide clear directions for students so they can effectively complete the assignment as you would like (and indicate whether to write the directions on the board, simply read them aloud, or any method you deem appropriate) and communicate the method and timing for turning in work (pass in at the end of class with your name in the top left hand corner, finish for homework and bring to class tomorrow, turn in to me with your name on it and I will return it to you tomorrow for completion in class, etc.), and where the substitute should leave the assignments for you to review and grade upon your return to school. See appendices 2f-2L for samples of lesson plans for substitute teachers. Along with the lesson plans include the following:

1. Schedule of classes
2. Bell schedule for the school
3. Bell schedule for non-standard schedule days (assembly, pep rally, early release or staff development schedules, should these apply at any point)
4. Fire drill procedures and map from your classroom
5. Emergency and extreme weather procedures

Do not leave a video to watch! This can provide the potential for zzzzzzzzzz and talktalktalktalk and, if you're not careful, kisskiss and sneakout-sneakout. Do not leave the responsibility for running a rehearsal to a student or student teacher unless previously discussed and mutually agreed-upon. When all is said and done, the certified teacher or substitute must be responsible for all discipline. It is not recommended that you include a packet of hall passes, as this will promote their being used. Include a short paragraph that states the customary policy you have adopted for use in your classroom regarding hall passes to minimize disputes between students and substitute teachers. You may also want to include a copy of your choir handbook, marked to this page, to which a substitute may refer as needed.

It is common sense to take a method and try it.
If it fails, admit it frankly and try another.
But above all, try something.
—Franklin D. Roosevelt

Go!

- ➤ Conducting

- ➤ Concert Dos and Don'ts

- ➤ Memorization

- ➤ Contests and Festivals

- ➤ Programming Themes
  and Variations

- ➤ Enrichment Opportunities
  for Students

- ➤ The Blessing of Added Extras

- ➤ Identifying Prospective
  Audiences

➤ Conducting

Down, left, right, up…

The effectiveness of our conducting and how it looks to others is important but should not engulf one's every waking moment. We've heard the tale of the student teacher that approached a supervising teacher immediately after the last number in a big concert. With students running everywhere and parents waiting to congratulate the choral director and student teacher, the student director's mind was focused on only one thing: "How did my conducting look?" In the end, conducting boils down to three things:

1. Do what works for you.
2. Observe the effective conducting of others.
3. When in doubt, dance, at least with your hands.

It is distracting to flail about wildly. Don't steal the focus from your singers. The audience came to hear the choir, not to see you conduct. If your movements aren't helping draw the best from your singers, you're doing the wrong things. The point is to hold things together and hopefully make them better. Don't get all wrapped up in the beauty of a conducting pattern at the expense of failing to fully connect with your choir and the music. There are excellent workshops and master classes with some of today's most notable conductors. Seek these out and learn from the best. Books and videotapes are also available to assist you in polishing your conducting technique. Resources that you might find helpful include:

Adler, Samuel. *Choral Conducting: An Anthology*

Busch, Brian. *The Complete Choral Conductor*

Decker, Harold and Herford, Julius. *Choral Conducting: A Symposium*

Demaree, Robert and Moses, Don. *The Complete Conductor*

Green, Elizabeth. *The Modern Conductor*

Hunsberger, Donald. *The Art of Conducting*

Moe, Daniel. *Basic Choral Concepts and Problems in Conducting*

Neuen, Donald. *Choral Concepts: A Text for Conductors*

Phillips, K. *Basic Techniques*

Ross, Allan. *Techniques for Beginning Conductors*

Rudolph, Max. *The Grammar of Conducting*

If you think you can, you can. And if you think you can't, you're right.
—Mary Kay Ash

➤ Concert Dos and Don'ts

It ain't over till the fat lady... puts away the risers.

Each concert your choirs perform requires extensive planning and rehearsal. Beyond rehearsal you are responsible for a plethora of non-musical details. Working on a careful timeline you can keep up with the music, technical considerations, and the multitude of other concert-related details on your to-do list. Acquire a working knowledge of equipment and theater terminology so you can "speak the language" when communicating with your theater colleagues.

Planning for what you need

You shouldn't need to hunt down a music stand for the guest oboist five minutes before curtain time! Let's look at what needs to get done, and when.

Scheduling

Scheduling meetings are generally held in the late spring with the faculty members who will need to use the theater during the following year. While the fine arts department uses the theater the most, your school will also make its stage available to other groups. It may be scheduled by the PTA, community organizations, other schools, or rented out to outside groups seeking a meeting location. Departmental presentations and theater classes may be held in the auditorium during various periods of the day. Prior to the beginning of each school year, you and the other fine arts teachers should make sure that all major concerts, rehearsals, set-up and strike times are clearly marked on the calendar.

Consult the school master calendar in selecting dates for the choir so you do not schedule against major athletic events, tournaments, induction cere-monies, or other school functions. Know who handles the master calendar as well as who controls the theater schedule. If you don't need all the times you reserved the preceding spring, have the courtesy to make the appro-priate changes on the theater schedule so others can use the available time. If a concert is cancelled, be sure to make this change on the theater and school master calendars. (You don't want to be the conductor who learned that several supportive board members came to the school for the concert that you cancelled.) See appendix 3a for a sample school year calendar.

Do not assume that the stage will be available for a spur-of-the-moment rehearsal, or that you can set up your risers at any time. Know what you need and arrange for it specifically with the appropriate people. Be prepared to negotiate, share, and rethink your original needs in an effort to live peaceably in the land.

Please check your school calendar (and the calendars at your feeder schools) before scheduling a concert. This avoids parents being divided between multiple events on the same night, and the perception that you focus only on what's going on in your school and with your choir. It also prevents inevitable conflicts between activities like baseball playoffs, track meets, and debate tournaments. Creative planning will help you find the days and times that are least problematic for your rehearsals and concerts.

Arrange for all personnel necessary to be present for choral rehearsals and technical run-throughs so your concert will proceed smoothly. This includes requesting theater tech students to work lighting booth, spotlights, ropes, and sound. Include ushers and your own equipment crews for before, during, and after the concert.

If the piano needs to be tuned, schedule time on stage with nothing else going on in, and around the theater. Coordinate with the tuner so their availability matches your reserved times. It is always preferable to tune a piano after it has been moved into place for the concert.

Know your responsibilities for locking up the venue and take them seriously each time you use the theater, even for short periods of time. The specialized equipment therein can be prohibitively expensive to replace if stolen or damaged.

Lighting

Determine the specific lighting you wish to use: the number of spotlights, overall lighting scheme, any mood lighting for special numbers, special effects, house light schedule, etc. and secure trained and experienced staffing from your theater tech teacher. Always include these "technical

*The technical needs of the performance must
be thought through step by step!*

wizards" in your program's acknowledgement section. These volunteer magicians provide a valuable service to the school's organizations and deserve much more gratitude than they usually receive.

Prepare a call sheet that lists everything that is going to happen on stage in chronological order. Begin with the house and stage lights before the concert, continuing through the beginning of the concert as the first singer walks on stage, and ending as the final curtain is pulled with house lights up. This call sheet will be an expanded version of your concert program, and should include announcements, welcome, planned comments during the evening, and specific instructions about what you want. The technical needs of the performance must be thought through step by step! After preparing the call sheet, highlight sound cues in one color and lighting cues in another. Use pale colors to make them highly legible in a dimmed light booth. (You may need a third color for ropes/backstage techs and yet another for backstage equipment crew, depending on your needs.) Suggested lighting cues:

1. Before concert: house lights up full, no lighting on stage (possible footlights on proscenium/curtain area if pulled).
2. Blink house lights five minutes before stated concert time.
3. Blink house again three minutes prior to concert.
4. Take house down to half one minute prior to concert.
5. Dim house to darkness as stage lights come up.
6. Spotlight any soloist or speaker at the downstage standing microphone. (Specify if the speaker will walk into the spotlight or if the spot cue is visual, illuminating the person already standing at the microphone.)
7. Dim stage lights between choirs and raise house lights (minimal change, more for mood; careful that there is sufficient light in house and on stage for singers to see where they are going).
8. At the conclusion of the final number and all bows, bring up house to full while dimming down stage to dark.
9. House stays at full for twenty minutes, dim to half for an additional fifteen minutes to encourage audience to gather outside while stage lights are brought up and equipment is cleared from stage.

It is important to note that if you run lighting cues prior to the concert on a time schedule as noted above, make sure that you and your singers also run by that same schedule. Singers should be in place on stage and seated in the house or holding areas at least seven minutes before concert time. You should be backstage, ready to go on at least five minutes before the concert begins. It is less than thrilling to have the curtain pulled to thunderous applause for an empty stage.

Sound

Make a list of sound equipment you think you may need and consult with your theater director, who can help you assess the best placement for microphones as well as what type(s) are needed. Know and understand terms such as "omni-directional," "uni-directional," "cordless," "clip-on," "hanging," and how each type of amplification might work to your singers' advantage. Consider the need for amplification of narrators, speakers, soloists, and perhaps some choirs as a whole. Remember to keep microphones turned off except when being used in rehearsal and performance!

Prepare a sound cue call sheet for each technician, similar to the lighting and backstage technicians, and remember to reserve time in your schedule for technicians to set up for the concert on your behalf, uninterrupted. Most things that need to be done for set-up cannot be accomplished easily if singers and technicians try to share the space.

Climate control in the theater

Know who controls the scheduling of heating and cooling in your building, and be certain you have access to the person who will control the temperature in the hall if you are not doing it yourself. Excessive heat or cold on stage and in the audience can spoil an otherwise wonderful performance. If possible, learn to override the system yourself in case there is ever an emergency.

When in doubt, go with a cooler setting. Providing proper climate control can be very expensive in a large venue, so setting the thermostat to a comfortable level may seem excessive. However, the hall will be filled with audience members for the concert and each will be generating additional warmth. With stage lights on, your singers will carry an additional burden of heat. If finances were not a consideration, seventy degrees Fahrenheit would be a conservative comfort level for most people.

Seating and holding room arrangements for your singers when not on-stage

It is recommended that all singers be in the choir room for warm-up no later than forty-five minutes before a concert. To help take attendance accurately you may want to post a sign-in sheet for each choir in different parts of the choir room, clearly visible to students as they arrive. Posting a copy of each class roster for students to sign is easiest for transferring later into your grade book or computer. Each student should sign independently, in his or her own handwriting. At the specified report time, student leaders can take down the sign-in sheets and secure them for you. After this time, an honest and responsible choir officer should sit by the door and write names and arrival times of latecomers on a list. This page should be secured on your behalf so you can take this information into consideration if you grade the concert. Deducting two points per minute tardy works well for grades and encourages promptness. Obviously, give leeway for true (and documented) emergencies.

An alternate method of assigning report or warm-up times is to schedule each choir individually with director, working backward from curtain time in fifteen to twenty minute increments so that the last group to warm-up goes straight to the stage as the first performing group. This allows your (mostly) older, more advanced singers who can drive themselves reporting at the earliest time(s) so that parents of younger singers can bring them and stay for the concert with a shorter wait time. By using multiple rooms (such as the choir room and band hall) this can work especially well if an assistant director is warming up one group while you work with another.

Both systems as described above provide adult direction and supervision of all choirs, and with either system, students reporting early prevents tardiness to the concert itself. Warn students well in advance to leave all purses, coats, and other valuables at home or locked in the trunk of their cars. This prevents your choir room from being an opportunity for theft during a concert. When it becomes known that nothing is being left in the choir room, the chance for theft will diminish.

After warm-up in your choir room, dismiss each choir accompanied by a parent, teacher, or volunteer after they are lined up in correct order. Singers should sit in the same order they will use for the first song they will sing on stage.

If space allows, reserve blocks of seats in the concert hall for your groups when they are not singing on stage. Rope off reserved rows of seats for your choirs in your preferred method: affixing a "reserved for choir" placard to both ends of reserved rows, running masking tape or rolls of crepe paper down both ends of rows, or using existing professional roping materials to cord off rows. This keeps students in order, organized, and quiet, especially if an adult, there to assist in case any emergency should arise, is seated with them. Lag time is eliminated if choirs do not have to travel between a holding room and the stage. This also limits scheduling other large rooms and the inevitable clean up involved for each. Most importantly of all, it gives choir students the opportunity to hear and support all choirs in the department. Arrange student seating for optimum traffic patterns in getting on and off stage during the evening. Consult your order of program, placing choirs on opposite sides of the theater so one group exits stage right as the next choir enters stage left. Your audience will appreciate the lack of dead time, and even thirty seconds is an eternity when students are filing on and off risers. The crowd will be impressed by your planning and concert finesse. The first and last singers to get on stage for each choir are important. Put responsible, experienced students in these key spots.

If insufficient seating is available for student seating in the theater, holding rooms should be secured well in advance of the concert by asking teachers if you may use nearby classrooms. Remind students not to touch anything in these rooms, move any furniture, write on blackboards, or put anything in garbage cans that will probably have already been emptied for the day. Adult presence in each holding room is strongly advised. Student leaders and accompanying adult for each choir should have students in place and silent backstage before the preceding group's final number. Plan for no down time between choirs on stage!

Some concerts segue from group to group by using a student soloist or small group to perform a song between choirs. Always audition these students! At the audition, music should be performance-ready, including memorization and accompaniment. Judge each singer's vocal quality, memo-

Plan for no down time between choirs on stage!

rization, and appropriateness of the selection for inclusion on the concert. This works particularly well for seasonal concerts and your final concert of the year, using senior soloists. In the case of seniors, consider student effort and give singers the benefit of any doubt. Your highly polished All-State students will have future opportunities to sing, but the rank and file members of your groups may never have the chance to perform a solo after their high school years. Whenever a senior audition is credible, consider giving these students an honored moment with their solo.

Remind students that they will be staying for the entire concert, regardless of the order in which the choirs perform. If possible, listening to the other groups should comprise a portion of the evening's concert requirement and be noted accordingly. Address individual needs in advance with those students who need to arrive late or leave early in order to participate in other approved activities that overlap the concert. When a playoff game is scheduled against the longstanding choir concert performance, it is sometimes possible to have your cake and eat it too, if you are flexible. More than one choir has had a singer/athlete appear on stage in football or baseball uniform, coming straight to a winter or spring concert.

Concert etiquette

Common courtesy isn't so common any more. If we educate our students about concert etiquette, we teach future audience members for generations to come. By requiring singers to be present throughout a concert, you minimize parents' standing by doorways, waiting to get a jump on the departure traffic. A final number for combined groups can make for a great ender as well as an additional reason for all to stay.

Although it may seem obvious, students need to know that gum, drinks, or food are prohibited in the theater, and that there should be no talking or noise during a performance. All cell phones must be turned to vibrate or off. A concert creates a world of sound and any extraneous noises are distracting from the musical sounds made on stage. Even whispering in a well-designed acoustical hall will be too loud for keen listeners. This includes "shhhhhh-hhhh," a sound even louder than the ever-dreaded unwrapping of the cough drop. Remind students that feet and legs do not rest over the seat in front of them, occupied or not, and restroom visits during the concert should be reserved for unusual emergencies.

Only three expressions of approval or disapproval are appropriate during a concert. The first is to applaud if the performance is done well, or the performers have put forth their best effort. Second, an audience member may stand up and applaud ("standing ovation") if the performance is incredibly well done, or third, in an extreme case of a poor performance, or one done in bad taste, an audience member may withhold applause. Teach students to hold their applause until the end of multi-movement works. A gentle request of the audience to observe this may also be helpful. Responses that are appropriate in one venue are often inappropriate somewhere else. Too often our students' experiences have been limited to pep rallies, athletic events, and rock concerts. It is our job to educate our students about traditional concert etiquette.

Flash photography and any out of seat photography should be prohibited, although video recordings are less obtrusively made from parents' seats or specific areas you reserve for this purpose. Bear in mind that the recording of copyrighted materials may be prohibited. Check current law relative to what you are taping and the use for which it is intended.

Consider limiting the seating availability to your audience based on house capacity and expected audience attendance so most people are sitting in one overall area. This could be as simple as blocking off a balcony.

Some directors have tried providing a room with free childcare for children under age five, particularly during extended concerts during which recordings will be made. It is unfair for the choirs' performance (and recordings) to be potentially marred by a crying baby or thoughtless parent. A trained babysitter (or three) in a child-proof room may be a potential solution, and you may want to make a short, friendly statement in your concert program, for example: "Tonight's performance may be a little long and quiet for our youngest audience members. To help us have the best quality recording possible, we appreciate your consideration if your young ones should begin to stir." You might take an opportunity at some point in the year to teach your choirs that as they grow up, they should remember how much performers and audience appreciate a quiet venue. See appendix 3b for a sample program insert concerning concert etiquette.

Sound shell and risers

Be sure to reserve the sound shell and risers, whether they are housed on or off campus. Provide adequate storage for multiple sets of risers for optimum care and access, and arrange for crew to transport and assemble the shell and risers under your direction. After the concert, schedule workers to take down shell and risers, and transport them back to the storage area. Ensure that all equipment used is safe and as up-to-date as budget will permit. Teach singers not to lean against, or touch the shell. There are a number of multi-step risers available including rolling, seated, standing, platform, and foldable. Be familiar with how to set up and strike your risers so you are able to teach students proper set up and take down. If you are unfamiliar with a piece of equipment, ask colleagues who are experienced with your type or brand of risers about potential pitfalls, dangers, or problems in use, set-up, or striking. Have your crew "walk the risers" to be sure they are secure for the choirs. Instruct students about the dangers inherent in using equipment improperly. The ramifications for the risers and shell being poorly assembled can be monumental.

Work crew

Form a group that will be responsible for setting up and striking your equipment on stage throughout the year. The leader might be a choir officer ("equipment manager") or other responsible student. Consider letting the remainder of your crew be the top freshman and sophomore choir students, developing leadership and continuity for future years. The variety of tasks, light and heavy duty, provides appropriate opportunities for students of varying physical strength to help as members of the work crew. Crew work can certainly be a basis for extra credit for hard-working members.

The crew leader should know all dates and times for setting up and striking, particularly whether you've reserved the stage for an extended time or fragmented times and dates. Prepare a checklist of things that must be done. If you tell the crew exactly how you want things placed, they will know how to please you and will work until they do. You are ultimately responsible for your students' safety whenever they work with equipment and prepare the stage. Particularly for the first concert of the year, you should personally work with your crew to show them how to set up the shell properly and ways to center the risers more easily, working alongside them to demonstrate the various tasks they will perform. The setting up and striking of the stage should be organized and methodical. Always leave the stage swept. Be prompt in using and clearing the stage in consideration of your colleagues' needs. Striking after the concert clears the stage soonest and gets your choir room set up again for the next day if the risers came from your room. However, it takes students out of post-concert exuberance and into work mode immediately, and while still in choir uniform! Find what works best for both your singers and colleagues.

Ushers

The tone for the evening is set by the professionalism and courtesy of your ushers. Instruct student ushers on appropriate concert attire for the occasion. This might be "dress up" for formal concerts, or "costumed" for theme concerts, but should be uniform if possible. Ushers might be students unable to perform, new to school, academically ineligible, students from the other fine arts in your building, or feeder school students serving as an "honor group." You might also use Booster Club parents, reserving their choice of seats for them in the house. Ideally, have two students stand at each entrance door to the concert venue. Assign individuals to specific locations, using the friendliest ushers at the most trafficked locations. Ushers should open the house thirty to forty-five minutes prior to the concert. Until this time, it is good to keep the hall closed to the audience for last minute checks on stage. As the audience arrives, the stage and curtains should be set for the opening of the concert. Maintain a uniform practice on this so your audience will learn what to expect and arrive accordingly.

Instruct the ushers to greet each patron on arrival as they hand out the concert program. Be sure that the ushers know in advance where the programs will be kept prior to the concert. If audience members have arrived before the opening of the hall, have one usher specified to hand out programs to those already seated, along with a warm greeting. Ask ushers to be prepared to offer special assistance to elderly, physically handicapped or other patrons with special needs. Ushers should remain in place at their assigned doors for at least fifteen minutes after the concert begins, assisting latecomers in finding seats between numbers, or choirs, as you prefer. After this time, ushers can be seated in reserved seats at ends of rows closest to their door, so they can open doors both at intermission and at the end of the concert. Ushers should thank audience members for coming as they exit the hall, and after the audience has cleared the hall, pick up any programs left in the house and bring them to a central location in the choir room.

Piano placement

Teach your crew to move the piano slowly to avoid damage on the way to and from the stage. Always have more help than you think will be necessary for this so all doors can be held open and all sides of the piano can be protected from brushing up against anything that might scratch its surface. Tell your crew where you would like the piano placed, and which direction you prefer it to face. Directors sometimes consider whether they are left or

Remind students that the piano is an instrument,
not a piece of furniture.

right handed in this choice, as well as whether the piano lid should open up to, or away from, the choir. Most feel that the choir needs to hear the piano and choose to open the lid toward the choir. Always check for desired balance between choir and instrumental accompaniment from several positions in the theater. Monitor choir and piano balance carefully.

Keep the piano covered when not in use. Always keep the key cover down and dust the piano prior to every performance, both lid and opened surfaces. Avoid wiping dust into the piano's interior. Remind students that the piano is an instrument, not a piece of furniture, and never allow folders or other items to be placed upon it. Never permit food or beverage near the piano, not even bottled water. Only the director and accompanist should play the piano on stage. There are only so many choruses of "Heart and Soul" and "Chop Sticks" a choir director should have to endure. Head it off at the pass.

Getting on and off the risers

As has been said before, that first and last impression is a lasting one for the audience, adjudicators' panel, or casual observer watching your choir get on and off the risers. There is a direct correlation between the way a choir has prepared to sing and how they are taught to address the stage for a performance. Adjudicators often note they can predict how a choir will sound in performance by observing the way they enter the stage. Observe other schools' choirs to see if you don't agree with this. Getting on and off the risers does not have to be militaristic or stilted to be effective. It does need to be organized and exacting. The most common way of getting on risers is to ask students to walk to the end of the lowest riser, turn away from the audience toward the back row of risers, and walk straight up the end of the risers until they arrive at their row. There should be no diagonal ambling, no creative paths. Once at the end of their assigned row, the student should walk into place, turning toward the audience after arriving in the proper spot. Each subsequent row of students will follow suit.

There are two basic schools of thought on the order in which students should get on the risers. A few directors have the first row take its place, with the other rows following, but most send their top row on first, working their way toward the bottom row so that the first person on stage becomes the last person to leave the stage.

Opening with an antiphonal number might warrant approaching the stage from two different sides and ascending the risers from opposite ends. Another way to do this is to take the two choirs up side by side. Pairs of singers walk to the center of the riser, walking alongside one another up to their assigned row, then turning in opposite directions and continuing until they reach their performance place, and so on. Processional entrances may be fashioned in the same way.

More advanced, or larger choirs sometimes take the stage from both directions simultaneously, with every other row approaching from opposite directions. This is fast and impressive. (If you've got a serious "cast of thousands" choir, please consider doing this. An endless line of students meandering onto the risers captures audience attention with the same passion as watching paint dry.) Students should walk on the balls of their feet, making the least possible sound. Crashing, thumping noises are less than melodious and can be avoided. (Speaking of squeaks, make sure riser hinges are oiled periodically as necessary.) Uniform pockets, if any, should be free of coins. Each singer should remember precisely where he or she stands, which riser, and where on that riser. This responsibility rests with each individual singer.

In order to space singers so that each can see the director (and the audience can see them individually) through a "window," space them accordingly. There are at least two ways of doing this. In rehearsal, have each student place their hands on the shoulders of the two singers on the row in front of them. Their right hand will go on one student's left shoulder, with their left hand resting on another student's right shoulder. This begins at either stage right or left, and works across the risers in kind, forming appropriately sized windows for each singer. This can also be measured out by having students put their hands at their waists with elbows extended to the side (touching elbows with one another) to achieve effective spacing. Begin with the center of the row and work outward. Every other row will be lined up between the row two levels down.

Another way to space singers involves each row of students lining up directly in front of the preceding row, so students are standing directly in front of, and behind each other in vertical rows. A discreet cue is then given, such as a nod of the head or the turn of the director to the audience, and every other row takes one step in the direction of your choice. This places the choir in a windowed order. Regardless of the system you choose to space

*Remind your singers that a performance begins
when the first student walks onto the stage.*

singers, practice it until it becomes effortless. Choirs should have rehearsed in such a way that the choir takes its place symmetrically from the audience's prospective. Please directors: do not "scooch" your choir over with little hand movements to get them from an off-center "amoebae formation" to a more effectively spaced symmetry on the risers. This just lacks class, and gives the appearance of a novice or haphazard group.

Remind your singers that a performance begins when the first student walks onto the stage. Hands should remain naturally at their sides the entire time they are performing on stage. No hands behind backs, no hands clasping each other in the front, no hands clutching the sides of a dress or front corners of a jacket; no "adolescent awkwardness." (Hands looking for someplace to be rather than just hanging naturally at the side. Making reference to this nickname often helps encourage teenaged singers to keep their hands still because they don't want to be considered either adolescent or awkward.)

In between songs, minimal movement is encouraged. An individual singer's movement is magnified in the eyes of the audience. Fixing a hair clip or adjusting a cummerbund seems innocuous enough but draws audience attention away from the group. Remind your choirs that while one singer brushing the hair from their face is simple enough, if you multiply it by the number of singers on stage who may alternately take turns brushing, touching, picking, or scratching, they will produce an unwanted visual effect. Teach students to place weight equally on both feet, resting slightly more to the front or ball of the foot. In addition to looking bad, standing more on one leg than the other will eventually cause the singer to shift weight. Demonstrating this for the choir shows them how dramatic a movement this really is from the audience perspective. Weaving or moving about nervously is annoying on stage. (Try calling this the "wee-wee wiggles." You'd be amazed how still a choir member can become when asked if they need to be excused because you've noted they have "the wiggles." Works like a charm!) While minimal movement is encouraged, singers should avoid physical stiffness, feeling free to move with the music as appropriate to the style without exaggeration. "Statuary" should be reserved for parks and pigeons.

Order of taking the stage, first to last, is students, instrumental soloists and page-turner (if any), accompanist, and finally, director.

Miscellaneous stage items

Music stands and chairs for instrumentalists needed at the beginning of the concert should be placed on stage before the concert begins. Other necessary equipment should be organized in the wings on the side closer to their eventual position. Observe how the professionals at the symphony move chairs, stands, and pianos with amazing efficiency.

Correctly position the director's music stand or podium and set up music stand lights (if needed) with accompanying snake, cords, and plugs. Arrange to borrow these from band, orchestra, or theater colleagues if you do not own these in the choral department.

Students will generally perform by memory. If folders are used they should be with the students as they enter the hall. Always carry folders with the opening side up. (This keeps music from falling out of folders.) Folders should be carried in the same hand at a uniform level by all singers. The director's folder may be placed in advance of the concert on the podium or music stand. A responsible student can do this for you prior to taking their place on the risers.

Soloists or instrumentalists should be in the wings well in advance of their place on the program, tuned and ready to go. Minor tuning on stage is common but prolonged tuning is an avoidable time lag.

It is possible that the director will need certain items backstage during the concert. These typically include bottled water, throat lozenges, breath mints, or a handkerchief. It may also include your car or choir room keys. Keep some extra tissues and cough drops backstage in case Paul should need to blow his nose or Dottie need to quiet her cough before walking on stage.

Asthmatic students may want to place their emergency inhaler backstage for use as necessary. The same would apply to diabetic students or others with special needs. Facilitate and assist with these issues privately. It is essential that you are personally aware of all singers' special health needs and difficulties. This confidential information is available through your school nurse. Students are often embarrassed about having a special need so you may need to make personal contact and appropriate accommodations for them rather than waiting for them to come to you. Handle such issues discreetly in a relaxed, accepting way so students are confident that whatever makes them unique or challenged is not a problem to you in any way. Educate yourself on any special needs a student may have and know when you should seek aid in case of an emergency.

Prepared remarks

Each concert should have a specific opening and closing planned so there is structure throughout. This may or may not involve spoken remarks. If you choose to open with speaking, prepare a concise welcome and keep acknowledgements, comments on music and recognitions brief. The audience is there to hear singing, not speeches. Some directors prefer to let the music alone speak and choose not to talk on stage. Others welcome the audience after the first selection. Still others speak (or have someone speak for them) in advance of the concert. Be professional in any choice you make.

At some point during the final concert of the year, it is gracious to recognize the parents of your singers. Have them stand at their seats to receive a round of applause for their support, transportation, and funding of their sons' and daughters' participation in choir. Do follow by asking all grandparents of singers to stand and be recognized. These can very tender moments, especially for the proud (and unsuspecting) grandparents.

A fine tradition is the recognition of seniors toward the end of the final concert of the year. It is a tremendous honor to call each senior's name, including brief comments such as where they will be continuing their studies, intended major, and any noteworthy honors achieved (such as All-State Choir, Valedictorian, Salutatorian, etc.) When a name is called, that senior approaches the front of the stage (from the risers or their seats, depending on which choir they are in), and forms a line across the stage. This must be practiced! Hold a seniors-only rehearsal to run through this, scheduled well in advance. Some schools include an underclassman presenting each senior with a rose as they come forward. Organize names so that seniors take the stage alternately from opposite sides, giving each person a special moment with minimal lag time. Your comments require only eight to ten seconds per singer, and this can be deeply meaningful to the students. The order of senior recognition might be:

Alphabetical
- Random (which has the benefit of giving you a second chance if you miss someone's name in alphabetical order)
- Starting with the most accomplished, awarded, or longest tenured senior in your program to the newest member, giving the most involved students the most stage time
- Starting with the newest or least involved of your students and working up to your most involved and accomplished senior.

Be private about using the third and fourth options. All students want to think they were the most accomplished and worthy.

Some schools have a tradition of inviting alumni to join the choir on stage for a traditional closing number. If you do this, add a sentence in the program so these graduates will be prepared, and include this on your call sheets for technicians. When this time comes in the concert, step to the microphone and invite choir graduates to join the choir on stage. If you are starting this tradition for the first time, get word around to key graduates that you will be doing this. Thereafter they will come on their own and, usually, in increasing numbers. This tradition is an opportunity to demonstrate the continuity of the choral program and its continuing place in the hearts of graduates to current students. It also honors past singers and forms a stronger alumni support base.

Another tradition involves calling the parents of senior students to stand by their singer for that same traditional closing number. (If little sister or grandma also wants to come up, let them. Exclude no family member.) Mention this to your students in advance so they can let their families know. Along with everything else, folks need to know their cues so things will run smoothly. The curtain then closes on the mass of people on stage or curtains remain open as the concert either dissolves into hugs and greetings, or you indicate students lead off in rows.

Acknowledging applause

After the end of a song, pause for a moment to let the moment settle and audience begin to applaud. Most directors will then walk to one side, extending their arm and gesture to the choir. If a second acknowledgment is needed due to extended applause, the conductor turns to the audience in place and bows alone. At the time of a first bow, plan to acknowledge these individuals as appropriate with a gesture of your extended hand: accompanist (should stand at the piano, facing the audience), individual soloists (step forward from the risers), any special instrumentalists or guest performers (step forward from place), the composer of the work, if in attendance. The order of the above bows should be tailored to the individual

---

Remind students that applause is the audience's show of appreciation and approval.

---

work and magnitude of contribution. Discuss bows with the choir and other individuals so everyone knows what to expect in advance.

Some directors have the entire choir bow, bowing with the conductor at the same time and tempo. Singers should count to three as they descend, head bowing to look toward their shoes rather than keeping their face up to the audience. If the choir has been facing in at an angle, they will need to face forward before bowing.

Remind students that applause is the audience's show of appreciation and approval. When singers smile in response, it says, "You're welcome. Yes, it was very good, wasn't it! We liked it too, you lucky audience!" Choirs with funereal faces suck the joy from the air; few audience members want to vigorously applaud people who appear to be suffering.

"It happens;" What to do if a singer becomes ill on stage

Overriding all other concerns and considerations, your priority should be caring for students' safety and well-being. No stage or venue is more important than an individual singer. A director who demonstrates poise and compassion in an unexpected emergency garners respect from an audience. Know what to watch for symptomatically as your students sing. Cold sweats, singers staring blankly, ashen skin tone or flushed faces can spell trouble. No one will know if you mouth the words, "Are you okay?" as you look at a particular singer.

At the beginning of the year, become aware of any student health issues that you need to be aware of during a concert, trip, or competition. Know recommended procedures for first-responders for all medical events that might reasonably occur on stage. Most audiences will include a nurse or other health care professional that will quietly come to your aid. Any student with an active illness or condition that might reasonably be expected to be a problem should not take the stage. When appropriate to the situation, these students might be able to serve as ushers. Asthmatics may want to keep an emergency inhaler backstage, if not on their person.

Pregnant students may be more susceptible to fainting or nausea. Handle individual needs as appropriate for each student.

To help prevent fainting, instruct students to avoid locking their knees, bending them discreetly between numbers. They should keep eyes focused and remain mentally alert. "Zoning out" can precede fainting if students are nervous or emotional under concert pressure. It is an old wives' tale that standing too long under hot stage lights causes most fainting. The first moment a student is on stage is the most likely time for a problem.

Prepare your choir for what to do should a health emergency arise during a concert. If feeling sick, a choir member should sit down in place. If feeling better, stand up and continue. If not feeling better, ask another student for help getting off stage between numbers. A nearby student should alert the director if additional action is warranted. If a student starts to sway or fall, have students on either side help lower the student to a sitting position or hold them up as best fits the situation. If nausea is imminent, the student should leave the stage immediately, without any notice or delay. A designated adult can meet the student in the wings and attend to their needs by accompanying them to the restroom and notifying custodial staff if needed. Encourage your students to be creative problem solvers. Singers should learn to think on their feet and care for each other.

If (and we hope this does not happen to you) a student should vomit on stage, handle the situation professionally with as much poise as you can muster. Obviously the concert must pause while the affected student is helped from the hall. Custodial help must be secured immediately. Refreshing the stage should be done with curtain closed if possible. If not, announce a brief intermission so the problem does not spread to others. The audience and choristers will understand and appreciate your intercession. Don't fret over having an imperfect event. No concert is perfect so take that weight off your shoulders before stepping on stage. In the end, it's the heart with which you worked and the joy of life through music that you brought to the stage with your students that matters, not whether every program was folded perfectly or if a singer didn't cough on a rest!

Concluding a concert

First and last impressions are most important. You want to have an ending with finesse rather than a hand wave and "see you" as the ants flee the hill. (Exception: after mass choir endings or pulling alumni or parents of seniors on stage in the spring, you may end up resorting to a tasteful anthill or some semblance thereabouts.) If singers perform in front of the curtain line, they should file off stage. If they are behind the line, the curtain should be pulled before singers turn to leave the risers. With much equipment and many singers on stage, the audience should be discouraged from coming up to mingle. This can also delay the striking of the stage by your crew and the eventual departure time for your theater technicians.

If your Booster Club chooses to meet in conjunction with concerts, it should be in a separate location following the event. It is more expedient to hold the meeting in the concert hall but a less than satisfactory way to welcome the audience. Do arrange for that separate room. It is also good to note that meetings before concerts have the downside of your being busy and unable to attend.

Concert recordings

Do not underestimate the value of a quality recording as a teaching tool and treasure for your individual students and their families. Secure all necessary equipment and personnel to make a recording of the entire concert, including a video recording when appropriate. Your equipment might be choir-owned, personally owned, owned by the school or district, borrowed from a local church or community group, or rented. Never borrow something you can't afford to pay for if broken or stolen.

Take a music bath once or twice a week for a few seasons,
and you will find that it is to the soul what the
water bath is to the body.
—Oliver Wendell Holmes

➤ **Memorization**

A piano vamp can buy you time for only so long...

To use music or not to use music for the concert, that is the question! Whether 'tis nobler to be assured the music and text will flow forth without a memory glitch, or for both conductor and singers to be free of the page, truly expressive, creating the most complete communication both with voices and eyes; this is the stuff of which wise choices are made. Memorized concerts suggest greater mastery of the music, are aesthetically more pleasing, and can be more musical. Internalizing the music provides a powerful ownership of expression for your singers. Be aware that the more skillful your choir is at sight-reading, the more difficult it will likely be for them to memorize a piece of music because they will require fewer repetitions for mastery. Keep in mind that memorization goes beyond the rudiments of pitch and rhythm, and extends to dynamic markings, tone, phrasing, and all other musical aspects of a work. If you choose to perform from memory, always practice and drill from memory so there are no surprises on stage!

There are reasons why it is preferable to conduct by memory. Make your choice for each concert based on what will bring forth the best from your choir. However, be prepared to conduct from memory if you expect your singers to sing from memory. You must set the standard and hold yourself

---

If you choose to perform from memory, always practice and drill from memory so there are no surprises on stage!

---

as accountable as you hold your singers. Communication on stage is reciprocal. Eye contact between the conductor and the singers is key to superior artistic creation and meaning. You may still have the music before you, even if you choose not to look at it. Turn the pages, with or without visual reference. Averting a possible train wreck due to the director's access to the score overshadows the benefits of leaving the music in the wings.

Rehearsal activities for memorization

1. As the choir is singing, ask singers to sit in place if they forget a passage of music or text, visually showing who is weak and where. Singers may stand again when they are able.

2. Moving one by one down the row, ask each student to contribute the next word of the text. An error means sitting down. The last person standing wins. (This is tedious, and harder than creating the text in phrases and sentences.)

3. Randomly quiz students on the next section or phrase of text at a place you've stopped.

4. Direct the choir to hum or sing on a monosyllable while one section sings the text. Take turns with different sections demonstrating text mastery. Create competition between your sections. This can run between a number of rehearsals and create positive group spirit.

5. If room permits, begin with all singers standing on the top row of risers. As they sing, they will grade themselves on their own errors. Each time a singer makes an error they will:

   1st error: face backward on the top riser.

   2nd error: face forward on next riser down.

   3rd error: face backward on the same riser.

   4th error: face forward, another riser down.

   This continues until the student is facing backward, standing on the floor level. Thereafter, be creative about where they should go and what they should do. You might have them go behind the risers, face backward, sit, or sit backward. The last person standing closest to their original place on the top riser wins.

6. "Run the gauntlet:" Students stand in two rows, facing one another, with about five feet between them. As they sing, any time they make an error they will step forward (in between the rows), face left and run down the row until the end, then run behind their row until they come back to their original position and stand again where they were. You can also try a variation of this from the risers. If a student makes an error, they step forward, walking down the risers to floor position, turn right and run around behind the risers, until they have made a complete circle. Then they turn toward the risers and walk back up to their assigned place. This can produce mass hysteria and abundant laughter as entire sections are running around the risers. This can be a great change of pace in the middle of a rehearsal or a fun moment from which to be released at the end of class. (One more variation would be to have the choir standing in a circle with "mistake makers" running around the outside of the circle for each error.)

7. While a recording of the song is played, students sing silently, mouthing their part to test their mastery, or give sections a minute or two to drill memorization by chanting the words together. This can become very humorous as well as vigorous when sections compete with one another to "get it" and be heard.

8. In songs with multiple verses that are easily confused, have a key word (and possible hand prompt while conducting to match the word) to remind students of the order of verses. Be careful not to promote dependence on these cues as a memory crutch.

9. Create a "dance" for the music according to the text. (This is incredibly significant for polyphonic pieces from the Renaissance for a host of other reasons!) Create hand motions or limited physical movements for the entire work, and practice singing the piece with the dance. Try "doing the dance" and just mouthing the words. (This works especially well in the hall at contest before taking the stage, to silently reinvigorate the musicality and memorization of a piece.)

10. Creating a "dance" also works particularly well with songs in foreign languages. By matching movement to the meaning of the text, you offer students additional depth of meaning to the words. Examples of matching movement to meaning might be the touch of a finger keeping the beat to the head ("knowing the word of the law"), or the palm tapping over the heart ("I am miserable, there is only pain in me").

11. If you need an additional written grade for a choir, give a written test either by having students provide the text to a particular verse or by giving them a "fill in the blank" test that you have prepared. Assign only a particular song or section of a song so memorization practice can be spread over a period of time.

12. Provide practice recordings for students' use at home.

13. Check the choir's memory of the score by asking them to turn the pages by memory without looking at the music as they sing.

14. If a choir's best efforts still result in spotty memory, have them hold their music (inside uniform folders) and refer to it only during emergencies. Sometimes just holding the printed page releases a singer's fear of forgetting what comes next. Give your students permission to make an error in text in favor of pressing on toward memorization; dwelling on errors will discourage efforts to improve. If one student needs to hold a folder, all students need to hold a folder. Sporadic placement of folders on the risers looks unsatisfac-

tory and tempts singers to look down to other folders, taking the conductor out of their line of sight. If part of a concert can be sung by memory, great! Students may hold their folders at their sides uniformly until needed, opening side upward.

My heart, which is so full to overflowing, has often been solaced and refreshed by music when sick and weary.
—Martin Luther

➤ Contests and Festivals

Something has to go in that trophy case...

Competition can serve a very constructive purpose in the schools in much the same way it does in the marketplace. Well-organized, equitable contests may be used as one measure of how things are going in your choirs. Ideally, they should provide helpful feedback to the choir and its director. This may take the form of rating your choir according to a fixed standard of accomplishment or ranking your choir against other choirs entered in the festival. Don't allow your students to get overly inflated by success or overly defeated by an adjudicator's critique. Directors can use festivals to improve their programs, build spirit, set tangible goals, and provide a great destination to which a choir can travel.

A word of caution, however: Be careful not to spoil the beauty of art by overemphasizing choral competition. The wonderment and heightened communication created by music making can too easily get lost in the shuffle. It is best to focus on the joy of singing and let the assessments be a simple tool and nothing more. To spend a year in a quest for trophies and come away with only some cheap plastic and metal to show for your work is a waste of time. Compare trophies to the potential of developing deeper artistic meaning and integrity through the choral art and your focus will become clear. Let's get ready for that festival, shall we? ("Festival" will be used hereafter, but refers to all festivals, contests, and competitions in which your students might sing.)

Selecting Literature

Selecting literature is the bulk of the work when preparing for a festival. You need exactly the right "frame" for your picture. Don't be tempted to frame your choir with the frame that fit last year's picture, or even the one from last semester. Your choir "picture" is in an ever-present state of change so this step may take a lot of time; plan ahead! Effective literature selection, based on an honest and thoughtful assessment of your choir's strengths and weaknesses is at least sixty percent of the battle. It is better to put the time necessary into choosing the right pieces for a group than trying to fix things that just can't be fixed later on.

Know the festival rules and abide by them. Don't get disqualified or penalized for not following competition directives. Is there a prescribed music list from which you must choose? If so, choose the most fitting selections listed for your choir. If not, choose music that will show off your group's good points and mask its weak areas. If you don't have low basses, don't choose a song that needs a sustained pedal point. Accept this limitation and proceed on to the next piece on the list. Are you considering a piece that is perfect except for that one chord spread from here to eternity, the parts of which you hope to cover with fifteen freshmen? Not the perfect piece for this day, not this time. Even a short moment of agony will stick in the judges' ears. If the ideal song for your choir requires a good twelve

Know the festival rules and abide by them.

weeks to truly master and you have only nine weeks until festival, don't consider it! Would you serve chicken that was "mostly" cooked? Take academic grades and eligibility into consideration for those festivals and contests that use them to govern participation. If the past grading periods suggest that you will lose certain numbers of students, choose music that can be successfully mastered and performed with the reduced personnel. If everyone earns passing grades and can travel to the festival, so much the better for your choir!

Aim for a balanced program, and choose selections that fit within the time limits provided by the festival. Mix fast and slow tempos, historical periods, keys, and homophonic vs. polyphonic so your program does not feature three slow contemporary selections: D major, d minor, D major. Trust us, this can happen without sufficient planning. Try to avoid programming more than one piece by any one composer or arranger in the same group. Consider contrasting styles and languages. In an ideal world, you would open and close with an upbeat dazzler, a slower, more lyrical work in the middle. In the real world, choose your music with this in mind, but place your best number first, the second best number last, and your weakest tune in the middle. Finally, consider the hour of the day at which you will be singing the program. This is particularly true in tenor-bass choirs, if scheduled first thing in the morning.

If a song isn't progressing after a week or two and it has that doggy sound that you know won't ever truly shine brightly, replace it with another piece. Don't waste precious time pushing uphill on a steep incline. Remember that as festival season approaches you will have two opposing forces at work in your choir: vastly improved abilities to learn and master literature along with lessened attention span and focus on "the serious stuff" toward the end of the year. Know your choir and use your best judgment accordingly.

Festival procedures

Learn everything you need to know on behalf of yourself and your choir. Singers' interest may revolve around where the bathrooms are, when they get to eat, how long they have to wear their uniforms, and the names of other choirs that will be singing. The other haunting question for students is "who leads off" in getting on and off the risers, and in which direction. Answer these questions and most of your singers' fears may be relieved. You will also want to become informed about the entire contest and share most, if not all, that you know with your singers. Learn which choir precedes and follows yours. The greatest student fears often hinge on the unknown. Therefore if you inform your choir of the rules, how long they have in the warm-up room, where they can leave their purses, etc. all in advance, they can give their full focus to singing when at the festival.

Learn about the warm-up room, including any time limitations for use, if a piano will be available, and which row leads out in which direction from the warm-up room to file onto the hall's risers correctly. Make sure your students know how they are coming and going during each segment of the festival. Include any warm-up traditions you may have and set the students' minds at ease with your calm and focused resolve.

Be sure to familiarize yourself with the concert venue. In addition to knowing how you will enter and leave the stage, know when, or if, applause will be permitted and who your announcer for the festival will be. Check on the number, style, and placement of risers on stage (especially if it differs from the warm-up room), and what kind and quality of piano will be provided. Arrange for stands for instrumentalists if needed, and ask if the festival will make an audio or video recording of your performance.

Be certain instrumentalists, equipment, and instruments are in place prior to beginning your performance. You may want to spell names or foreign words phonetically on an index card for the announcer in advance. List title, composers or arrangers in performance order as well as the name(s) of the conductors. You'll want to be familiar with the sight-reading room, including all rules and regulations, student sight-reading standing formation (if different from one or multiple concert formations), and which row or side leads in. A lack of scary surprises makes for a good day.

Judges' copies of the music should be clean and free of any student or director's markings. Number all measures individually. New or never marked music is best for judges. Clip the music together in performance order for each judge and place all music for each of your competing choirs into a separate envelope. Each envelope should be marked clearly with your group's name and performance time.

Post-performance, know where you and your choir may go if ratings are posted. You may choose to direct the students to a public posting to learn their scores and results, or you may decide to have them report to a different area so that you may do all the revealing of results yourself in your way. Prepare your students for any ratings they might receive. Be a gracious winner and a good loser. Remind singers that there are no "losers" in choir. They will have heard this from you a thousand times before but a gentle review is usually appropriate. Allow your students to be joyful without being offensive.

Be a gracious winner and a good loser.

Particularly when you've traveled a distance for a particular festival, please build in some time for students to listen to choirs from other parts of the country. They will learn so much by hearing and observing, and appreciate peers from schools and communities different from their own. Before leaving the contest venue, take time to personally thank your judges, contest host, contest chair, and any other festival personnel. It is considered gracious to do this after a festival has concluded.

Festival Checklist:

- Reserve all buses in advance and complete all paperwork as appropriate. Don't forget to get the check processed to give to the driver or mail to the bus company according to the arrangements you have made.

- If a meal or snacks are appropriate, know where you will stop and how to get there. Make sure students have time to plan for the amount of money they will need. If your group will be eating together in one establishment, give the restaurant ample notice to prepare sufficient food and appropriate staffing. Speak with the manager and ask for a discounted price per person in light of the group sales you will provide. (This might be as simple as charging regular price at a pizza buffet, but the beverages are included for free, for example.) Most managers will work with the prices in order to gain your patronage. If your plans involve grabbing a fast food lunch, park your buses in easy walking distance to at least three different restaurants to which they can disperse. An adult should accompany students to each of the establishments. Do not situate your buses in such a way that students have to cross major streets in order to get to all venue options.

- Depending on the time of day and length of time at the festival, you may need to purchase bottles of water for the singers. Water fountains are not all created equal and may not be readily available when a student needs one.

- Learn who the adjudicators are for the festival. Students, directors, and parents like knowing something about the judges such as their professional choral backgrounds and where they are from. This helps frame the constructive comments that will be given orally or in writing from each.

- Know and observe all contest entry and payment deadlines, and secure all medical release and parent permission forms.

- Allocate sufficient time for gathering at the school, traveling, meals/snacks, listening to other choirs, and returning to school, but do not abuse your school's trust by causing students to miss more classes than is absolutely necessary. In the short term, removing students from school may seem tempting for extra rehearsal, warm-ups, or simply to please some of your students. In the long term, you do students a disservice in the make-up work they will face upon return as well as taking advantage of the professional trust accorded you by faculty and administration in your school. Festivals may come and go, but trust and respect as a professional in your building are lasting and significant, worthy of your best efforts as a choral director.

My grandfather once told me that there are two kinds of people;
those who work and those who take the credit.
He told me to try to be in the first group;
there was less competition there.
—Indira Gandhi

➤ Programming Themes and Variations

How to avoid life in the ruts and ditches...

A creative choral director keeps programs infused with life and variety for the singers. There are many ways to vary what you do in class as well as vary the performances you will present in a given year. Typical times when new music may be presented include Fall Concert (early October), Winter Concert (December, preceding winter break), Choir Festival or Contest (late March or April), and Spring Concert (at the end of the school year). These dates are usually pretty firm, self-imposed markers on the calendar to help you pace your work and provide a timeline of performances for your choirs annually. However, the formats those concert use can be varied to keep things interesting, constantly exposing your students to new information and musical experiences. Why not try some of these? (See appendix 3c-3g for sample programs.)

Join forces with your school's band or orchestra for a special concert

Any time you involve more than one discipline, planning needs and potential complications escalate. However, this is a perfect opportunity for an instrumental and choral group to present a short group of stand-alone pieces, culminating in one or more works in which the instrumentalists accompany the choir. While most often done in December, with the school orchestra presenting the string accompaniment to several selections from Handel's *Messiah*, there is no reason a joint concert couldn't be presented at any time of year. This is particularly opportune for advanced groups that may have concert-worthy literature ready while beginning and intermediate choirs are taking more time to learn new works. A joint concert could be as simple as "From Sea to Shining Sea" type pieces. It could also provide performance possibilities such as Orff's *Carmina Burana*, *Song of Democracy* by Howard Hansen, or any number of Vivaldi works.

As you plan a joint concert, consider the musical difficulty of both instrumental and vocal parts. Insure that both groups can master their parts and have a positive musical experience together, and see the benefits of school musicians working together on a common program, learning more about what the other does and developing increased respect for other artistic disciplines. Many band and orchestra parents may never have attended one of your concerts. Similarly, this may be the first time your choir parents may be hearing a performance by your school's band or orchestra. Utilize all publicity tools available to both groups for the best audience and public relations possible. Seek a year in which to do this when both vocal and instrumental students are working at a similar level. The year of the school's dynamo orchestra may well be a rebuilding year of predominantly younger, less skillful students in the choir.

Join forces with another school's choral department for a special concert

In some choral departments it has become a beloved tradition to present a joint concert between two top choirs, neighboring or not. This gives students a chance to meet their peers at other schools and to see another campus's singers as fellow singers, not competitors at a festival or contest. It can breed goodwill between schools that sometimes may only know sporting rivalries

If choirs are reasonably well matched in size and maturity, consider a program of double choir works. This affords singers an opportunity to sing music that might otherwise be difficult to perform within the home school's choir program. There is a host of extraordinary works for multiple choirs and most can be put together with a reasonable amount of rehearsal. You may seek a venue that features opposing choir lofts or balconies to add a spatial component to the concert.

Form partnerships with community orchestras and bands

Your community may have a semi-professional orchestra or band that might benefit from a partnership with an area choir for joint performances. This provides a group of seasoned instrumentalists to accompany the choir while presenting the band or orchestra to a wider audience.

Theme concerts

Concerts built around a topical theme are standard fare in December, when holidays and family traditions are celebrated. This thematic approach to programming can be an interesting way to present any concert, building a central theme around which all texts revolve. This leaves open the opportunity to represent all periods of music history and a variety of styles with an interesting common thread to the performance. There are countless themes that might be used. Here are just a few ideas to get your imagination started.

Love
American history
Patriotic
Around the world
Carols from around the world
Nature/ seasons
Flowers
Songs from Childhood
Water Music (rivers, lakes, sea chanteys)
Geography (songs about your state or region of the country)
Humorous
Songs of the night
The history of music through choral works
Texts from one poet or group/nationality of authors
Celebrating music itself ("In praise of song")

Special guest choirs

Perhaps you might bring variety to your concert season by inviting a guest choir to perform on your program. Program carefully to keep the concert within a desirable length. Guest choirs might include groups representing other schools in your community, such as the middle school or elementary choir. If you invite one school, you need to provide similar invitations to the other choirs in your area to insure that there is no perception of favoritism. Hosting a feeder school on your concert as "special guest performers" spotlights these younger students with a larger audience on the high school stage. Your audience will come from a larger pool of parents and your future recruitment will benefit as these guest singers get older and remember positive experiences with your choral program.

Why not host a guest choir from another state or country? This can result in a reciprocal arrangement in which your choir will house and feed a choir on tour for a period of days, and then at a subsequent time or following year, your choir may travel to stay with their new friend in their home city, state, or country. This requires substantial planning but can be very rewarding, particularly on an international level. Most families are willing to host a foreign student for a few days and most principals are amiable to letting these students "shadow" their adoptive choir member throughout the school day as your singers attend classes. The traveling choir provides its own transportation and can be featured in a stand-alone concert or in conjunction with an existing concert on your school schedule.

Form a faculty/administration choir and include it on one of your concerts. (Careful! This can become a very popular tradition.) You'll be amazed how much talent lurks within your faculty members. Or, form a parent choir! This can become a near instantaneous tradition. The parents love it and their kids love it as well!

The ever-popular Broadway musical

Producing a musical shouldn't be seen as a concert substitute but as a separate performance opportunity for interested students. This type of project is best undertaken by a team of fine arts professionals who agree to plan, sponsor, and rehearse while instructing students in this uniquely American art form. Some schools grant academic credit for the intensive work hours involved in musical production for actors, technicians, pit orchestra, and student directors. If you produce a fine arts musical, the workload is shared and students receive specialized training by experts in their individual disciplines.

Choose a musical that fits your projected performers, not necessarily the musical that one or more directors have recently seen and loved on Broadway. You have got to have a potential Emile DuBecque to choose "South Pacific," a wonderful Jim for "Showboat," and a captivating King in order to perform "The King and I." Think about the number of female and male roles realistically and try to find a musical that mirrors the students who will be auditioning. Some roles can be played regardless of gender, appearance, height, etc. Other roles cannot be so flexible.

Be realistic about how much your directorial team can undertake in addition to their class loads, upcoming festivals and contests, and concerts already on the schedule. Some musicals are easier, require less scenery, and can be costumed more affordably.

Make certain you read the script carefully, cover to cover, to insure that the stage version of the musical is as appealing as its movie adaptation may have been. Be sensitive to community standards and choose only those musicals that can be comfortably attended by children, grandparents, clergy, and the members of a diverse community. A musical might be considered appropriate if potentially offensive language or content can be changed or omitted, but these changes are technically illegal by most rental agreements. When in doubt, make wholesome choices. Never perform any musical or part thereof without a legal contract for which you will pay royalties. (For more information, see copyright law, chapter five.)

Announce the title of the musical selected for production only after it has been approved by your administration and both parties have signed the contract. It should be noted that a contract could be rescinded if a national touring company is formed and scheduled to perform within a given radius of miles and dates. (There is nothing you can do to either prevent or change this in the unlikely event this occurs after your school has committed to a particular musical.) Musicals can be expensive to produce. (Very expensive!) Make sure the fine arts department has a plan for funding all costs.

Our minds are like our stomachs; they are whetted by the change of their food, and variety supplies both with fresh appetites.
—Quintilian

➤ Enrichment Opportunities for Students

A rolling student gathers no moss...

In every choral program there will be students who want to go above and beyond basic course requirements. These students will devote their time and energy to a variety of opportunities designed to develop their talents to a greater degree. You are encouraged to offer appropriate curriculum enrichment for those students whose talent, interest, and time should be encouraged in an enhanced or accelerated fashion. It is said that the whole is greater than the sum of the parts. We submit that the whole of your choir will benefit appreciably by your nurturing and motivating your students to participate in as many individual and small group projects and competitions as possible. As each individual singer develops vocally, musically, and personally, your choir becomes all the richer.

Solo and ensemble contest participation

Solo and ensemble contest provides individual singers the opportunity to develop vocal technique while exploring literature for solo voice. It encourages poise, self-discipline, memorization, and responsibility. It may cost you a free Saturday and a chunk of additional work, but it benefits your students as performers. This will, in turn, have a significant impact on your choir. Remember this when the chips are down and you are tired.

To prepare for solo and ensemble participation, become familiar with any applicable prescribed music list of vocal solos or ensembles appropriate for

As each individual singer develops vocally, musically, and personally, your choir becomes all the richer.

each individual student. Consider vocal range, maturity, music learning ability and experience when choosing literature for individual singers.

If private voice teachers are involved in preparing students for solo and ensemble contest, be sure they know all rules, procedures, and limitations on who may perform from which tier or list of solos (if any). Remember that you are the choral director and have the final responsibility for the entry and preparation of your students. Voice teachers are there to help your students, but when the results of the day are posted for all to see, they are a reflection on the school, director, and students.

Know and observe all entry deadlines, completing all forms and paper-work neatly with correct fees attached. Plan for acquiring a school or district check in payment for fees well in advance of the deadline. If you have special needs for scheduling considerations based on the number of accompanists involved, student conflicts, or other constraints, explain them briefly and clearly in a note attached to your original entry. Many contest hosts will schedule a competition with an eye toward honoring special needs and requests if they are known well in advance. It is considered unprofessional and inappropriate to ask for special considerations once the contest schedule has been made, except for emergency. Plan ahead and communicate this to your students and their parents.

If the contest your students have entered sends blocks of time to each school for which you will schedule individual solos and ensembles, schedule individual entrants with an eye toward honoring student scheduling conflicts and assigning no more than one soloist singing a particular song within a block of entries for a particular judge. If you should have any duplication of literature, assign two students singing the same solo to two different adjudicators. Avoid scheduling younger, less experienced voices directly following the more mature voices in your choir. Students who sing a solo and participate in an ensemble should be scheduled far enough apart to give sufficient time to go from one event to the next without panic. By the same token, if a singer's solo were first thing in the morning, you would not want to schedule their ensemble entry for the last entry of the day. Appendix 3h and 3i include sample solo and ensemble schedules.

Prior to the contest day arrange transportation to and from the contest site. Arrange and schedule accompanists. If you are an accompanist yourself, make certain you do not try to play for more students than you can manage, both musically and schedule-wise. Please make sure that you have sufficient accompanists to serve all singers. Even the finest musician cannot be in two places at one time. Relying on a handful of pianists for a large number of solos can result in a contest running woefully off schedule, making it even harder for accompanists to move from room to room. Ideally, an accompanist should be scheduled for a group of five to eight soloists with one particular judge before moving to a different room and group of soloists. This keeps the contest moving more smoothly and your accompanists from running themselves ragged unnecessarily.

Confirm that each student has rehearsed at least twice with the accompanist, and make a point to hear each soloist or ensemble personally at least once. Instruct students in how to stand and how to hold their hands while performing, and where to stand in relationship to the judge and piano. Meet again with any entry that still needs improvement. Use professional judgment in advising a student whether the degree to which he or she has mastered their song is appropriate for a particular event. Contest is designed to be a positive learning tool for students, not to crush students' spirits. You may want to gently guide some students to wait for a future contest to sing their solo, as appropriate. Be sensitive to your students' feelings when discussing this.

If class time permits, ask singers to perform their solos and ensembles for the choir. Choose a student to serve as "judge" for each one, and include asking questions the student should be prepared to answer. Judges commonly ask a few questions of each student upon entering their room to sing. Students should be ready to state their name, grade, school, name of director, and title of the song they are performing. They should also know the historical background of their piece, its meaning or message (particularly if it is in a foreign language), and the composer's name and short biographical facts. Different students will enjoy acting out the part of the judge, some gruff and others friendly, which prepares the soloist for the unknown at contest. This reaps great benefits for the competitors in practicing "battle conditions" of singing under pressure (in front of the class) and having to look a judge in the eye while performing. The class also benefits by hearing vocal literature from various historical periods and composers. Some classes might be able to write positively worded "critique sheets" for the singers as they perform, reinforcing their listening and evaluative skills in basic vocal areas. (These critiques could also serve as a daily grade for the choir.)

Consider scheduling a recital about a week ahead of the contest so students can sing for their parents and friends. This gives them an additional opportunity to deal with stage fright and the chance to sing their song for more than one occasion. It also gives them a date for which to be ready and polished in advance of the actual competition.

If a singer is suffering from stage fright, practice "playing contest" additional times with them, whether it be singing for the night janitor or a passing faculty member or maybe one of the band students until they have left their fears at the choir room door. Singers perform best when they have developed this measure of confidence before others. This also gives faculty, staff, and administration a chance to see your good work in action and allow students to show others what they are learning.

On concert day, if room monitors are used to negotiate traffic in and out of judging rooms, give each a copy of your students' names in contest order organized by judge's room. Monitors can check off names and know that they all come from the same school. Make sure to note any DNA (did not arrive) cancellations due to illness, emergencies, or lack of preparedness, so the contest will not wait for a student who will not be appearing. A DNA list should be supplied to the contest office as well as the door monitors.

The singer should enter the room with an original copy of his song for the judge to use, all measures neatly numbered. If the song appears in a collection, place a paperclip or bookmark in the appropriate page so the judge can easily turn to the correct solo. Judges' rating sheets can also be used as bookmarks. Ideally, it is nice to have enough copies of music that students singing from the same volume in different rooms have enough original judges' copies to go around!

Singers should wait until the judge speaks to them before speaking or singing. Often a judge is still writing comments about the preceding student when the next singer enters the room. If this is the case, the student should wait to approach the judge until acknowledged. It is always gracious for the singer to greet the judge and smile. Singing is supposed to be a positive endeavor, not an act of suffering. In most contests, music must be committed to memory by the singer. Ideally, students should be singing by memory at least a week prior to the contest. One successful rendering does not a sure thing make.

While dress is rarely specified for a solo and ensemble contest, it is highly recommended that students dress as though singing for a contest is an important event because it is! Whether your students wear their choir

---

*Singing is supposed to be a positive endeavor,
not an act of suffering.*

---

uniforms, nice dresses and suits, neatly pressed dress shirts and ties, or skirts and blouses, they should "dress up" for contest. Students should always present themselves in the most favorable light. This invaluable experience will reap substantial benefits when it is time for job interviews, presentations, and giving speeches.

The singer should look or nod at the accompanist to signal readiness to begin. Even if the choral director is the accompanist, the role of student and teacher changes to soloist and accompanist in the judge's room. Students should be prepared to assume this role appropriately and understand the responsibility to take control. Students should sing to the judge, maintaining eye contact with the judge as the audience. This should be practiced with a "pretend judge" before contest day because this is a learned behavior that improves with practice. If looking directly at the judge unnerves a student, ask them to try looking directly above the judge's head for a more comfortable focal point. At the end of the song the student should remain in place until the judge indicates otherwise. Some adjudicators will want to speak to the students, while others will exclusively write their comments. It

---

Consider putting interested students into trios, quartets, or madrigals as appropriate.

---

is your job to tell students to be prepared to accept whatever mode of critique the judge utilizes. Students should be prepared to re-sing any portion (or all) of their song if asked, demonstrating any changes or improvements the judge may have suggested.

Remind your students that when a judge looks up at the end of the song and says, "thank you," it means, "You're done... goodbye." This response to a song is rarely an indication of anything negative about the performance or the personality of the judge. It is usually a reflection of a tight schedule. At that point the student should smile and say "thank you" and quietly leave the room. Courtesy and poise under pressure are useful life skills to learn. Judges commonly continue to write as a singer leaves the room and usually need to retain the music to refer to finish writing comments. For this reason students should not wait for their music after singing. A monitor will periodically retrieve rating sheets and music. Make sure both the name of the student and school are written on the cover of the music so it can be correctly filed.

If this is a contest at which directors "check out" at the end of their performer's scheduled day, do so in a timely manner. Thank all monitors and hosts for their work, as theirs is often a tedious and thankless job. If possible, send a follow-up thank you note to the host school's choral department and ask your singers to sign it. When it is your turn to host an event, you will appreciate these small tokens of thanks. After the contest, include student names and awards in your choir publicity venues as appropriate. Offer special commendations for unique achievements or awards. Return all student-owned music to the appropriate singers.

Ensemble singing is a tremendous enrichment for choir members. Consider putting interested students into trios, quartets, or madrigals as appropriate. Some directors allow students to form their own groups, but this has the potential to put vastly dissimilar voices together. Friends may sound great when mixed in a large group but not as good when singing one or two on a part, when the size of voice and keenness of tuning become more noticeable. For these reasons, you are in the best position to place students in the most effective groupings according to voice, appropriate level of musicianship, and skills needed to successfully compete in a small group.

You will need to teach students how to stand in a semicircular formation in order to perform without a conductor. Tell them how to position themselves in relationship to the piano (for pitches) and the judge. Provide practice opportunities to enter the choir room and sing for you, changing where you are sitting each time so they learn to adapt to different room arrangements. Each ensemble will need a student spokesperson to announce the title of the piece and composer. A different student in each group should be prepared to give the starting pitches at the piano. (There are some laughable anecdotes about problems doing this under pressure. Please have students practice playing the correct pitches in the appropriate octave.) A third student should be responsible for being able to explain the meaning or message of the song. Dividing up the tasks in this way shares the leadership. Student attire should be "Sunday best" clothes unless the choir uniform is worn. Avoid shorts, jeans, t-shirts, sweatshirts, tennis shoes or sandals. Dress for success, not for school or a ball game.

The All-Region, All-District, and All-State Audition process

Just as solo and ensemble contest benefits your choral program by improving its individual members, so does student participation in the All-Region, All-District, All-State Choir process contribute directly to building your program in size and quality.

Acquire the list of music to be auditioned for the coming year as soon as it is released and distribute it to your choir. This gives them the opportunity to purchase the packet of audition music and get a head start. Distribute any rehearsal and historical notes from your regional, district, or state organizations so your singers may mark their music accordingly. If a half note is to be changed to a quarter note followed by a quarter rest in measure seventeen, it is best that your singers know that and mark it accordingly from the very start. Set deadlines for students regarding memorization if it is required. Find out the locations and costs for summer camps that will help students prepare for auditions.

To help students take this responsibility seriously, establish policies and procedures for attending rehearsals and coaching sessions. Post open coaching slots on your door starting with the earliest time after school, directing your students to sign up for coaching in pencil, not pen, on a first come, first served basis. Request that students needing to cancel erase their names at least twenty-four hours prior to a scheduled coaching session with you so another singer may take the time slot. An alternative is to ask students to be responsible for contacting the last student on your posted list for the day to fill their empty time slot so you do not have to sit around and wait needlessly. Make this easy for yourself as well as your students. Students with a regular schedule of football, band, or play practices directly after school will need to know alternatives for coaching times. Decide how many times per week you will allow the same student to sing for you. Remember that a student needs time in between coaching sessions to practice and correct errors before singing for you again. There is no point to singing the same mistakes, thus wasting coaching time while reinforcing the errors themselves.

Hold ample sectional rehearsals to help your students prepare their individual voice parts. Working in sectionals rather than individual sessions is the best use of your time. Be wary of substituting individual sessions for those unwilling to attend group sessions. In addition to working on the literature, provide opportunities to drill competitive individual sight-reading skills. This is very different from choir sight-reading in a group and can rattle many students in the process. Help students develop their skills and poise under pressure by practicing competitive sight-reading regularly.

Maintain a schedule of goal masteries throughout the preparation process so students do not procrastinate in their preparation. Listen to all music to be auditioned, perhaps on a rotational system, rather than the songs the student prefers to sing or performs better. Zero in on weaknesses and strengthen them! Set goals for your students in each coaching session, such as, "Next time I hear this song, I don't want to hear any of the same mistakes. You may make new mistakes, though I hope not, but make sure you completely eradicate these errors or weaknesses before our next session together. Our goal is by the time you get to audition week, I will have to work hard to find any imperfections in how I would want to hear this song performed if I were your judge. Make me work hard and struggle to find a mistake or anything unpolished."

Simulate battle conditions several times prior to audition day. This can take the form of a mock audition at your school, using volunteer monitors, or setting up a room as it will be per contest procedures. Singers should become familiar with singing behind a screen, using a music stand versus holding their music (if they so choose), and singing their best under pressure. The fewest surprises or new variables present on audition day for a singer, the better. Rehearse every part of the audition as closely to the real procedure students will encounter as possible. You might consider having a neighboring school join you for mock auditions so each director can be a "fresh set of ears" for the other school.

In much the same way you prepare for solo and ensemble contests you will need to fill out all contest forms in a neat and timely manner, and attach any scheduling conflicts to the original entry. Know your region, district, and state rules like the back of your hand! Make sure your students know all rules that apply to them, including costs involved and the schedule of the day including the total time of involvement. Make certain you and your students understand the audition process, the announcing/posting procedure, how many are auditioning in their section, and how many will advance to the next round of competition. Plan for appropriate transportation, and meals and snacks.

Establishing and maintaining a private voice lesson component to your choral department

When considering a private voice lesson program in your choral department, assess student and parent interest in providing voice instructors through your school. Proceed by posting openings for voice teachers on appropriate web sites, college school of music bulletin boards, etc., and ask colleagues which teachers they use on their own campuses.

Interview and select teachers for this position carefully, in the same way you would for an associate or assistant director. (See chapter five for more on interviews.) Bad voice lessons are worse for your students than no voice lessons at all. Check references and credentials carefully. Remember that any potential difficulties will become your problem. The buck stops with you for everything relating to your choral program. Therefore, it is in your best interest (as well as that of the students) to insure that all voice teachers maintain a professional relationship with students. Professional distance, dress, and deportment are critical when these instructors work with students. They must be able to collect and receipt cash and checks in an effective manner, because if they cannot do their own bookkeeping, it will become your bookkeeping. Avoid becoming involved with the financial dealings associated with voice lessons. Other than informing your teachers about all district guidelines, fee limitations, and deadlines, you would be wise to let all matters about fees rest with the parent, student, and instructor. Unfortunately, if things go awry, you are the final authority in your choral department, so organize your voice lesson program with great care to be self-maintaining without bloodshed. You have plenty of other important matters to worry about!

Have all candidates sing for you as part of their audition. If they don't have a pleasing voice, their students are unlikely to develop one either. Personality and ability to relate well to young people does matter. Voice teachers must be able to positively interact with students, parents, any district personnel involved in the process, and you. Be certain to check with your school district regarding any forms, background checks, fees, and medical requirements that might apply to these individuals. It is common in most districts to require a criminal background check and a TB test before working with your students. Let applicants for this position know that this is common procedure for all adults (including parent volunteers) in our schools these days. Can a prospective teacher serve as accompanist for their students? If not, you will also need to hire a bevy of accompanists for recitals and competitions. Be aware of this potential additional expense.

Secure a location in which a piano, mirror, and a cabinet or file can be placed to serve as a voice studio. It is ideal if this room can be locked when it is not in use so teachers can leave materials there between lessons. Be sure that this area will have working air-conditioning and heat as appropriate. When first establishing your program, assist voice teachers with scheduling students for lessons. Be clear that students cannot miss classes in order to attend voice lessons and that hall passes may not be written by the instructor for running over schedule. Provide all necessary information on fire drill procedures, bell schedules, and school calendar, including days with non-traditional scheduling, early release, and holidays. Establish clear boundaries about the use of school phones, copy machines, and teachers' lounges, and arrange for parking on campus in the faculty/staff lot.

To interest students in studying with an instructor, you may want to ask the instructor to sing a mini-concert of three songs in addition to speaking briefly about their background and goals as a teacher. This gives your choir a good overall impression and helps you match students with particular teachers. When possible, have a male voice instructor work with male students and female instructors teach female students.

Include your voice instructors in choral department communications on a regular basis to make them feel a part of the staff. Strive to maintain a positive relationship with your voice teachers, providing a comfortable atmosphere to work in. Happy voice teachers feel more a part of the organization and give of themselves more freely. Invite them to participate in choir activities such as chaperoning trips, attending banquets, and dropping in for choir parties. Place their names on your list of holiday card recipients, also celebrating their birthdays or other personal occasions.

If your choir as a whole is having a particular vocal problem, consider hiring your voice teacher to teach a vocal master class with the choir or a particular section. You might invite your voice teachers to periodically lead the choir's warm-ups, if they are willing. This increases their visibility and inclusion in the choir program if it is not perceived as extra work or unpaid duties.

Investigate the possibility of funding vocal study scholarships for deserving students whose ability to pay is limited. (Free lunch program lists for the school can be consulted in determining where financial need is the greatest in your program.) The booster club is an ideal group to work with when funding such partial or full voice scholarships. Some districts have a policy in place that requires you to provide free lessons for any students unable to pay for them if lessons are offered through the district on school campuses. Be aware that this can have huge financial implications depending on your choirs' demographics and the size of your program.

Keep in mind that voice instructors may be working only part time for your program, and may have other positions teaching or performing in your community. Be considerate of this when dealing with schedules and asking for extra time.

Choir camps and workshops

For students with a few free days in the summer, camp can be a wonderful way to get started on All-District, All-Region, and All-State music before the rigors of the school year begin. This is especially true for multi-talented students whose time outside school is spread between more than one activity; AP classes and the projects they require, and various sport teams that practice during nearly all hours you might schedule sectional rehearsals. While camp is not a substitute for your work with students, it can give students a tremendous head start on the year's competitions. While others are beginning to learn correct rhythms, pitches, and how to pronounce medieval Russian, your students will come back to school energized and ready to check the accuracy of their work over the summer.

There are countless summer camps that provide vocal, choral, and musical opportunities for your student's growth during the summer months. Style-specific offerings include a number of show or swing choir camps throughout the country that feature classes on vocals, use of the microphone, choreography, stage presence, and auditioning. Barbershop music "harmony camps" have sprung up nationally to encourage young men to fine-tune their vocal skills while learning this exciting style of choral music. Seek recommendations for outstanding summer opportunities and share this information with your students and their parents!

Encourage your students to attend a camp that is well organized and supervised, taught by the most knowledgeable and experienced directors possible, with emphasis on sectional rehearsals and competitive sight-reading. It should be affordable, and geographically desirable for parent transportation. Speak with your booster club to see if it might sponsor several full or partial scholarships to summer choir camp for worthy students in your program who need assistance to attend.

If a group of students choose to attend a particular camp together, assist in arranging parent-driven carpools to and from camp. Consider attending camp yourself as a sponsor. This is a wonderful opportunity to learn the music yourself while enjoying the fun and frolic of "camping" with your choral colleagues. Good times are had and strong friendships are formed, both for students and their teachers.

> *Take chances, make mistakes. That's how you grow.*
> *Pain nourishes your courage.*
> *You have to fail in order to practice being brave.*
> —Mary Tyler Moore

➤ The Blessing of Added Extras

Adding sugar and spice and everything nice...

If variety is the spice of life, it can also be the key to a vibrant choral program. By planning carefully over a multi-year period, you can choose different "spices" to enhance the curriculum, goals, and activities within each school year. This gives students something new and different to look forward to and can serve you well in fund-raising, public relations, and publicity. Just as a cup of cinnamon would overwhelm a batch of cookies, so you will want to measure out these flavor-enhancers for your choirs so your choir's schedule (and yours) does not overtake you in any given year.

Madrigal dinners

What an opportunity to prepare a cross-disciplinary performance opportunity learning about the Renaissance through musical performance, costuming, scripted narration or dialogue, all while throwing a grand party and meal for choir patrons to enjoy! Madrigal dinners can be simple, or develop into a detailed and complex spectacle according to your preferences, preparation time, and interest. It can serve as an excellent fund-raiser for your program and a wonderful learning tool. An army of students can be assigned to serve as period characters, jousters, court jesters, jugglers, madrigal singers, lute players, and you might even let one of your more confident "hams" be the village idiot. Whether you choose to develop period costumes over several years or try it out on a smaller scale, madrigal dinners allow students the opportunity to learn about one of the most significant periods of world history. You will likely find eager support and allies from your colleagues in the history and English departments, and perhaps your principal or Dean of Instruction would be willing to serve as the King or Queen of the Kingdom for the evening. Your drama director may want to involve several theater students working on period accents as coaches for your choir students, or participate as performers themselves. The possibilities are endless. In addition to creating your own, you may want to save time by purchasing pre-packaged scripts for madrigal dinners. These usually include a sample menu, costuming tips, a script, and suggestions for everything from musical literature to how to greet patrons at the door.

Dinner shows

This is a simple premise that can also double as a fund-raiser by providing a meal and entertainment for audience members. Tickets can be sold in advance or at the door, though a careful eye toward advance sales can help you estimate the amount of food you need to prepare for the evening. Keep the menu economical and simple to prepare so ticket prices can be affordable and still generate a profit for your department. You might choose a number of menu themes from Italian to fancy desserts to La Fiesta. See appendix 3j for sample dinner menus. If possible, arrange to donate any leftover food to the local community soup kitchen or shelter. This can be a valuable lesson in using resources wisely, and promotes community service.

Your school may require you to use one or more cafeteria workers or involve the school dietician in order to give you access the kitchen. This is for your protection as much as theirs. Build any additional cost for this into your budget. Student help in set-up and clean up is essential. Tables can be inexpensively covered with borrowed tablecloths or rolls of butcher paper. A candle or simple table centerpiece can add to the ambiance at dinner. Strategically place garbage cans for use by patrons to encourage bussing their own tables.

Entertainment for the evening can be a formal presentation by choirs, small groups, soloists, or a mixture of soloists and smaller ensembles. This is a perfect opportunity for solo and ensemble contest singers to perform publicly. Plan for lighting and sound equipment as needed for the evening. Consider providing platforms for a portable stage so diners can see performers more easily.

Coffee houses

This is a simple way to provide an evening of entertainment as well as a dessert and beverage to your supporters and the public. Serve donated and homemade desserts and an assortment of specialty coffees, teas, and soft drinks to patrons while presenting non-stop student entertainment.

Faculty/Staff/Administration choirs

You cannot begin to imagine how much musical talent resides within the walls of your building until you put out the word that you're forming a faculty choir to learn a few pieces for an upcoming concert. If you can decide on a rehearsal schedule that is sufficient to bring a few easy numbers to mastery by the concert date and timed so that interested colleagues may attend, this can be more fun than a barrel of… science teachers! Select literature that focuses on unison and two-part singing until you know if you've got a powerhouse group of ex-choristers in your ranks. Let the music be light with perhaps one novelty number for maximum audience response. Many directors have tried this out using "Kids" from Bye, Bye Birdie. This tune affords a number of one-line solos sung or spoken, and showcases personalities that may have been long hiding under academic cloaks for years. Open this door for your audience but be careful, you may create an instant tradition!

Alumni choirs

Alumni treasure the opportunity to return home to sing together in their former school choir. Depending on the length of your tenure in a particular school and community, the choir may be multigenerational. It will surely be a combination of college students and working adults, so your best scheduling for an alumni choir will likely be at the end of a semester, in December

Alumni treasure the opportunity to return to sing together in their former school choir.

or May. Diverse geography of singers will necessitate two (or three, maximum) rehearsals of music suited to short preparation time by singers who may be professional musicians or rusty choristers from years gone by. If you have featured a treasured song every couple of years, consider including that title on the program. Your current students will benefit from seeing and hearing your alumni come back to perform in countless ways. If possible, have the alumni choir join your current choir on stage for a final number, perhaps your traditional closing number, if you have one. This is a very meaningful homecoming for choir members, past and present.

Parent choirs

Ever wondered where some of your students' flare for drama started out? Want to know the source of Yolanda's vibrato or Jordan's propensity for talking on the risers? Meet the parents! Forming a parent choir for a special number or two on the spring concert can be a ticket to hilarity and a major dose of fun for you! Send home a flyer and e-mail, inviting moms and dads to be a part of the concert. Establish at least four rehearsals to prepare this grown-up version of your students. You will discover a wealth of talent and enthusiasm and will likely have formed a tight army of ardent supporters of your program by the time the concert rolls around.

So many of our dreams at first seem impossible,
then they become improbable, and then,
when we summon the will, they soon become inevitable.
—Christopher Reeve

► Identifying Prospective Audiences

Don't hide. We seek!

Any number of groups would enjoy a performance by one of your choirs. You may have some choirs that do not have the same opportunities to present short concerts as your more advanced singers. With a little publicity, you can effectively develop a list of potential audiences in your area and match them to the groups you have in any given year, providing them with a variety of short concert opportunities.

In developing a group of audiences for whom you may schedule concerts, consider sending out a letter of introduction on behalf of your program. Many community program directors do not know that the local school has a group (or groups) that will perform free at their venue. Be prepared for the phone to ring off the hook after your letters arrive. If a venue has an appreciative audience in close proximity to your school, it may be possible for you to take a group there each semester, always changing the literature performed if not the group itself. These are perfect opportunities for younger and less experienced singers to know the joy of performance! In some cases, you may also find audiences that are best suited for your more advanced singers. Once you have sent your letter announcing your group's availability, wait for audiences to contact you. It may look awkward (or desperate) if you call them to follow-up. If groups are seeking high quality entertainment, they should contact you.

Residential facilities for senior citizens are consistently welcoming to student performing groups. Residents are too often confined to a building filled with other older people and welcome the arrival of younger people for a visit. Contact the Activities Director to schedule a concert at residential senior facilities. Smaller choirs and ensembles can be accommodated more easily here, and other performers do not visit many of these audiences routinely. Prepare a fifteen to twenty minute performance stressing up-tempo numbers. Include popular songs during the generations represented by residents when possible.

Before the concert have an informal talk with your performers about aging and the place music (and music therapy) can have in providing a positive environment for residents. Explain that some audience members will be able to clap but others may not. The lack of applause does not mean that a song was not appreciated, but more often is because physical or mental faculties are compromised in some way. Students will learn to find satisfaction in a toe that taps or lips that form the words to a text being sung.

Remind students to walk against walls, not blocking doorways, so residents may move easily in and out of their rooms. Students also must be quiet at all times out of respect for residents who may be ill or sleeping.

Many children's hospitals have careful regulations governing visiting groups, but most are grateful for small groups singing in their lobby or presenting short, child-centered music for patients and their families. Often you will not have a piano available and should consider singing *a capella* or using pre-recorded accompaniment. If you do use pre-recorded accompaniment, make sure to practice with the recording! Students accustomed to live backup can become easily confused when using a recording. Contact the Director of Volunteers, or Special Events Coordinator to schedule a performance at a Children's Hospital. Remind students that young children look up to "big kids" as heroes. Singers should be prepared to provide a welcoming smile and friendly spirit to all children for whom they sing. It can be difficult for young people to see critically ill children in the hospital. Maintain a policy of allowing any singer to excuse himself for a moment if there is something or someone making him uncomfortable.

Local elementary schools

Younger students enjoy up-tempo, fun performances by your "big kids." Involve them in a pass-the-microphone song or have a show choir go out into the audience and dance with willing students. This is a recipe for exciting young students about choir at an early age! To schedule an elementary school visit, contact the principal's secretary, PTA president, or school music teacher.

Ronald McDonald House

This venue can easily become one of your students' favorites. Here they will have the opportunity to sing for the families of seriously ill children in local hospitals. (Sometimes outpatient children will be housed at the Ronald McDonald House as well as their siblings.) Contact the Program Director or Director of Volunteers and prepare a fifteen to twenty-minute up-tempo program geared for children and their parents to enjoy.

You will want to consider that at any given time, the house could be filled to capacity or have only a few people present. Students should know in advance that the number of audience members could likely be smaller than the number of performers. Help your singers see the value in bringing musical entertainment to a group of any size. Be silent in the halls. Bedrooms are interspersed throughout the facility and there may be someone who just returned from a hospital visit who is trying to sleep.

Discuss the special stresses a critically ill child may present a family. Let students talk about how a musical program might lessen that stress for a few minutes.

Clubs and organizations

Look for opportunities to present your groups before audiences of businessmen, community leaders, and other groups that may be looking for an eight to ten minute opening for their meeting. It is always good to have a few patriotic numbers handy for these groups. Contact the president of groups that might include the Kiwanis Club, Rotary Club, Lions Club, Elks Club, Chamber of Commerce, VFW, PTA, and your School Board.

What we have once enjoyed we can never lose...
all that we love dearly becomes a part of us.
—Helen Keller

4

After All, They **Do** Call You a Teacher

> ➤ Grading Policies

> ➤ Paperwork

> ➤ Teaching Sight-Reading and Musical Literacy

➤ Grading Policies

How much do you weigh...?

In an ideal world, there would be no need for a grading policy in your classes. Students would flock to your room for the sheer exhilaration of learning, singing together in joy and harmony. Your job would be to share musical wisdom to your highly motivated choristers, satisfied that each rehearsal was a meaningful musical celebration of life.

Alas, we do not live in the perfect world and are charged with the duty of regularly assessing student learning and progress in a fair and concrete way. These assessments are important to students, parents, and school districts, and assigning grades cannot be capricious or mysterious. We need to construct a grading policy that rewards hard work, unbridled enthusiasm, leadership, attendance, and positive participation in concerts and competitions. How do we grade a student in a meaningful, uniform way that is educationally sound, rewarding the behaviors we most keenly value?

In days long gone, a general grade might be given based on participation. Today's schools will not (and should not) tolerate subjective or fanciful grading. Grades are as important in your music class as they are in any other subject. Arbitrary assignment of grades is an invitation to disaster the first time a parent asks why her son or daughter "got" a seventy-five in your class. Your administrators cannot support approximation in grading. Toward this end, begin by knowing your district policies and school guidelines. Hold yourself accountable to an appropriate, challenging grading scheme that has been made known to the students at the beginning of the year. Inclusion of your grading policy in your choir handbook puts your expectations in writing for all to see. Be aligned with your school's requirements so the principal or superintendent can support you if your grades are ever questioned.

Many districts use percentages in constructing grading policies, with a portion of the grade for summative work (exams, major projects), and formative work (class participation, daily grades). While we don't want to turn a participation class into a prison of bookwork, we must find ways to assign points and percentages to reward the positive behaviors and learning that makes a great choir. A good place to start in formulating your grading philosophy is this: "If a student is trying, he or she won't fail." Hard working students doing everything in their power to contribute their best will receive grades that reflect their effort.

Giving away automatic "100s" in choir undermines your credibility as a professional. If a student is physically present in your room, do they automatically receive participation or daily grades of 100? If not, how do you assess what was, or was not, done to substantiate a lesser daily grade? Should a student be able to pass choir without singing in concerts and contests? Is coming to class enough? Most directors structure their grading scale so that a passing grade can only be achieved by including contest and concert performance grades. Strive to find ways for students to have their own materials such as folders, music, sight-reading books, and music textbooks from which you can make and grade assignments.

Options for test (summative) grades
- Concert performances (grade based on demonstration of mastery through attendance and positive participation; can be extended or enriched by having follow-up activities such as listening to a recording or viewing a video of the concert for student critique)
- Contest participation
- Sight-reading tests
- Pop quizzes
- Theory tests and quizzes

Options for daily (formative) grades
- Folder checks, announced or unannounced (checking to make sure name is on cover, markings are penciled in music per director, sight-reading book and pencil inside, and measures numbered.)
- Random daily assessment using a checklist that includes things like good singing posture, correct vowel formation, breathing, etc.
- Having appropriate materials on the riser (pencil, music, folder, sight-reading material)
- Asking individuals for feedback: How was the blend that time? Were the altos balancing or still singing too loud? Look at the sopranos this time and tell me if you saw any poor vowels in this section. How could that have sounded better?

When a student or parent wants to discuss a grade with you, be open and positive. Always meet privately and have all documentation organized so you can speak to specific grades, strengths, and weaknesses that formed the basis for the number or letter on a report card. Remember that privacy laws protect grades. Do not compare grades with other students or speak about other students' grades beyond the student or parent at hand. If you've made an honest error, admit it and adjust the grade accordingly. Do not hesitate to admit a mistake, as we all make them at some point. By the same token, if the grade is correct and fair, hold fast and do not cave in to outside pressure. Documentation is important. If counselors or school administrators are included in a grading dispute, your careful documentation of curriculum mastery kept in written or in computer form cannot be overstressed. Never say, write, or do anything that might have negative consequences if taken to your administration, a lawyer, or the PTA. Be transparent in your honesty, motives, and fairness. Realize that if you make any type of exception or adjustment for one student, you must be prepared to do so for all students in a similar way.

Make-up work

While it is impossible to replicate a rehearsal or concert, students need a way of recapturing points or grades for an excused absence. These assignments must be meaningful and contribute to choral understanding and education. An excellent assignment for missing a daily rehearsal is found in appendix 4a. Assignments such as these can be included in your choir handbook and be self-sustaining if organized and explained to each class carefully. In this example students drill and demonstrate sight-reading skills in a way that can be done when not in class. Make-up assignments derived from state adopted music textbooks also have excellent chapters (and chapter questions) that can enhance student learning. Research on the composers and historical styles represented on a student's concert, along with an oral presentation is yet another potential make-up assignment.

Extra Credit

It is a useful to develop a system for rewarding extra work. Toward this end, offering extra credit can be a very useful component of your grading policy. Opportunities for extra credit might include concert attendance (band and orchestra concerts at your school, choral concerts at other schools, local symphony or professional performances), volunteering at district, region, or state auditions, solo and ensemble or choral competi-

---

Don't get bogged down in a flurry of paperwork.

---

tions, working on equipment crew, singing the "Star-Spangled Banner" at a school function or athletic competition, or singing with the choir at graduation exercises. It is important to remember that choir is a participation class, and necessarily, grades will be assessed differently in this class than in others. Don't get bogged down in a flurry of paperwork. Excellent rehearsals will produce excellent choral work; give ample thought to items that will work together to reward those things you know will mean the most.

Honors coursework

The topic of grades has an additional meaning to students who are striving for superior grade point averages and places at the top of their graduation class. Because of weighted honors class points, a "regular" class, like choir and many other elective classes, will render fewer grade points than an honors class, thus impacting a student's rank. You may consider the needs of these top academic students (and your desire to retain them in your choirs) by developing a plan for an accelerated curriculum as an optional part of your advanced choir. After securing permission through your school principal, you can offer Honors Advanced Choir to those who want to do the extra work that will lead to these coveted extra grade points. The students to whom this might apply are a valued part of any group. By developing a rigorous advanced placement program, you include an important segment of the student body. Appendix 4b includes a sample list of Honors Advanced Choir coursework requirements.

Music is a discipline, and a mistress of order and
good manners, she makes the people milder and gentler,
more moral and more responsible.
—Martin Luther

➤ Paperwork

*Things to do with paper besides wadding it up
and shooting hoops...*

Concert programs

Whenever possible, upgrade the quality of paper used for programs and vary the colors in keeping with concert themes or seasons. Be creative (but legible) with fonts. Some fonts are too "busy" to be clearly read by all patrons. Similarly, consider the size of fonts used, particularly in a darkened hall. Let the formality and style of the program correlate with the concert itself. Be wary of overusing cutesy clip art and graphics for more formal events.

When space allows, include current information such as recent awards, upcoming calendar of choir events, and lists of choir officers and choir members. Remember that everyone likes to see his or her name in print on a program! Pass around a rough draft of student names as they would appear for possible corrections or omissions before you prepare the final draft of the program. Acknowledge district staff on your programs. This might include your principal and school administrative staff, names of all fine arts directors who have helped with your concert or provided their students to help, school

It is better to recognize too many people than too few.

board members, central staff administrators, and feeder school vocal music teachers. It is better to recognize too many people than too few. Consider including a short lesson on concert etiquette. See appendix 3b for a sample program addressing this subject. Inserts tend to "drop all over the place." Avoid using inserts when laying out your program if possible.

Know all costs and deadlines for each of your printing options: school duplicating machine, the district print shop, or a professional print shop (possibly sponsoring your concert as a donation or discounted service). If printing is off campus, consider asking someone else to do the delivery for you.

Provide enough concert programs! A good rule of thumb to determine the number of programs needed is three times the number of performers. Leftover programs can be handed out to students the next day and can promote good public relations by sharing them with your administrative staff, feeder school teachers who weren't in attendance, and school board members.

Parent permission forms

Most districts have a standard form which gives teachers permission to take a student on a field trip for an educational experience such as a concert, performance, or contest. Never take a student off campus without parent knowledge and appropriate, signed permission slip. For groups that perform frequently, you may want to ask that parents to sign a "blank check" form which leaves the destination and date blank on an otherwise completed form. This may make things easier for parents, students, and the director, but if parents are uncomfortable leaving any line blank, be quick to give them a stack of forms to be completed individually throughout the year.

Keep these forms alphabetized by student last name. Increasingly, parent and student last names are different, so organize your forms alphabetically by student last name for easy locating as needed. Always carry these with you when you leave the campus with students and keep them readily available in a three-ring binder.

Medical release forms

A permission form allows you to take a student off campus. A medical release form authorizes you to get emergency medical care for an injured or seriously ill student. They perform two entirely different functions. Medical release forms are the difference between an emergency room doctor immediately rendering aid to an injured student, and having to wait an indefinite length of time until a parent can be reached by phone. When time is critical and the unexpected happens, it is imperative that you have correctly completed, signed medical release forms for each and every student in your choir when they leave campus with you. Hope that you never need to use these forms but be prepared in the event that you do.

A medical release form identifies student health issues, history, and allergies, and is critical to medical personnel in caring for a student. It also has health insurance policy numbers and pre-certification phone numbers for hospital staff. Use your school district form; do not place yourself in a quagmire of liabilities by creating your own. If your district has a short form and a long form, choose the long form for everyone's best protection in the unlikely event that such paperwork is needed. Discreetly carry a folder of medical release forms with you at all times, alphabetized by student last name. Be aware that these forms contain a great deal of very personal medical information. Never allow others to look at this information to maintain student and family privacy.

This form gives you legal proxy to act in the parent's absence if medical care authorization is required. Most hospital emergency rooms will not treat a student without this form until a parent can be reached. This is a weighty issue and not one to be entered into lightly. If a student is injured or has a health problem while off campus with you, call the parent immediately while making your way to the nearest appropriate medical facility with the student. If you're unsure if an injury is worthy of emergency room treatment and expense, if possible let the parent choose how you should proceed. Keep documentation of time and content of calls should a question later arise.

Always accompany the student personally to medical help. Do not send a parent chaperone with the student. As the district employee, you are the person the form designates as having the power to get medical assistance for this student. Always carry the original copy of the form. The signed, notarized original is the only legal document that will allow care to be rendered. Take your medical release forms with you whether you are going two blocks to the nearest elementary school, or on a two-week concert tour of Bavaria. We do not have the luxury of scheduling emergency time and location.

When a student reaches their eighteenth birthday they can legally sign many documents for themselves. However, many districts still consider students minors in the area of student travel because they are under the supervision of a teacher, and not independently leaving school on their own.

Media release forms

Be aware that parental permission is legally required in most locales before using a student's photo for publicity purposes such as inclusion in newspapers, newsletters, flyers, etc. Investigate local procedures and policies about this and secure all necessary permissions prior to using students in publicity photography. See the South Bay Choir Handbook in appendix 1b for a sample media release form.

After silence, that which comes nearest to
expressing the inexpressible is music.
—Aldous Huxley

➤ Teaching Sight-Reading and Music Literacy

Help stamp out illiteracy. Teach those singers to read!

Just like reading words, reading music is a learned skill. Anybody can learn to do it to some degree, refining and improving skills with training and practice. People who are unable to read and write the printed word are seriously limited as they make their way through life. Singers who are unable to read music and basic music symbols are seriously restricted in their ability to negotiate and function within a choir. Give a singer a fish and you... give him a fish. (You know where this comparison is headed.) Teach a singer to read music and you open the window on the wide world of music. Teach them to read and read well! What follows below is an overview of how to address sight-reading with your choirs. In the big picture, this book's authors believe: Sight-reading is our friend!

A plethora of sight-reading pointers

Teach rhythm, then melody, and then harmony. This sequence fosters confidence, pride, and spirit because the director is insuring success. Sight-read EVERY day, no matter what. (The only exceptions might be the day of the big concert when the class period is spent without music, on stage, or the day after University Interscholastic League contest because, if you've done it right, you and they are on the floor, prostrate and listening to your tapes in serendipitous bliss.) Pressed for time and the PTA performance is tomorrow? Sight-read first. Kids whining that they don't want to? Sight-read anyway, with a cheerleader's spirit. Have a positive attitude! Sincere, positive attitudes and enthusiasm will spread through your choir like wildfire. The

---

Give a singer a fish and you... give him a fish.

---

fact is, you can succeed and should succeed (no reason not to!) and WILL succeed, if you so choose. Make it into a game they can win and enjoy. If you allow yourself a reason not to sight-read you will find more reasons not to sight-read, and will never allow students to gain true success and confidence in this most important musical skill.

If you are enthusiastic about sight-reading, your students will be enthusiastic about sight-reading. If you downplay its importance or aren't comfortable sight-reading yourself, your students will mirror your lukewarm attitude.

If you're a weak reader, or lack confidence, practice daily on your own. If you don't see what the big deal is, read the research, talk to other successful directors, and get on the sight-reading bandwagon. Every minute spent on sight-reading with zeal, humor, vigor and energy is many minutes you'll increasingly save during rehearsal. Strong sight-readers can do so much more in rehearsal. Skill builds on skill; confidence leads to more confidence, and anything learned about sight-reading is immediately transferable to the literature you're working on for performance. Few get excited about coming to your class today to sing those eight measures of the bass part twenty times in a row to get it right. Imagine if they could "get it" in ten repetitions, or eight repetitions, or eventually, no repetitions! You and your students will enjoy rehearsals far more when you make sight-reading a daily activity.

Construct daily warm-ups that use various intervals, choral patterns, and particular skills students will encounter in their sight-reading or concert literature that day. Appendix 4c provides aural helps for identifying specific intervals. Sight-read on the second day of class (The first day doesn't "count" since periods are so short, roll takes forever, etc.) and throughout the year, including the last day of class and every day in between! If you cease sight-reading after contest, you imply that it was only learned to earn a rating or impress the judges rather than learn and constantly improve a basic music skill. You do not want to read these things on your sight-reading comment sheets from contest: "find a system and use it every day," "drill the basics," "keep at it," "good potential, "all students should be participating/concentrating/using hand signs," etc.

If you are enthusiastic about sight-reading, your students will be enthusiastic about sight-reading.

There is always room for improvement. If your students can sight-read with technical precision, take it up a notch and sight-read with artistic interpretation and dynamics. Dynamic markings not printed in the sight-reading music? What a perfect time for students to demonstrate their creative understanding of phrasing and artistic variety by creating them as the music dictates. If they're already skillful at this level, use a scrambled riser order to foster more independent reading and do so without losing artistry and musicianship.

Teaching far beyond the test

To improve sight-reading in your choir, practice sight-reading unaccompanied for the best results. As learners advance, begin to add rests, including entire measures that are tacet. The ability to learn to sight-read is not tied to intelligence or talent. All students can learn to sight-read. Students learn differently, with different skills and habits. Base initial teaching on the tonic "home," from which we relate all other pitches. Relate tonic to the dominant " away from home." For slower learners, do up to sol is easy to differentiate as high and low.

We can observe that the sight-reading skills of most students fall into one of two groups. In the first group (the "ones") are students who pick things up immediately and sight-reading falls into place with ease. They sing on the beat and can fit rhythms in between the beats. In the second group (the "twos") students need more help in gaining these skills. They are followers, singing behind the beat and singing notes separately, not relating as well to the pulse. Standing and singing posture also affect sight-reading success. "Ones" tend to bounce their bodies and eyes with the music and beat, moving their eyes constantly when sight-reading. "Twos" tend to retreat into the music, using poor posture, leading to an attitude of defeat. "Ones" know how to mark their music much as a conductor would. "Twos" are messy or haphazard in marking their music. Finally, while listening to music, "ones" hear specific details in the music like changes in dynamics, the shape of a melodic line, etc., while "twos" hear more generalized sounds.

Build tuning and inner listening by occasionally having students sight-read by alternating singing one measure aloud with one measure silently. If there is a "train wreck" in an exercise and the students laugh, directly after the laughing is the BEST time for teaching! Students are relaxed and receptive, so get your best licks in on the material at that moment. Teach students how to "get back in" if they go astray in their reading. Recovery is often a key skill!

Many students do not believe they will ever be able to learn to sight-read. Knowing this will help you understand their initial lack of motivation, and their amazement and joy when they do "get it" and learn to read. Appendix 4d-4f contains examples for student assessment in mastering sight-reading skills. Remember, you and your students CAN sight-read, sight-read well, and have fun in the process! Sight-reading is our friend.

Sight-reading materials

Some materials we have used successfully include:

- Appleby, William. *Sing At Sight*
- Crowe, Lawton, & Whittaker. Oxford Folk Song Sight Reading, books 1-4
- Vandre, Carl. *Sight Reading Fun and Four-Part Choral Trainer* (SATB)
- Carlisle, Marcia, Hemmenway, John, Leach, Marybelle, and Wehrung, Mary Nan. *Keys To Sightreading Success*
- *101 Bach Chorales*
- Jones, Henry, Mary, and Marilyn. *Songs For Sight Singing*
- *Essential Elements*, Hal Leonard Publications
- Hymnals

Individual sight-reading, especially for competitions:

- McGill, Stan and Stevens, Morris. *90 Days to Sightreading Success: A Singer's Resource for Competitive Sight-singing*
- McGill, Stan and Stevens, Morris. *18 Lessons to Sightreading Success*

Additional materials:

- Heffley, Rosemary, Land, Lois, and Wimberly, Lou Ann. *A Cappella Songs Without Words*
- Eilers, Joyce, and Crocker, Emily. *Patterns Of Sound*
- Lavender, Cheryl. *Rhymes, Raps, & Rhythms*
- Eilers, Joyce, and Crocker, Emily. *Choral Approach to Sight-Singing*
- Crocker, Emily. *Essential Sight-Singing*
- Eilers, Joyce, and Crocker, Emily. *Sight-Singing for SSA*
- Williams-Wimberly, Lou Ann. *Sing A Cappella*
- Whitlock, Ruth. *Songs for Sight Singing*
- Munn, Vivian. *Songs for Sight Singing*

You will find many other publications designed to assist in teaching sight-reading to singers on choralnet.com as well as publisher and music retail store websites.

Tips for using sight-reading materials

Begin by teaching rhythmic reading first, then melodic reading, each separate from the other. When your choir is able to read confidently in unison, begin to include harmonic exercises and materials with ever-increasing complexity, length, and numbers of parts until they are sight-reading in as many parts as the majority of their octavos.

Hymnals are an excellent resource for sight-reading material. There is no issue with sacred texts when you use your preferred system of sight-reading: moveable do, fixed do, or numbers. Hymnals can be purchased new, or acquired from a local church for free or next-to-nothing. Ask your singers to approach the appropriate person at their place of worship to inquire if

---

Hymnals are an excellent resource for sight-reading material.

---

there are, or will be, any hymnals available to donate or sell to the school choral department. Due to potential damage and wear it is suggested that these not be borrowed. Our experience has been strongest with straightforward four-part hymn writing as found in Methodist, Episcopalian, Presbyterian, and Baptist hymnals.

Try writing short examples, melodic or rhythmic, for daily sight-reading. These are great for "bell-ringers," exercises that students can work on independently while forming on the risers before the tardy bell; and can drill specific weaknesses you have previously identified. Rhythm sheets are easy to write and photocopy, and may be reused year after year if filed according to difficulty. Devise warm-up drills or reading based on passages from the literature you are currently rehearsing in class. This gives singers an immediate benefit.

The Bach *Chorales* can be used by advanced high school choirs eager for an extra challenge beyond the literature they will likely encounter in a sight-reading competition. The chorales include difficult intervallic reading in all parts as well as an increased use of chromaticism and fermati.

Superior sight-readers in choir will consistently use hand signs as they read. Superior choirs will have one hundred percent of their members using hand signs. Once students master them, hand signs strengthen reading concepts at a faster pace. We urge you to use the Curwen hand signs (see appendix 4g) as you sight-read in your choir on a daily, one hundred percent participation basis. Students will think they look "goofy" (and some days they might), but the kinesthetic component is beyond dispute. Tell your singers the hand signs are moral, legal, honest, and maybe even "goofy" on Tuesdays, but they work! They will have to trust you on this point for a goodly while but they will thank you in the end, we promise!

A Comparison of the Three Major Options: Which Sight-reading System is Best for You?

A rose by any other name still has some thorns...

Sight-reading using numbers, pros:

1. Easiest to teach initially because they are familiar. Numbers are easy to think about both ascending and descending.

2. Intervals are easy to "see" because a student has a concept of the relative size of a third when compared to a fifth or a seventh.

3. There are only seven numbers, the octave being a repetition of number one, eight tones higher.

4. Any pitch can be the tonic.

Sight-reading using numbers, cons:

1. The vowel sounds when singing numbers one through seven are essentially ugly. ("uh, ih, and eh" being the offending numerals.) With sustained pitches, students generally sustain one on "uhhhhhh." Six uses the "ih" sound and se-ven uses the "eh."

2. Accidentals involve polysyllabic names that blur rhythms and can be hard to sing rapidly. ("Seven-sharp," even when "seven" is routinely contracted to "sev'n.")

3. It is more difficult to form a mental image of relative minor. ("In ms. 72, we will be singing in the key of six?")

4. Modulations can be difficult to explain and understand.

Sight-reading using moveable *do*, pros:

1. Vowel sounds of solfege syllables are pleasing to the ear. They will support your work on tall, open, rounded vowel sounds.

2. There are only seven basic note names to learn: do, re, mi, fa, sol, la, and ti. Many students will have already heard these from The Sound Of Music.

3. Existing hand signs correlate to the solfege, providing a kinesthetic way to reinforce learning.

4. Any pitch can be the tonic.

5. Altered pitches have monosyllabic names (fi, ti, leh, etc.) and are rhythmically precise to sing.

6. Relative minor can be easily explained by "singing in the key of la, with la as the tonic."

7. Modulations can be explained easily. For example, "In ms. 54-78, our tonal focus will be around mi."

Sight-reading using moveable *do*, cons:

Moveable *do* does not develop a strong sense of relative pitch because the tonic can be any note of the chromatic scale.

Sight-reading with fixed *do*, pros:

1. Fixed *do* affords singers the best opportunity to develop a strong sense of relative pitch because C is do in all keys, D is re in all keys, E is mi, etc.

2. Solfege syllables contribute to quality vowel sounds.

3. Altered pitches do not need to be renamed.

Sight-reading with fixed *do*, cons:

1. Fixed *do* takes substantially longer to master due to the frequency of using accidentals' pitch names.

2. Fixed *do* is not as easily transferred from choir to choir because it is the least used system.

Each system has advantages and disadvantages. For a variety of reasons, both authors recommend using the moveable do system. We are conversant with all three systems but both of us prefer the use of moveable *do*. However, studies show that all three systems can be effectively mastered if used consistently. Attitudinal zeal is vastly more critical to sight-reading success than which system you choose.

Music literacy

Part of our job as choral directors is to teach the language of music. The terms, symbols, and basic notational systems used in writing music are essential to interpret a printed choral score. It is wise to review music theory basics each year (even in rapid fire review), including:

- The lines and spaces of the staff
- Treble clef, bass clef, and a general explanation about the history of the other clefs
- Note values
- Dynamic symbols and their meanings in both Italian and English

- Common tempo markings
- Ledger lines and spaces
- Key signatures
- Musical symbols including accents, marcato, legato, phrase marks, breath marks, first and second endings, D.C. al fine, D.C. al segno, repeat signs
- How to construct a major scale using whole and half steps
- Relative and parallel minor
- Terms like melisma, tessitura, timbre, and hemiola

Once taught, these symbols and terms should be used regularly in rehearsal, leading to greater musical understanding and pride in musicianship. Test student mastery of these concepts throughout the year. Two good music literacy resources are Vocal Connections by Ruth Whitlock, and *Music Reading Unlimited* by Vivian Munn.

Taking Care of Business

> Copyright Law for the Choral Director

> The Art of the Interview

> Teacher Observations and Evaluations

> Professional Resources

➤ Copyright Law for the Choral Director

"Jailhouse Rock" only really worked well for Elvis...

Purchasing music for choirs is expensive. Budgets never seem to increase and prices seem to inch ever upward. We know that composers and arrangers should be fairly compensated for their work just as we are compensated for ours. Nevertheless, it's the bottom of the ninth, the bases are loaded, and you need music. What will do you?

We contend that doing the right and lawful thing is always your only choice. It not only keeps you out of court, but also demonstrates to your students a respect for composers, arrangers, music publishers, retailers, and the law. It is important to know that it only takes one report of using photo-copied music to set in motion an inquiry by the publisher. This puts your job at risk and causes professional embarrassment and personal liability, and takes just one report, just one time. Some publishers hire private investigators to document infringement prior to notifying you or your school. Before you set the school copy machine ablaze to save money, learn the law and know that your district wants you to stay above it.

An excellent source for copyright information may be found at http://www.copyright.gov/. There are also free government publications you may request to become informed about everything you need to know on this topic. A synopsis of pertinent areas that affect choral music educators can be found at the Music Publishers Association website: www.mpa.org.

Sometimes copyright law impacts our work in ways that don't involve a copy machine. It governs what we can and cannot do in areas that include recording choirs for student use or for sale, performing copyrighted materials in particular venues, writing your own choral arrangements based on published music, and performing material from Broadways musicals. Consider the following real-world examples. Do you know the law regarding each of them?

Photocopying:

Q: A state-adopted textbook, loaded with great choral literature, is heavy and cumbersome for students to hold. You photocopy the work you're teaching so it can fit in students' folders. After all, you own a full set of the books so you're not dodging costs. Can you do this legally?

A: You may only reprint copyrighted material with the permission of the publisher.

Recording:

Q: Your recent competition performance was stellar and even other competitors commended your choir's fine work. To commemorate this outstanding performance, you purchase CDs with your own money and make a copy for every singer so their families can hear the performance. Is it legal to do this?

A: If the music is under copyright, you must acquire a mechanical license or receive permission directly from the publisher. See www.harryfox.com.

Q: The recording of your choir's performance of the Mozart *Requiem* is stunning, so much so that a local church wants to use it as the background music for a series of tapes it is producing. Can the church use your recording? Was it legal for you to have made the recording it in the first place? Would it make a difference if the requiem were by John Rutter?

A: The Mozart *Requiem* is in the public domain and does not require a mechanical license or permission from the publisher unless you are performing a copyrighted arrangement of the work. The church may use the recording with your permission. If John Rutter composed the work, you may not use it without a mechanical license or permission from the publisher.

Arrangements:

Q: You plan to do a medley from *Little Shop of Horrors* from the published arrangement you bought. However, "Somewhere That's Green" isn't included, and you want to do the entire "You'll Be A Dentist" instead of the short part in the medley. Can you make these changes and perform it in good stead?

A: To make an arrangement of any copyrighted work, you must have the permission of the publisher.

Q: Your students just love a particular song on the radio but there is no published arrangement available. As a gift to them, you write an easy version that is perfect for their ability and range and will destroy all copies after the performance. Can you do this legally?

A: To make an arrangement of any copyrighted work, you must have the permission of the publisher.

Broadway musicals:

Q: Your school paid royalties to Tams Witmark for this year's school musical. The buzz around the community is so strong that tickets are already a sell-out and you've added an extra matinee show to accommodate the demand. Is this legal?

A: To add a performance to a licensed musical, you must contact the licensing agency.

Be informed. "I didn't know" won't hold up in a court of law.

Q: The musical was such a success that people who came want a copy so they can watch it nightly thereafter. You figure this is the easiest fund-raiser that ever fell in your lap and sell videotapes for twenty dollars and DVDs for thirty dollars. Is this legal? Would it be different if you gave away the recordings and no money was involved?

A: You may not videotape your performance without the permission of the licensing agency regardless of whether you sell or give away the DVDs.

Be informed. "I didn't know" won't hold up in a court of law. As choral directors we are expected to know and uphold the law with regard to copyright. It's not as difficult an area as it may seem once you learn the basics. We may be tempted to cut corners when we think "no real harm" will come of our actions. Cutting corners when it comes to copyright is illegal and can have staggering consequences. Do the right thing.

Real integrity is doing the right thing,
knowing that nobody's going to know whether you did it or not.
—Oprah Winfrey

➤ The Art of the Interview

How to hire and be hired...

Whether you are seeking a job or interviewing an applicant, there are many factors that impact the hiring process. Those seeking applicants are looking for an individual who will excel in a particular position while also acclimating well to the department and school community. There are numerous factors to consider.

When interviewing, keep all questions pertinent, avoiding all references to factors that might be considered discriminatory by federal law. Things that are prohibited from being considered in the hiring process include age, gender, race, national origin, disability, pregnancy, and religion. More information regarding job discrimination can be found in federal law: *Labor, Title 29, The Civil Rights Act, title 42*, chapter 21, and *Equal Opportunity for Individuals with Disabilities, Title 42, chapter 126*. It is important to note that compensation for teachers is based largely on years of experience and number of academic degrees held. School districts can afford to hire several less experienced teachers for the salary it would need to pay a highly skilled teacher with many years of experience. This places a district and personnel director in a tough position when hiring the best candidate legally and affordably. Whenever possible, allow ample time to post a new position for exposure to the largest number of potential job candidates. This would include district postings as well as job notices on your state Music Educators Association, ACDA, and choralnet.com websites.

Ask the same questions of all applicants. This provides similar information about each candidate and leaves the committee's leanings uncommitted if candidates compare notes post-interview. When interviewing by committee, make sure the group knows who will lead the conversation and questioning. All parties should dress professionally. Observe the applicant's attire and grooming, noting how they choose to present themselves. Look applicants in the eye when speaking to them. Observe whether they look the interviewer(s) in the eye or not.

Be honest with the applicant in describing the job. It is unprofessional to exaggerate strengths or omit weaknesses in a position and may result in a bitter attitude when both are viewed more accurately after an applicant is hired. Describe the level and caliber of students in your program, the teaching schedule, including extended school day time demands, and perks, if any, such as payment of convention expenses, reserved parking spots, or free lunches. Discuss specific duties such as working with middle schools or feeder systems, team-teaching opportunities, and your own expectations as well as those from supervisors, administrators, parents and others who impact the position. Supply information about the anticipated salary and other monetary compensation, and give a general explanation of employee benefits.

Listen carefully when applicants express concerns, demands, expectations, limitations, or other issues. Interviewing is a two-way street. Applicants want a job and those hiring want the right person for the job. Don't present yourself as desperate or too selective, which could discourage good applicants. Be respectful of an applicant's time. Any interview lasting more than an hour is usually time wasted by all. Make interviews concise and productive, filled with information relevant only to the job vacancy and applicant.

Treat applicants fairly and leave them wanting the job.

Do your homework on each applicant. Read resumes and applications, check references and be knowledgeable about each applicant's abilities and past work experiences. Be certain all committee members, if applicable, have access to an applicant's folder of information. Note those individuals selected as references for the candidate. If a teacher lists references from colleagues ten years ago and has omitted principal, fine arts director and department chairman from their last two jobs, you may see a red flag waving to be investigated. You may have contacts in the choral music field that can help you form a better picture of a candidate. Look for the most current, honest, specific information possible.

Treat applicants fairly and leave them wanting the job. By the same token, do not make any formal or informal comments that might be considered an "outcome" to the interview process. Usually the district personnel director or principal will make any final decisions and contacts. Keep all committee deliberations and comments in the strictest confidence.

When hiring an assistant or other professional, always keep your program in mind. Make decisions based on what is best for the students, school, and community, rather than on your own preferences or allegiances. Consider the advantages of having a balanced team if there will be more than one director, and make a note of personalities, temperament, and the ability to work together.

When you are an applicant, remember that by studying a resume a prospective employer can glean information about the candidate's ability to prepare paperwork in a timely, crisp, professional manner. The resume also provides insight into how a candidate might prepare a concert program, exam questions, parent newsletters, and so forth. During the interview a candidate's speaking abilities and sense of humor come to light. Table manners and etiquette (it is not a coincidence that many second interviews take place over coffee or lunch), as well as appearance, attire, personal grooming and cleanliness are important. The adage "if you want to know about someone, take a good look at the condition and care they give to their shoes" has some merit.

Be aware that past legal entanglements may surface. (Criminal history is always checked as part of the hiring process.) You may be asked why you left your previous position (avoid talking poorly about a past supervisor, principal, or district), and other questions about stability in your employment history. When hiring new directors a district would expect an anticipated five to seven year commitment. They will be wary to commit to an individual who changes jobs after one to three years repeatedly, knowing that this will not provide continuity or growth for a program.

Present a positive attitude and keep your private life private. Districts do not want your private life to enter into the workplace any more than you want the district intruding on your privacy at the end of the workday. Toward that end, make life choices in such a way that private things remain private both in your interview and work. Presenting a readily acceptable wholesome persona in the workplace will serve you well.

Tips for successful job interviews

- Always allow enough time to get to your interview. Arrive early to impress. Build in enough travel time for traffic, stopping for gas, finding a parking place, locating the room in which your interview will take place, and that last minute stop to "powder your nose" before going in.

- Be well groomed. Get the haircut before the interview if you're on the fence about it. Lean toward the conservative.

- Offer a strong handshake and maintain eye contact. Introduce yourself in this way to everyone on the interview committee.

- If you are a gentleman, please wait for the ladies in the room to be seated before you sit. Open doors, say please, etc.

- Never chew gum or arrive with food or beverage in hand.

- Thank your interviewer(s) before you leave. Follow up with a thank you note sent the same day to show your interest in the job.

Questions you might expect

1. What are your greatest strengths?

2. Do you have any weaknesses?
   (Everyone has weaknesses. By saying that you have none, you show yourself to be a liar or a fool. Choose which one(s) you feel are appropriate to mention, and be honest. You're "selling" yourself at this interview, not someone else. If the school hires the "fake" you for the job, won't they be surprised, and won't you be miserable, when the "real" you arrives for work every day.)

3. Would you please tell us a little about yourself?
   (Remember that you are being evaluated on what you choose to say as well as how articulate you are in saying it. Be able to condense your life, education, and career goals in positive little packages prior to the interview.)

4. Why did you leave a particular school or job?
   (Be careful not to air "dirty laundry.")

5. Why did you choose to become a teacher?

6. Why did you choose choral music as your field of specialization?

7. What other courses are you prepared to teach?
   (You will be asked to differentiate between "prepared to" and "certified to" if this is asked.)

8. Why do you want to teach at this particular school or in this area?

9. Please describe what a typical class period might look like if someone dropped in to observe your choir.

10. What was the last book you read?
    (Answer thoughtfully. There are some really good, really bad, and really false answers that can be given here. Choose carefully but remember they're more interested in whether you can read and do read.)

11. Please tell us about any special talents you may have.
    (These may include the ability to speak other languages, coach the fencing team, etc. Being well rounded is a plus for any teacher.)

12. Are you willing to teach on more than one campus each day?

13. What are your experiences in, and attitude toward team-teaching?

14. Are there any questions you wish we had asked you?

15. Do you have any questions you'd like to ask us?

Questions you might want to ask

1. Could you please describe your choral program at the present time?
2. Is there a district curriculum I will be using?
3. Does this position involve the production of a musical?
4. Can you describe parent involvement in the school, and in the choral program specifically?
5. May I see the choir room?

A final note about employability

With ever-spiraling health care costs, health insurance is a major and critical expense for school districts, representing a substantial amount of funds and financial benefit to all district employees and, hopefully, their immediate families. This is done at low or no cost to you and can easily represent an additional third of your salary if you are married with one child. With this in mind, all employers have a growing interest in the health of prospective employees and school districts are no different. People who are overweight, smoke, or have lifestyles prone to promote certain health issues may be assumed to be potentially unaffordable by the provider of district health insurance. If you smoke or are heavier than your doctor feels is healthy, you may want to give careful thought to making healthier lifestyle choices. Beyond societal opinions and prejudices, smoking and obesity are costly issues in regard to health care in every school and district nationally. "Hiring healthy" saves money for employers. Put the odds in your favor as much as possible.

➤ Teacher Observations and Evaluations

The teacher giveth grades, the teacher receiveth a grade...

Whether you are a novice or experienced teacher, administrative observations are important to your evaluation as a district employee. Both formal observations and informal "walk-throughs" by one or more administrators and outside evaluators may be used to assess your strengths and weaknesses as an educator. The diligent work, planning, investment of countless extra hours, and visibility involved in conducting a masterful choral program soars far above expectations. We must carefully document our work so those who interpret it may have every reason to find that we are exemplary teachers, worthy as a model from which others might learn.

*Evaluation day is a dangerous time to pull
something new from your bag of tricks.*

Some observations may be announced in advance. If you are going to be visited, place a chair where you hope your evaluator will sit for best view of your work and student response, as well as out of traffic patterns that might interrupt a normal class period. Have a notebook of lesson plans to present to your evaluator, organized in chronological order with the current plan on top. You may want to keep an accumulative notebook that could be reviewed at the end of the year by your evaluator. Documentation to save might include concert programs, letters of commendation from parents, community members, and students, and clippings from newspapers, professional journals, and other publicity. Also include special education modifications, rehearsal components aligned with standardized testing content, and service projects involving the choir.

Remember that your observer will only be in your class for a limited period of time. With this in mind, put your best foot forward and focus on those planned activities and rehearsal techniques which best demonstrate the items noted on the appraisal form. For this particular class period, feel comfortable aiming questions at specific students, and use activities and pacing which is tried and proven for you. Evaluation day is a dangerous time to pull something new from your bag of tricks. Observations reward teachers who give constant feedback and adjust work to match goals. Use a kinesthetic mode for demonstrating a particular aspect of the music, engaging students both cognitively and physically. A solid, well-paced choral rehearsal fits into the majority of appraisal systems perfectly!

In advance of observations, identify a student who will unobtrusively slip off the risers and greet any visitor while presenting them with a music folder (so the evaluator can follow along) and your evaluation notebook. If you are in the middle of class, acknowledge your visitor and continue with your work. Evaluators look for work in progress and will appreciate your on-task teaching.

The conference that follows some observations will provide an opportunity for your evaluator to identify the strengths and weakness he or she sees in your work. Accept criticism gracefully and say "thank you" for praise. Display a positive attitude and body language. Avoid fidgety hands and poor posture. Don't be defensive, and always look your evaluator in the eye. Be prepared to explain the contents of your evaluation notebook if asked, and to present your own strengths and weaknesses as appropriate. Talk about exciting plans for the future and upcoming concerts or projects, and above all, be enthusiastic about your program. At the end of the conference, thank your evaluator and extend an invitation to visit again at any time. Be sure to save your copy of any formal assessment documents for your records. Maintain a welcoming attitude toward any observers or evaluators. Show off your fine choir and teaching!

From school district to school district across the country there are a number of common denominators evaluators will look for when assessing effective teaching. The choral director has some distinct advantages in being able to demonstrate these teaching behaviors within a traditional rehearsal. Here are some ways various professional development and appraisal systems are worded, and examples of how you can shine in rehearsal.

Domain I: Active, Successful Student Participation in the Learning Process

1. Engaged in learning
2. Successful in learning
3. Critical thinking/problem solving
4. Self-directed
5. Connects learning

Demonstrated by: choir on the risers, everybody participating, all students doing their hand-signs during sight-reading, students able to answer questions about the key signature and location of do-me-sol of the tonic chord, student led sectional work on sight-reading example before it is sung as a class, students able to critique what was right or wrong about an aspect of performance, students understanding what is happening in class, students mentally and visually "tuned in."

Domain II: Learner-Centered Instruction

1. Goals and Objectives
2. Learner-Centered
3. Critical thinking and problem solving
4. Motivational strategies
5. Alignment
6. Pacing/sequencing
7. Value and importance
8. Appropriate questioning and inquiry
9. Use of technology

Demonstrated by: quality lesson plans, student ability to determine what is wrong in a given passage and how a section or the choir might solve it, keeping rehearsal varied and moving forward, task orientation to time use, well worded questions to students, using technology for sight-reading examples and individual student drill on basic theory at computers before or after school.

Domain III: Evaluation and Feedback on Student Progress

1. Monitored and assessed
2. Assessment and instruction are aligned
3. Appropriate assessment
4. Learning reinforced
5. Constructive feedback
6. Relearning and re-evaluating

Demonstrated by: effective and fair method of determining grades, meaningful assessment tools, re-teaching areas of weakness, cyclically reviewing and building upon foundational concepts, correcting rhythms, notes or other aspects of performance for immediate feedback and correction by the choir as passage is sung again.

Domain IV: Management of Student Discipline, Instructional Strategies, Time and Materials

1. Discipline procedures
2. Self-discipline and self-directed learning
3. Equitable teacher-student interaction
4. Expectations for behavior
5. Reinforces desired behavior
6. Equitable and varied characteristics
7. Manages time and materials

Demonstrated by: teaching bell to bell, absence of discipline problems due to effective class pacing and focus of students, setting high expectations and modeling concentration and smart use of time, praising good work in individuals or groups, having materials organized and a routine established so that time is not wasted in transitions, fairness with students and positive interaction.

Domain V: Professional Communication

1. Written with students
2. Verbal and non verbal with students
3. Reluctant students
4. Written with parents, staff, community members, and other professionals
5. Supportive, courteous
6. Verbal and non verbal with parents, staff, community members, and other professionals

Demonstrated by: progress reports, ability to draw reluctant students into full participation in a positive and enthusiastic way, parent newsletters, positive relationships with parents, staff, and community members in all dealings, pro-student and pro-school attitude, diplomacy in both written and spoken word, calling parents before potential problem behaviors become chronic or serious.

Domain VI: Professional Development

1. Campus/district goals
2. Student needs
3. Prior performance appraisal
4. Improvement of student performance

Demonstrated by: coordination of lesson plans with overall achievement and testing goals of the school, knowing, accommodating and modifying individual instructional plans for special needs students, measurement of student progress in mastery of curriculum.

Domain VII: Compliance with Policies, Operating Procedures, and Requirements

1. Policies, procedures, and legal requirements
2. Verbal and written directives
3. Environment

Demonstrated by: following school rules, prompt attendance at all faculty and departmental meetings, conforming to all district policies and procedures, taking direction from supervisors, maintaining a healthy and positive teaching environment in your classroom.

Domain VIII: Improvement of Academic Performance of All Students on Campus

1. Align instruction
2. Analyzes state testing indicators
3. Appropriate sequence
4. Appropriate materials
5. Monitors student performance
6. Monitors attendance
7. Students in at-risk situations
8. Appropriate plans for intervention
9. Modifies and adapts

Demonstrated by: making all possible connections between your curriculum and other subject areas for maximum cross-curricular learning benefits, teaching new concepts in an appropriately sequenced order, assessing student progress consistently to monitor that you truly are teaching and not just talking or demonstrating in front of young people, noting attendance problems and finding ways to encourage and follow up with those students who are missing class, using all tools possible to intervene with at-risk behaviors or discipline problems, knowing how your subject matter equates to state testing areas and indicators so you can make special effort to reinforce those concepts.

Competence, like truth, beauty, and contact lenses, is in the eye of the beholder.
—Laurence J. Peter, *The Peter Principle*

➤ Professional Resources

Dial A = 440 for help...

Whether you're seeking information, music, ideas for fund raising, or equipment, there are countless resources available to you. Never feel stranded or lacking a strong support system of colleagues, no matter how geographically removed you may be from other choral educators. Help is as close as a phone call or keystroke away!

Professional Organizations

American Choral Directors Association (ACDA)
National and divisional ACDA conventions are held throughout
the nation.
www.acdaonline.org

State Choral Directors Associations
State conventions are held annually. Research other states' choral
conventions and attend one
in another state periodically to "compare notes" in your profession.

State Music Educators Association (MEA)
Conventions are held annually. This group sponsors All-State Choir
competition and performances.

Music Educators National Conference (MENC)
This group is a national association for music education.

International Society for Music Education (ISME)
This group provides an international network for music educators.

Music Teachers National Association (MTNA)

There is a veritable cornucopia of resources available for choral professionals and students. Included here are several that have been helpful to us
in the past.

Online Support

Choralnet.com
An incredible treasure chest of resources for the choral musician,
featuring everything from discussion groups to areas where questions can
be posed for answers from any number of international responders, from
parodies of Christmas carols to works by women composers – you name

it, choralnet has got it, free! This web address will also lead you to countless others that serve as helps to choral directors and students alike.

Books

Bodymind and Voice by Leon Thurman and Graham Welch
Brain-Based Learning by Eric Jensen
Choral Conducting: A Symposium edited by Harold Decker and Julius Herford
Choral Conducting: Focus on Communication by Harold Decker and Colleen Kirk
Choral Therapy by Lloyd Pfautsch
Complete Guide To Teaching Vocal Jazz by Stephen Zegree
English Diction for Singers by Lloyd Pfautsch
Group Vocal Techniques, by Frauke Haasemann
Harvard Dictionary of Music
Mental Warm-Ups for the Choral Director by Lloyd Pfautsch
Translations and Annotations of Choral Repertoire, Vol. I: Sacred Latin Texts by Ron Jeffers

Videos and DVDs

Charles Nelson, *The Voice*
Robert Shaw videotapes
Paul Salamunovich, *Choral Perspectives: Chant and Beyond*
Weston Noble, *Achieving Choral Blend Through Standing Positions*
Weston Noble, *Choral Perspectives: Perpetual Inspiration*
Donald Neuen, *Choral Excellence: Choral Techniques and Methods*
   Vol. 1: *Energy, Beauty, and Placement*
   Vol. 2: *Individual Section Characteristics*
   Vol. 3: *A Unified Approach to Vowel Formation*
   Vol. 4: *The Power of Words*
   Vol. 5: *Rhythmic Interest and Forward Motion*
Donald Neuen, *Choral Excellence: Artistic Musical Conducting* (2 volumes)
Linda Spevacek, *The Choral Director As Voice Teacher*

Music Advocacy

Americans for the Arts, www.artsusd.org
Arts Education Partnership, www.acp-arts.org
Community Arts Network, www.communityarts.net
Cultural Policy & the Arts National Data Archive, www.cpanda.org
Gaining the Arts Advantage: Lessons from School Districts That Value
   Arts Education, www.peah.gov/gas/index.html
Keep Arts In Schools, www.keepartsinschools.org
SupportMusic.com, www.supportmusic.com
VH1 Save The Music

Periodicals

Choral Journal, ACDA's professional publication
Your state MEA journal
Your state's choral directors' association professional journal

Groups and organizations relating to particular aspects of working in choral music

ASCAP (American Society of Composers, Authors, and Publishers)
CASA (Contemporary A Cappella Society)
Chorus America
Harry Fox Agency
Music Library Association
National Endowment for the Arts
NATS (National Association of Teachers of Singing)

A word about professional conventions and workshops

It would be difficult to overstate the importance of attending your state's MEA convention each year. Workshops filled with pertinent topics are excellent opportunities for professional growth and development. Local staff development credit may be offered for attendance by some school districts. Attend concerts by choirs throughout your state, hearing groups that inspire you and give insight into your own work at home. Meet your colleagues and arrange sharing sessions over a cup of coffee during breaks. Visit the exhibit halls to see what is new and different in everything from printed music to resource books to fund-raising products to classroom decorations. The list of benefits for attending convention is seemingly endless. Save your money and go! (Your district may even have methods of partially funding and facilitating your attendance.)

Another professional goal might be to attend an ACDA national or regional convention, meeting directors and hearing concerts by groups from across the nation and abroad. Your state ACDA convention is an excellent opportunity to choose and select music for the coming year, meet and compare notes with colleagues, and network about job openings.

The important thing is not to stop questioning.
Curiosity has its own reason for existing.
—Albert Einstein

6 How to Get Along, and Play Well With Others

> ➤ **Building Your Support System**

> ➤ **The Recruitment and Retention of Choir Students**

> ➤ **Effective Publicity and Public Relations**

➤ Building Your Support System

Rome wasn't built in a seven-period day...

As you seek assistance and support from those around you, be aware of district policies and procedures so you stay within the existing chain of command. Know your own building's policies and procedures like the back of your hand and heed them! Be nice because it's a great way to live, not because of what a person or group can do for you or your choir program. There are sandwiches to be shared, jokes to be told, and friendships to be forged!

The care and feeding of your choir booster club

An organized group of parents interested in volunteerism, leadership, and hard work on behalf of the choir can be an invaluable asset to any choral director. It can also become the third ring in Dante's *Inferno* if it runs amuck. With this in mind, remember that the basic function of a booster club is to positively support the efforts of the choral director and the choir program. While an autonomous group in many ways, its agenda must be your agenda, and its goals must be an outgrowth of yours. If two roads diverge in a confused wood and you are headed one way while your booster club prefers the other way, you will be sorry that you missed one unified path. In forming, or tightening up the structure of the booster club, it is important to have a constitution to provide clear structure for the organization. Work together with parents to form a scholarship program, fundraising wish lists, chaperoning needs for the year, etc. Always attend booster club meetings to ensure that your agenda is theirs, and so that no project gets going without your nod, eliminating the time lag between their ideas and your approval. Regular attendance also shows your respect for their work, volunteerism, and time. (See appendix 6a-f for a sample booster club constitution and other related forms.)

Officers and committee members should reflect multiple grade levels and choirs. This facilitates carry-over between years and helps the booster club support all choirs and their activities, not just a top group. The choir booster club is not synonymous with "parents who long to be full-time fund raisers." Please see parents and supporters as more than a source for money. Learn to delegate. Student volunteers can do some projects, and some projects can go to parents. Things may not always get done exactly as you would have done them, but you may find new ways of doing things refreshing, and maybe even better! Many hands make light work and a happy choir director.

Show your appreciation for your booster club and all volunteers often. Do this in your newsletter, by email, or with a handwritten thank you note. Always give trip chaperones a T-shirt as a token of your appreciation for their traveling with the choir. They will wear them proudly.

Spread the wealth (of hard work) around.

Get to know the parent volunteers connected to your work with middle school students. This is a great opportunity to welcome them to your booster club in the future as freshman parents. Word of mouth between parents gives you visibility in the community at an adult level. Supportive, enthusiastic adults are invaluable in countless ways!

Your principal and administrative staff

Work hard to maintain a quality program without creating extra work for your administrators. Work cooperatively and communicate frequently with parents to deflect letters and phone calls to the office. Never let your principal be blindsided by something that has happened in your program. Yours should be the first account of any incident or controversy so the principal has time to process the information without the immediacy of a parent on the other end of the phone or outside an office door. Work professionally and successfully. Be a team player, attending other school events beyond the fine arts and volunteer for committees and other tasks shared by the faculty.

Invite your administrators to your concerts. While the schedule of events to attend administratively is staggering, it is always nice to be included. Invite your principal to be a guest singer, Santa, or narrator for an important concert or program and always include your administration in concert program acknowledgments. Ask students to deliver a choir T-shirt to each administrator as a way of saying "thank you" for all they do for the choir throughout the year. Be generous with your time in providing choirs for your principal's service club and district programming needs. Ask your principal to introduce your group. Prepare singers to serenade your principal (and other staff) on their birthdays. Pageantry is such great fun!

The counseling staff

Provide lists of choir students for the following year to your counselors in a timely fashion. The end of year pace in their office is grueling, so any special effort you can make to work ahead of schedule will be appreciated. Turn in easy to read choir lists of who goes where, either alphabetized by last name or color-coded according to choir. A spreadsheet format works well for this. Include student identification number, grade, course number, and any other information that will make the job easier. During your auditions, it will take extra effort to keep up with student identification numbers from feeder schools, private schools, and new students; use this opportunity to complete your work rather than ask the counselors to search for bits of information on their own. Fight the urge to be unreasonably demanding with schedule changes. Make it easy for them to schedule students in your choirs.

Point out that choir can be beneficial for reinforcing language skills of students new to English, can provide socialization for special-needs students, and how incredibly good it is for many kinds of students to be in choir! Show your appreciation to your counselors periodically by singing for their birthdays, leaving them an apple and a note, and don't be afraid to get creative. They will either counsel students to take your classes or not, to think favorably about choir on your campus or not. Give them every reason to like you and want to promote your work. Sometimes counselors only hear from a disgruntled student with a bone to pick with a teacher. Let them know you and all your students. Be visible!

Feeder school teachers

Feeder school choirs do not exist solely to populate your high school choir. It is offensive to elementary and middle school teachers for colleagues to view them as a means to an end regarding recruitment. They build and maintain valuable music programs and appreciate your support. Visit your feeder school teachers regularly. Listen. Sometimes, a listening ear is better than all the advice in the world. Offer help. Your students can help with choreography and teaching parts at the middle school choir camp, you can hear solos and ensembles before contest for helpful critiques, or offer to do their program layout at the last minute when they are pulling their hair out! Please, don't only visit them sheepishly directly before middle school auditions. Be available throughout the year. Invite feeder school teachers to accompany your students, and attend your feeder schools' choral concerts regularly.

Invite your feeder schools to perform on your campus by having a different "special guest choir" at different events or concerts throughout the year. Include younger students in roles for musicals and other presentations. Youngsters who have performed in this way are likely to join your groups when they get older. Invite your feeder school teachers to work with your groups in sectionals, as "practice judges," hearing solos and ensembles for critique, or to conduct a rehearsal. Most middle school teachers welcome the opportunity to work together to provide skillful, experienced musicians teaching in your district with all age levels of students.

The PTA

Become a member! When at all possible, acknowledge requests for performances and be available to sing at meeting and events. Take advantage of the PTA newsletter for posting upcoming events as well as offering applause for award-winning groups and individuals. Be aware of potential funding available for items unbudgeted by the school and district. Sometimes there is money available through the PTA for equipment and supplies that cannot otherwise be secured.

Your esteemed faculty

Support fellow faculty members and always speak positively about all colleagues and their courses. Be a team player. Work across curricular lines on committees and projects, showing active interest and support beyond the fine arts wing of the school. Work cross-curricularly with faculty members. Combine a music history lesson with the AP English teacher's presentation on Shakespeare. Bring CDs and information to geography, sociology, and history classes, or any subject! Offer your resources (and yourself as a teacher) to the faculty. You can spice up their lessons, connect music's importance with the rest of the curriculum, and improve your visibility in your building.

Encourage students to do well in all classes at all times.

Look to your faculty as an instructional resource when you need help. Consult world language teachers for pronunciations. Your physics teacher can shed light on harmonics and tuning, and your history faculty can share insights into world events relating to a piece of music the choir is studying. Teaching across subject lines help unify the curriculum and shows students how the sum of parts makes an educational whole.

Do not beg for grade changes to keep students academically eligible to participate in choir activities. Play fair. However, work fervently and consistently to promote academic success on behalf of students to avoid issues of ineligibility. Release students from your rehearsal to attend tutoring sessions when alternate times or dates are not available. You might even consider offering a peer-tutoring program within your choir to match weaker and stronger students in specific academic subjects, to help keep choir grades up. Encourage students to do well in all classes at all times. This is positive for students, teachers, parents, and the choir as a whole.

Prepare singers to perform "The Star-Spangled Banner" for sporting and official school events like games, pep rallies, assemblies, and honor organization initiation ceremonies. You could use individuals, groups, or the entire choir! Consider letting a highly responsible student maintain a calendar of singers, venues, times, and event names as well as appropriate dress for each; some may even post reminders for your singers when their big date is coming up and provide a substitute singer in case of illness or emergency. Audition singers in advance so you know which singers might best suit particular occasions and venues. Seek out musically talented faculty members for inclusion in concerts, instrumental or piano accompaniment, or critiquing student performers. Consider forming a faculty choir for a special event, and always invite faculty and staff to attend your concerts.

Band and orchestra colleagues

It is regrettable that in some schools choral and instrumental directors do not get along well. If you are aware of some potential areas of conflict, it is easy to improve the odds that peace and harmony can rule in the land. Potential areas of conflict may include sharing rooms among music staff members. Allow other directors to use the choir facilities within established guidelines. In reality, your room is school district property and not yours exclusively, so it behooves you to be nice about sharing. Set reasonable guidelines for using each other's rooms, materials, and equipment. Effective planning will reduce potential differences during combined events and projects. Jealousies about budgeting, salary, and staffing between choir and band and orchestra colleagues serve no useful purpose.

Show support for your instrumental colleagues by keeping the lines of communication open. Ask band and orchestra directors before asking a student instrumentalist in their group to play for your choir. Invite your instrumental colleagues to play on a concert or competition trip. Offer your singers when the jazz band wants to explore charts with vocals. Ask the band or orchestra director to drop by your rehearsal to offer a quick critique of a particular contest or concert piece. Volunteer to accompany or chaperone for your instrumental colleague's students and be supportive of their fund-raising activities. Buy that attractive band candle!

Theater/drama director

Plan ahead when sharing your school's theater, both during and outside traditional school hours to avoid conflicts with shared facility use. Work with the theater or drama director to identify theater tech students willing to provide support at concerts and other performances. Plan well in advance and provide a copy of the program with lighting and curtain cues clearly marked and highlighted. Make sure to include theater tech students (and their director) in your program acknowledgments! Because they work behind the scenes, they are often overlooked and under appreciated. Include theater or advanced speech and debate students as narrators, announcers, or for help with set design.

Who really runs your school?

Too many teachers see custodians and paraprofessional staff members as an invisible part of the school's inner workings. Oh, WRONG! The head custodian runs your school! They can turn on the air-conditioning when there's no key or code and the auditorium is stifling. They know exactly how many cafeteria tables can go outside for a garage sale and where you can find some screws for the broken music stand. Most importantly, your custodians, day and night, work the same hours you do! You're never alone when the custodian knows you're in the building and will look out for you.

Similarly, your principal's secretary and the front office secretary run your school! From knowing everyone to having the secret code to the hidden copy machine, these good people are right up there with Bach and Mother Theresa. Hold them in high esteem, sing for their birthdays, remember them with flowers during Secretaries' Week, share choir T-shirts, and thank them with your every breath. Be considerate in giving ample notice when you need their help; if they hit a time snag, be patient. Don't take advantage of a good-hearted custodian or secretary! If we are quick to ask for help, we must be equally fast to say "thank you" and show our appreciation to all those with whom we work. Invest in some boxes of thank you notes and use them liberally.

I've learned that people will forget what you said,
people will forget what you did,
but people will never forget how you made them feel.
—Maya Angelou

➤ The Recruitment and Retention of Choir Members

Or, as those great ancient philosophers,
The Bee Gees, once said, "Stayin' alive, stayin' alive..."

Increasingly, education is turning to the world of business as a model of potential new trends, strategies, and effective tools to strengthen our schools. As we annually reach out to potential new members for our choirs, we would do well to look to the business sector to see how successful marketing works for them, and how we can use these strategies to make our efforts more effective. Traditional ways of reaching out to potential new members include:

- Flyers and signs posted around school, classrooms, feeder schools.
- Audition forms in counseling offices and proudly displayed in the hall outside the choir room.
- Cleverly written, "ear grabbing" public address announcements.
- Listing choirs offered in course catalogues and scheduling materials.
- Contacting transfer students with choir on their transcripts.
- Targeting students needing a fine arts credit for graduation.
- Inviting budding actors, musicians, and performers who want to complement their stage skills.
- Seeking out students who need a place to belong and positive reinforcement in a can-do classroom.
- Scheduling enthusiastic choir member visits, performances, and public address announcements at feeder schools.
- Providing information packets (including audition form, general information about choir, Q&A sheet of common misconceptions and ways to work through schedule conflicts) in all feeder school counseling offices and choir rooms.
- Volunteering to assist with concerts or events at your feeder schools.
- Inviting student leaders to audition for choir.
- Welcoming your students' friends in the choir room when appropriate.
- "Working the halls," casual conversations with students (and downright collar-pulling) by savvy directors.
- Helping students prepare schedules to include choir, particularly those who have multiple talents and are involved in several organizations.

- Asking colleagues on your faculty to point out potentially gifted or interested students.
- "Fill your own shoes," while you'll explain that nobody could ever fill your graduating singers' shoes, perhaps each of them could recruit two or three promising singers who could one day develop to fill the void they will be leaving in your choir.
- Creating a choral department website, and visibility on the school website, updated regularly with upcoming dates and events as well as recent awards and activities.
- Ads in sports programs, school newspaper, yearbook and other local media that is respected by the student body.

The power of word-of-mouth advertising

Even with all these methods of publicizing your program and educating your community about what your choirs have to offer, the fact is that the most powerful tool of all does not appear on the above list, and that powerful tool is word-of-mouth. The business sector has conclusively found that for all the money invested in traditional advertising, word-of-mouth is the most effective way of reaching a potential audience. People tend to give extra credence to the opinions of those known to them, people they trust and believe. Looking to this business model, we would do well to realize that the perception of, and participation in our choral programs rests squarely in what one neighbor says to another about the school musical, or a conversation at lunch between students about their classes. Perception becomes reality, and even if we have one of the best choral programs in the land, perceptions will determine how the community defines our program and the value placed on it.

The fact is that conversations are already taking place, whether we like it or not. People are talking about you and your choirs all over your school's attendance zones and beyond. This reminds us that each rehearsal, trip, concert, and garage sale, everything we do with our singers, translates into potential conversation that will ripple out to the public with lasting results. No number of signs or pamphlets can substitute for this potential treasure chest of endorsements. No "happy camper" speeches can repair the negative buzz already out there. This is an outgrowth of what we do every day, and is a part of our social fabric. We share opinions, as do the students, their parents and friends. The trick is to promote your singers in such a positive and infectious way that word-of-mouth about your program catches fire throughout your community. Your audition materials and PA announcements will just add fuel to that fire. It has been said that if people aren't going around talking about what you're doing then you're either not doing it well enough, often enough, or publicly enough.

Could this mean that having the best choral program at your school isn't enough? Yes! The truth is that perception IS reality. If your choirs are the aesthetic wonder of the hemisphere, it still counts that people feel they are the best and that choir is a fine place to be. Word-of-mouth will sink or float your boat. It is still important for the choir to perform a brilliant concert directly before students make their scheduling choices for the coming year. However, it will be what the students told their friends and neighbors after rehearsals and classes that will make the final difference in who signs up for choir and who doesn't.

Retaining existing singers in choir

Remember that while recruiting new students is essential to the health and life of a performing organization, so is the retention of current students in the program. Building choirs around returning students is a key to choral excellence, and provides experienced musical leadership to newer singers. Student retention in a choral program can be affected by a number of things. Issues that might affect scheduling decisions may include:

- How much extra time is required outside the traditional school day. Be respectful of students' time, always.

- Financial cost of participation. Devise creative ways of assisting students in paying for expenses so that the ability to pay never keeps a singer from your risers.

- Graduation requirements, and limited number of elective choices. Be informed about what is required. Be flexible in helping students find ways to keep singing.

- Student burn out. Model balance to your students by having a life outside the choir room just as you acknowledge that they, too, have a majority of their lives outside the choir room.

- Conflicts with the director. Conflicts are a given, no matter how nice we are. How we handle those conflicts with students and their parents will affect student retention.

- Fear of auditioning. Strive to have at least one class that any student may take without audition. This may take the form of a humming anthill at times, but from these choirs have come many enthusiastic and gifted singers. When you spot talent at the beginning of the year, there will always be the opportunity to pull a student aside and ask them to sing for you. For feeder schools, offer auditions in a practice room at the student's home school to make auditions closer and easier for all.

- Parent preferences or demands that students concentrate on "solid" subjects.

- Director indifference or burn out. Be passionate about what you do! People respond to energy and zeal.

- Feeling alone or excluded from the group. Build a social aspect to choir to assist students in making new friends and wanting to bring others to your groups. Make choir a fun, safe, welcoming place to be.

When recruiting students it is important to remember to be honest. Don't promise things your choir program can't deliver. Be positive about all the fine arts, and do not recruit students away from band and orchestra. Be respectful of your colleagues and their work. Students with multiple talents will find a way to schedule choir. On the other hand, if a band or orchestra student is choosing to drop that organization and auditions for choir, discuss this privately with your instrumental colleagues prior to placing the student in your group. Be respectful of other directors and their groups as well as being transparent about recruiting. Your newest soprano might be their only oboe player. They deserve inclusion in the loop.

Consider giving additional weight to continuing upperclassmen when placing students in advanced groups. Honor their experience and dedica-

Work equally hard to retain singers as you did to first recruit them for choir. Unlike the swallows of Capistrano, they don't necessarily return each winter.

tion to your program when considering auditions that are similar between students. However, do not be held hostage by a student who threatens to quit choir if they aren't placed in a particular group. This "all or nothing" type of attitude is detrimental to an organization. Beware the student who, after audition results are posted, emotionally explains that their schedule will only "work" if they have choir during third period. Most of the time you will notice that this scheduling conflict just happens to be with a student placed in your intermediate choir with only your top group's class period open for an elective. Consider these situations carefully. (See appendix 6g and 6h for sample audition forms.)

If a student's four-year plan does not appear to have room for participation in choir throughout their high school years, encourage them to begin as freshmen and stay as long as they can. If you get them now, there's a greater chance they will want to continue and use summer school or other creative scheduling to facilitate staying with choir until they graduate. Students who plan a scheduling hiatus until they are upperclassmen may be attracted to something else along the way and never join choir later on. Welcome your school's foreign exchange students to sing in your choir.

Include a copy of a student's report card to date as a requirement for auditioned groups. Student grades can be a strong indicator of work habits and academic dedication. They can also help you see a bigger picture with a student who might need to become involved in choir to help build confidence and motivation in their other studies. Realistically, a report card that shows multiple grading periods paints a clear picture of who is likely to be eligible for contests and extracurricular concerts. A singer with the best tone quality cannot benefit a group if the student is academically ineligible to participate for periods during the year. Consider including a student in a particular group on a probationary basis, pending grades through the end of the year. Some form of provisional contract with academically questionable students can be a beneficial both for the student involved and your group. Additionally, teachers will appreciate your valuing student work in their classes as well as your own.

Anyone who has never made a mistake
has never tried anything new.
—Albert Einstein

➤ Effective Publicity and Public Relations

Keeping the choir's name in lights...

Let there be no doubt. What people think of you and your choral department is important. How you and your program are perceived may affect funding, recruitment, more advantageous scheduling on the school's master schedule, donations, honor or special event concert invitations, staffing, and even whether a program can or should be cut back when finances are in a pinch. Commit to excellence in all things and use concrete ways to inform your school and community about your program.

Recruit a booster club public relations officer to serve as your mastermind for a yearlong program of advertising and information gathering, and appoint or elect a student public relations officer to work with them to advertise within the school. Choose the best mode of communication for each event you want to publicize. There are many ways to do this including school public address announcements, signs, banners, flyers, school, community, and city newspapers, and national media when appropriate. Consider taking an ad in the school yearbook and sports programs to publicize your choir.

Email is another form of communication to consider. Choir email lists can be compiled at the beginning of the school year and can be subdivided by choir, home and business addresses, student/parent addresses, and

---

Give your choir the same visibility in your school
as other fields of endeavor.

---

alumni addresses for more personalized communications, reminders, and advertising. District email should be uses sparingly. Use this for state or national honors only, or for those very rare occasions when something unique happens within your organization. Do not promote individual fundraisers or concerts via district email, as boxes will be clogged with like communications. Know policies and rules in your district prior to using district email lists.

Ask your principal if you may display recent trophies in one of the school's more prominent trophy cases. Keep the rest of your awards in your room. If there are no trophy cases available, ask your principal if one might be purchased when funding permits. Give your choir the same visibility in your school as other fields of endeavor.

Provide updated articles about recent awards and events in choir on the school's website, and develop a website for your own choral department. This can be informative, including grading policies, make-up work, and topics of interest to choir parents, as well as a place for showcasing contest winners, festival trophy recipients, and a calendar of upcoming concerts and activities.

*In times like these, it helps to recall that
there have always been times like these.*
—Paul Harvey

How to Do Stuff

➤ **Fund-raising**

➤ **Uniforms**

➤ **Music Library Organization and Maintenance**

➤ Fund-Raising

You can't pass the buck if you don't have one...

Money can be the bane of our existence. With it, we can acquire materials and equipment galore. Charter busses for field trips, fees, and travel expenses can be paid without a second thought. It's a useful tool and therefore, fund-raising is a necessary evil. And, any time your students are personally involved in earning money for the choir, they will appreciate it more. Money that mysteriously "appears" due to directorial heroics denies students the opportunity to reap the benefits of their own hard work. There are a number of ways to raise money:

- Sell something produced for student fund-raising.
- Provide a service.
- Sell acquired goods and services.
- Hold a raffle.
- Ask for it.
- Charge for booster club membership.
- Barter for it.
- Seek a company or corporate sponsor.
- Sponsor an event.

Before you engage in fund raising you must thoroughly, utterly, and completely know and abide by every small and large requirement and limitation placed on you and your group. These policies will come not only from your local building but also from your school district. Study them, and follow them to the letter and spirit of the law. Do not seek to circumvent any procedure or restriction. This can cost you your job.

Know how many fund-raising activities you can sponsor in a given school year, and if there are limits, do not exceed this number. In any case, limit yourself to two or three projects per year. It is best to make more money in limited efforts than for your singers to be constantly engaged in fund-raising. Singers join choir to sing, not to become salespeople. Plan and choose your fund-raisers so that a minimum number will produce the maximum result.

As non-profit entities, schools are limited in how much money they can carry over in activity funds from year to year. This is an enviable problem to have but can happen! Know your parameters and fund-raise accordingly. For multi-year efforts to purchase a costly piece of equipment you may need to make special arrangements with your business manager or principal. Ask questions and learn the policies. Your Booster Club's own fund-raising efforts on your behalf may or may not count against the number of projects you may do with the choir annually. Particularly when sales do not involve the students and take place off school grounds, it is possible for your parents to organize a drive that will benefit your program. Be aware of district policies regarding where parent-generated funds may be deposited (school choir account, separate banking facility, etc.), what accounting and auditing procedures must be in place, and any restrictions on how this money may be spent. Also be aware that interscholastic organizations that govern competition between school athletic and music groups may have restrictions about students' receiving any sort of financial benefit from such funds, such as meals provided, uniforms, or other garments purchased. As always, know the rules and follow them.

You will also need to consider if all monies raised go into one big account or into separate accounts for each student. There are many implications, philosophical differences, and motivations for doing either or both. Raising money for the group shows group spirit in a selfless, "one for all and all for one" fashion. It breeds energy and enthusiasm rather than individual greed. Establishing individual accounts can be complicated and time consuming.

Know the rules and follow them.

Once a singer "has" all the money they need in their own account, they are more likely to stop participating in fund-raising or work less actively. You will also need to provide additional funds for goods and services for the entire choir and choral department. It can less dazzling to sell candy bars to buy new choir folders or charter a field trip bus than to raise money for an individual trip fund. By the same token, you do not want to be in the position of having some singers ride a field trip bus for free and having to charge other members $2.61 for their share of the bus cost. If you run separate accounts solely, they must be non-transferable. Students must understand that any funds remaining under individual names at the end of the year remain in the choir fund for the group's needs, and are not refundable in cash to an individual singer.

Always do your banking by using the school's activity fund if possible, because this can provide legal protection for you in many ways. Your school's business manager, a district employee, will check your work before any deposit is made. This provides official verification of monies received and amounts recorded. Running all money through the school office does slow down the time it will take for the money to become available to you. This is not a problem if you plan ahead. It will also help you save money for your most worthy expenditures, as funds will be harder to get to. (Some schools maintain a petty cash fund from which you can withdraw a quick twenty-five dollars for a last-minute purchase. Find out about this.) The school will keep money safe over holidays, between years, and provide ending and starting balances each year. Make sure that your balance, if any, at the end of a year will be carried forward for the choir's use the following year.

Never, ever, ever leave any fund-raising money in your classroom! Do not leave money locked in your desk, in your office, or under a stack of dust-covered *Melodia* books. Know exactly how, when, and where you can deposit money and do it every day possible and as required. Holding money from one day to the next is asking for trouble. Do not ask for exceptions to this. Never take choir money home with you overnight unless directly told to do so by your building principal. (This might happen with a late night event, but even so, there is usually a night bank drop location or school safe your administrator can use until funds can be dealt with following day.) Know your business manager's preferred way of doing things and abide by it. This is a person who should be included at holiday times and birthdays with flowers, thoughtful gifts, or singers serenading in the office. School business managers work hard for little recognition. Be good to them. Whether you are required to do so or not, always sort money carefully with all bills facing in the same direction, and place coins in wrappers by type. Do everything possible to be organized, clear, and accurate. This makes the life of the business manager easier!

Pay all bills promptly and accurately, and keep meticulous records. Never require students to purchase unsold or undelivered products. It's just bad business. Never allow a student to give a product, ticket, or symbol of value without having payment in hand.

It is awkward to deal with bounced checks. Spare the student embarrass-ment and contact the parent or guardian privately, letting them know the check was returned to you. You know how easy it is to make a math error; you do it all the time yourself… make it easy for the parent to save face. Ask that they bring cash or money order for payment. Do not accept a second check and start the same process all over again. Some schools require cash only in these circumstances. Other schools no longer accept checks for any reason due to the high rate of return.

Bringing money to school is dangerous for students. In a world in which a convenience store clerk can be shot over eleven dollars, consider the target your singers become when they carry large amounts of money to school to turn in. Consider the vulnerable position it places you in as you receive these deposits. For this reason, ask students to be private about which days are turn-in deadlines and only accept money before school. Money carried around during the school day can be stolen from lockers and purses. It can fall out of a book bag or be taken from a student's pocket. Lock yourself in before counting money. Don't count it in front of your office window, with cash spread out all over your desk. Think! Carry money to the office in an old but rugged backpack or tote bag. Don't advertise by carrying a cash box without first placing it in a worthless looking exterior covering.

Some ways of raising money reap higher profits than others. You will want to get the best results for your group by considering the pros and cons of the type of fund-raising activity you choose.

Using professional fund-raising companies

Countless products are offered for sale through professional fund-raising companies. They include holiday poinsettias or greenery, gift wrap, specialty food items, greeting cards, candy, candles, magazine subscriptions, bedding plants, and gift items, just to mention a few!

One of the biggest advantages to using a professional fund-raising company is that they do most of the work for you. One of the biggest drawbacks, however, is that fund-raising companies stay in business by splitting profits between themselves and your organization, using your students as their sales force. A fifty/fifty split has nearly become extinct. Sixty/forty percentages are more common, with the company taking the sixty percent. This means that your supporter's dollars are funding the company as much or more than your choir. Many parents wish they could just hand you five dollars instead of buying a product for almost twice that amount.

Other pluses to using a professional company are being able to take advantage of sales materials and the labeling, shipping, and handling of orders. Disadvantages to consider include the responsibilities involved for students in transporting and delivering the items once the orders arrive at school. (We should also mention that the arrival of a massive 18-wheeler at the door closest to your choir room is not a lot of fun either.) Once students have picked up their orders they will need to return to each buyer to collect payment and deliver the order. This doubles the time put in by students and can also present a dilemma when a buyer has moved or changed their mind about a purchase. Another consideration is collecting payment. Buyers may not have cash in exact amounts, or may wish to pay by personal check. Personal checks are bouncing in increasing numbers. This becomes a nightmare when school business offices must serve as collection agencies, with you as their primary agent. Students and parents should not be held responsible for buyer's bounced checks. Ultimately, many bounced checks must be entered as a loss to your group. This can make a meaningful dent in your profit margins.

Selling is another issue to consider. In order to broaden the buyer base, students will be tempted to sell door-to-door. In today's world, this can be highly dangerous and has come to the point that some school districts have banned door-to-door sales for school fund-raising. It's never as easy as a parent "leaving a brochure" on their desk at work. Coworkers may feel obliged to order and purchase items in order to maintain a collegial atmosphere in the workplace. This wears thin when Mr. Kadel's goalie son is selling chocolate bunnies, Mrs. Herbek's daughter must sell twenty rolls of wrapping paper, and Mrs. Hosteria's twins each have a brochure on her desk that tout the benefits of potpourri in every home. There is only so much "stuff" that parents can (or should) buy. There is a limit to how many times the same people at churches, Girl Scouts, and soccer practice can be approached. This is especially true when a congregation, club, or team has more than one member in your choir program. Keep these things in mind as you consider sales as a means of fund-raising for your program.

When dealing with wholesalers, don't gamble your profits. Take pre-paid orders. This type of fund-raiser has worked especially well with holiday poinsettias or greenery as well as bedding plants from a local nursery at the beginning of planting time for your location. Making this a traditional sale with your group, using the same wholesale provider from year to year can work very effectively.

Providing a service

Providing a service as a means of fund-raising costs little or nothing to you and your program. For example, singing telegrams for Valentine's Day would be one such service. Once your choir is organized, practiced, and available for delivery, orders can be taken from families, or with permission from your principal, from students during lunch periods. Options could include individual singers or quartets, a choice of songs, and even the inclusion of a carnation (or rose) for an extra charge. Prepare a price list of services including name and phone number of buyer, name and location of honoree along with time, choice of song from a limited list you provide, if a flower is to be included, price total, and name of singer who made the sale. This should be turned in along with payment. Performers should dress in a uniform way for easy identification and should not be sent into a stranger's home. Offer varied songs, so telegrams can be purchased for more than one type of relationship. Include songs that are more suited to friendships, parents, teachers, and so forth. Some ideas could include:

"My Funny Valentine"

"Never My Love"

"I Love You" (a bushel and a peck)

"Come Again Sweet Love"

"Ah Sweet, Whose Beauty"

"Sea of Love"

"Love is a Many Splendored Thing"

"I Wish You Love"

"Canadian Love Song" (When I'm calling you-ooo-ooo....)

Holiday carolers are another such service you could provide. Again, make sure you have the resources ready to do this. Bad carolers are not necessarily a bargain.

"Choir Servant Day" is another fund-raiser you could consider. Sell your singers' time for a specified amount, say ten dollars, in groups of at least two people, to provide services such as yard work, house cleaning, dog walking, or babysitting. Take an inventory of what students will do and develop a flyer to promote this endeavor. Have a parent volunteer coordinate jobs offered, accept phone calls to hire workers, schedule specific workers for particular jobs, and verify how much money was collected by the workers. This fund-raiser can be done on a one time, or regular basis. One more popular fund-raiser is to provide workers to staff a concession stand at sporting events at your school or in your community. This requires an organized schedule of dependable people and clear communications.

Selling donated items

Substantial sums of money can be raised through silent (or live) auctions of goods and services donated by individual companies, celebrities, and anyone who has a saleable item or service. Past silent auctions have offered staggering diversity and value; from homemade baked goods to Cancun condos for two weeks with staff. Students and parents can be organized into a small army to locate items for your auction. Have students think of what they know how to do to earn money that people commonly pay for: babysitting, detailing a car, cutting lawns, general yard work, tutoring younger students, or cleaning houses. The more invested students are in your auction, the better. (Some parents bid on their own student's house cleaning service just to marvel that they actually know how!) Encourage thinking "outside the box," and think big! Unique and costly items are often donated to worthy causes for the community goodwill derived, as well as the tax write off. Solicit donations from people and companies you know personally, and consider asking celebrities for donations. To do this, locate an updated book of

---

Encourage thinking "outside the box," and think big!

---

celebrity contact information, or check on-line resources to find names and contact information for movie stars, television actors, famous athletes, musicians and other celebrities. Divide the names and addresses by the number of students participating in the project, and ask students to write a form letter to each individual on their list, personalizing it by telling what school they attend, a little about their involvement and honors at school, and how much they would appreciate the celebrity donating any item they might spare to benefit their school choir. The letter should include the name and address of a responsible adult who agrees to receive, catalogue, and be responsible for all items. When setting up your auction, display all items on long tables. Presentation is important! Use tablecloths, a pen or two next to each bid sheet, and pleasing displays of goods, gift certificates, artwork, and whatever else you have for sale. There's no limit to the list of possible acquisitions for a silent auction. These are just a few:

- Gift certificates (oil change at the local gas station or speedy oil place, local restaurants, teeth-whitening from a local dentist, free flu shot from a local physician, flower arrangements, music or other lessons).
- Helicopter ride over your city.
- Hockey stick, puck, baseball, jersey, etc. from a celebrity sports figure or local athletic hero.
- Fung shui of one or more rooms.
- Gift baskets (these can even be made into a competition for which students or parents fashion a "themed" basket from a group of smaller items placed attractively in a decorative basket and covered by plastic and a big bow! Make sure each basket's contents are clearly visible and listed on the bid sheet.).
- Professional photography packages.
- Fun, "motivational" events (certificate that entitles the winning bidder to throw a cream pie at the director, shave their head, etc., think carefully before signing on the dotted line on this one).

Next to each item displayed, tape down a bid sheet with the item number, name, retail value (which may be "priceless" in the case of celebrity and one-of-a-kind items), name of donor, and a brief but catchy description of the item. Your bid sheet should also include the minimum opening bid at the top of the "bid" column, already in place before the auction starts, and the minimum bidding increment, and a place for people to print their name, bid amount, and phone number. At the end of the sale, the bidding sheets are taken up and high bidders are contacted. If this is done in conjunction with a performance or other event, encourage bidders to "pick up and pay" at the end of the auction; this means fewer phone calls and possible item deliveries by your students and parents.

Publicity and exposure to the largest number of bidders possible are the keys to maximizing bids. If only thirty people see the display of your one hundred and six items, they are going to get huge bargains at the expense of potential profits for your choral department. If you hold a silent auction in conjunction with a concert there must be enough time for bidders to mill about and bid, or improve their best price when outbid, and not interfere with the ongoing performance. You don't want Mrs. Cogburn to sneak out during a dramatic "Agnus Dei" to make sure she's still high bidder on the clog dancing lessons! With this in mind, a silent auction is better offered along with an event-a-thon of some sort that will attract a large number of people. A good example of a combined fund-raiser would be a coffeehouse with non-stop student entertainment, throughout which the silent auction would be open. Put flyers in teacher boxes or use multi-school emails so they can have the opportunity to bid on some terrific items that may be won at greatly reduced prices! Advertise what you've got by listing some of the bigger or more unique items and some of the gift certificates that have the most universal appeal.

Other donated items you might also consider selling include arts and crafts at a stall in your local city street fair or similar community event, or a choir cookbook with favorite "secret" family recipes donated for the cause. If you have secured the appropriate copyright permission you may sell CDs, videos, and DVDs of your choir performances.

Raffles

Before considering a raffle, know what is legal in your community and what is not, and stay well within the law. Figure in the price of professionally printed tickets, each with the same sequential numbers on them for ready identification as the winning ticket. Make sure your student turns in the drawing half of each ticket with their money. Ticket stubs must match dollars exactly! Typical big-ticket raffle items and sources include locally based airline roundtrip tickets, local car dealership donated cars, car rentals, or a vehicle lease. Raffles of smaller items are not as attractive to supporters. However, if you assemble a whole group of new items donated at moderate values, multiple winners can find themselves the owner of a new sewing machine, vacuum cleaner, set of luggage, or other items.

Asking for what you need

Begging is not recommended. It lacks class, looks desperate, and is expressly forbidden by most every school district. "Asking" however, could take the form of a request of the PTA, local school budget, district fine arts' office, as well as local corporations and sponsors. It could also involve applying for grants from foundations and organizations for specific things. It certainly is the most direct approach. Matching funds may also be available to you. Locate a list of companies and corporations that donate matching funds for employees. A donation could double if the donor works for one of these companies.

Booster club memberships

Another potential source for funds is to charge an annual fee for choir booster club membership. This can give families an avenue for cash donations if you offer a wide range of membership options, such as member, friend, sponsor, etc. A downside to this is the fact that you primarily want volunteers, supporters, workers, and chaperones as members of your booster club; you don't want to appear to be overwrought by financial needs which can drive parents away if they think all you want is their money. Additionally, this may exclude financially limited parents from joining if a token amount, or "free" membership, isn't an option.

Memberships could be free ("Count me in to work and support but I cannot assist financially at this time"), or begin at a reasonably token amount like ten dollars (or whatever might constitute "token" in your community), to memberships in the amounts of fifty, seventy-five, one hundred, and even five hundred dollars. You'll be amazed how many people opt to donate more than you ask for if you give them the option, and a tax donation form along with your thank you note. Remember that those who support your choir are not necessarily restricted to current parents of choir students, and that memberships should be offered per family, not per child, in the case of one family having multiple students involved in your program.

Grants from educational foundations

Learn how to write a grant proposal from someone who has successfully done so in the past. There is an art to it. Use their language, use spell-check in addition to a good proofreader, be neat in all work, and observe every deadline down to the millisecond. The *Directory of Foundations*, found in most library reference centers will list potential foundations in alphabetical order according to:

- Type of projects typically funded.
- Name and address of contact person.
- Examples of areas not funded (such as elective travel).
- Required format and deadlines for submission.
- How often applications are considered.
- Projected times of year for granting and dispersing funds.

Focus on local foundations. They are the most likely to fund projects in your area, and do not waste your time and stamps with mass mailing. Most foundations have specific geographic, financial, and demographic requirements that will be clearly stated on their websites and on all printed materials and application forms. Construct each proposal individually, tailoring it to the specific foundation you are apply to. "One size does not fit all" in submitting grant proposals. Be concise and specific in your request, describing specifically how funding will benefit your students. Be clear and precise about:

- What you want to do with the money requested.
- The reason you want to do this.
- The difference it will make to your program.
- Why you are the person and group who should receive the funding for this specific purpose.
- How you will measure whether the funding accomplished your stated project goals.
- How far-reaching this project may be, continuing beyond the year of funding.
- Your statement of commitment to the project or purchase for which you seek funding and its significance to the individual student, group, school, and community-at-large.

More information about grants can be found in the *Chronicle of Philanthropy*, and philanthropic and foundation websites such as www.not-for-profit.org, www.schoolgrants.org, www.grantsmart.org, and www.fdncenter.org.

Local special interest groups, corporate sponsors

Local special interest groups may contribute to the financial needs of a particular student representative of their group. Groups such as these might include the African American Chamber of Commerce, Hispanic Chamber of Commerce, local businesswomen's organization, teacher's credit union for a future teacher, etc. Also, most of us are familiar with adopt-a-school programs in which corporations donate employee volunteer time, funding, and goods for particular schools. However, many of us don't know that some companies and corporations also "adopt" organizations within schools, underwriting specific purchases or programs on a one time or multi-year basis. As long as the corporate world values the employee pool of the future by investing in the best possible education for your community's young people, there will be corporate sponsors. Various IRS tax laws and advantages are also a significant corporate donation motivator.

Barter

Some suggestions for bartering services include offering a mini-concert of holiday songs for a corporate party for a company who will underwrite your new risers, or invite the T-shirt printing company in town to add their business logo to the back of your choir shirts for a heavily discounted (if not free) price for your students' shirts for the year.

Hold an Event

This can have many benefits beyond earning money. Students develop *esprit d'corps* and genuinely have fun whether they are performing or serving up burgers, although proceeds can be unpredictable depending on date, weather, overlapping school events (as with an athletic event), or even what's on television that night. Some events can be so much fun that they are useful as a performance opportunity, earning profits or not. However, with limited time and profitable projects, you need to structure events to maximize profits while being enjoyable and useful. You will want to insure that what you spend to make the event happen does not exceed the profits. You can vary the type of event in order to stay creative and have the most fun for your patrons. Be sure to schedule an appropriate school venue (the most visible parking lot for a car wash, the cafetorium for the pancake breakfast, etc.) on an available date. Possible events for this type of fund-raiser include dinner shows, coffee houses, pancake breakfasts, skate-a-thon, walk-a-thon, sing-a-thon, bowl-a-thon, or anything-a-thon. Take pledges for each mile, lap, minute, or pin, and collect afterward, keeping careful records.

A choir garage sale can be held indoors or outdoors, run as a whole on behalf of the choir, or families can set up tables like stalls in an antique mall to benefit their own student for a big choir trip. Items must be pre-priced with student initials on it for identification. If you keep individual accounts on one big sale, offer different percentages according to how long singers work the sale, such as eighty percent of what your items brought in if you work all day, sixty percent if you work half day, forty percent if you drop off your stuff and leave. At a given time, any items that have not sold or taken home by students can be picked up by a local charity to benefit those in your community. Hold a mega car wash. Students take pledges per car they helped clean, and big signs and splashy colors identify the choir's FREE CAR WASH with donations accepted in a "donations" bucket (monitored) at the end of the line. This fund-raiser has minimal cost and large profit potential if your site is located on major arteries with easy access in and out. Most schools, businesses, and houses of worship will allow students to hook up their hoses and use their water for free. Other ideas include Bingo Night, Casino Night, Hole-In-One Tournaments and Basketball Tournaments. You might feature parents against students, faculty members against choir athletes, one school's choir against another school's choir (splitting the profits and ticket sales), or even your choir against your school's orchestra, band, or chess club.

Some final thoughts on fund-raising

Local restaurants may donate a percentage of their profits on specific dates and times to all patrons who mention your choir. Often, they will want choir members on site to generate enthusiasm, advertising for the establishment, or to work during those hours.

Some grocery stores chains have means by which customers can designate a set percentage of their purchases to benefit a designated non-profit group. Why not have this group be your choir? In all likelihood, some organizations are already signed up locally. You can join them. This will require your picking up some paperwork, filling it out with required signa-

Any honest money is good money!

tures, and then obtaining a number by which your choirs will be identified. Choir supporters, alumni, students, parents, and community members can then sign up to have their percentage go to your choir on a regular basis. (If a customer does not designate a donor-destination, these monies are additional profit for the store chain so it's free money to the customer and your choir!) A bonus to doing this is that most people will leave their designated non-profit as the beneficiary of this money even after their own singers have graduated from your school. This becomes a self-perpetuating source of funds, token though it may be. Any honest money is good money! See appendix 7a for an example of how to keep records and post accountability.

Offer a tiered system of donor acknowledgments in printed concert programs each year. Pattern this after professional music organizations, and read their programs to see which terminology fits your range of donations. Names might include gemstones (garnet, ruby, emerald, diamond,) termed (friend, supporter, sponsor, angel,) types of cars (Mercedes, Porsche, Lamborghini, Rolls Royce,) or any number of designations. Do not use negative terminology. Any donation is a good donation. The lowest category must still hold an honored title.

It is not as difficult as I thought it was,
but it is harder than it is.
—Eugene Ormandy

➤ Uniforms

No matter what they promise, one size does not fit all.

Ah, those repeated questions we have all known and loved: "This dress is so ugly. Why can't we wear something more up to date and stylish?" "Why is it a problem if I wear my big hoop earrings that have the cool macaw feathers hanging down?" "I wouldn't be seen *dead* in this at prom."

Oh, to have a dollar for every time the word "ugly" is used to describe choir dresses. Some choir members forget that the choir isn't going to the prom, or about how that fine prom dress would look when simultaneously worn by sixty girls, standing in rows, of every shape and size. In the real world we all know that "one size doesn't fit or flatter all." The finances involved in acquiring dozens of dresses preclude replacing gowns annually. Tux lapel cuts come and go but choir tuxes remain, at least as long as any three threads are still attached to one another. The answer to many questions is in the word itself: u-n-i-f-o-r-m.

Dictionaries tell us that uniforms are a style of dress that is distinctive, worn by members of a group and serve to identify that group by presenting an unvaried appearance. This is a tough one for students who value individuality, just as we all do. Being required to look alike may be a less frequent battle if singers understand the essential reasons why uniforms are worn at all.

Costs will certainly factor into what your choir wears as a uniform. When considering uniforms for your choir, determine who will pay for them. Will singers or parents, the school district, or your choral program buy the uniform? Other questions to consider include how long you plan to use a particular uniform, whether your school or district has a policy which requires all performing groups to wear the same style and color so the pool from which to draw uniforms from year-to-year is more substantial, and, if students provide their own uniforms, will they be expected to buy a new outfit every year they are in choir if they change sizes or groups.

Uniforms can be as simple as a choir t-shirt worn with the same color pants or skirt. If you are fortunate enough to have the funding, they might be formal black gowns and tuxedos. Other typical options might include robes, individual uniforms bought by students, using uniform colors (often black and white) for example, black pants or skirts with a white shirt or blouse. All black is usually more flattering than two different colors. Insist that skirt length is uniform (floor length is better than varying degrees of short) or consider formal gowns and tuxedos.

Most of us work in communities that include students from a variety of financial backgrounds. Let us not be guilty of keeping out any singer who wants to participate but is sensitive to their family's monetary limitations. We must keep costs manageable and be responsible stewards of money, whether it is ours, the choir's, or to be spent by individual families. Increasingly fewer parents sew, but using a trusted seamstress can be a solution to providing inexpensive uniforms if the volume of garments isn't overwhelming. Consider, too, that new garments will be needed in the future to match the ones you've already got. Can dye lots be matched so the "new" royal blue dress is the same royal blue as two years ago? Even two different dye lots purchased within days of each other can look as different as pink and green on stage. For these and other considerations, most choirs turn to reputable companies that specialize in making uniforms for performing groups.

If funding is available, the classic look of formal black gowns and black tuxedos is probably the most practical uniform choice and will give you the best look on stage for your money. These can be used for a number of years and remain in style as well as providing versatility in fitting different

Consider singers of various shapes and sizes to make a choice that is as flattering as possible.

students. Returning students may check out the same uniform if it still fits. Most of the boys will need to start from scratch in the fitting department each year they sing. In choosing a supplier for your uniform needs, make sure to use a reputable company that has experience in dealing with large groups. Changing suppliers after two or three years is a nightmare you don't want. Talk to your colleagues to learn where they bought their uniforms. Talk to vendors at professional conventions to learn about what is available, prices, lead-time between order, payment, and delivery, who does the actual measuring of students, and any warranty against defective merchandise.

Keep in mind that school spirit is great, but school colors in uniforms are usually the antithesis of great. Buy choir T-shirts sporting school colors but see the wisdom in "going classic" for formalwear on stage. When selecting uniforms accept input from a variety of sources. Include choir students and choir parents in an advisory capacity, with the director making the final decision. Consider singers of various shapes and sizes to make a choice that is as flattering as possible.

You will need to decide if you will permit students or parents to alter school-owned garments. If you do, uniforms will fit students better and everybody will be happier for the most part. On the other hand, once you've had uniforms altered, they become more difficult to catalogue and fit in future years since all your size nine dresses will no longer fit the same. In hemming, may students cut material from the bottom of the garment? If they do, the garment can never again be made longer. Hemming without removing any cloth from the cuff or hem length is recommended.

Give ample time for students to prepare for uniform check in advance of your first performance of the year. Have this date on your calendar. Check each uniform on the student, including correct shoes and appropriate hem or cuff length. Regarding hems, the hem should touch the top of the foot but not show the ankle or cover the shoes. Uneven hems across the stage are visually distracting and sloppy. Remind students that uniforms stored in a car trunk or school locker rarely look flattering. Hemming is done carefully with thread that matches the color of the garment. It does not involve a stapler, safety pins, or duct tape. Dry cleaning and your washing machine at home are not the same. We don't recommend using dry cleaning kits in your home laundry. If you're not sure if your uniform needs to go to the dry cleaner or not, it does.

When in uniform wear nothing at the wrist, not even watches or bracelets. Rings on fingers are fine, and earrings may be worn if either a small loop or stud. No necklaces, although uniform pearls can work well on stage, especially if all your choirs are using the same uniform and your advanced ladies get to wear their pearls. Discount shops and importers can provide strands of very faux pearls of the same color for a dollar or little more. Facial piercings are generally distracting to the audience and can be a barrier between the singer and listener in performance. When singers are approached individually in private, and respectfully asked to consider leaving off facial piercings for performances, they will invariably honor your request. If power posturing starts on the part of either student or director, you've lost the battle and set yourself up for skirmishes to come. Stay on the same side of the fence without adversarial attitude. (If piercings or other appearance issues are covered by school policy you are obliged to support the district dress code.) Do not wear perfumes, colognes, or scented hair-sprays in consideration of those on stage whose allergies will be triggered.

Students should provide their own shoes of solid uniform color, usually black. Disallow shoes with trims, buckles, and straps that shine or attract attention to them. Allow sufficient variety to accommodate different budgets and less available sizes. For gentlemen, black socks must be worn with black dress shoes. (Yes, people can tell if they are very dark navy or brown.) You might have to tell your gentlemen several times. Many may not own black socks. Black dress shoes are recommended, whether lace up or loafer in style. Black hightops with black duct tape over the white rubber trim are unacceptable. Black socks worn instead of shoes are unacceptable. For the ladies black shoes are recommended, flats or a low heel. One test of whether a heel or shoe is appropriate for a female singer is if she can stand in them comfortably for an hour and a half. If you prefer not to have open toes, sandals, or some other type of shoe, address this and when you draw the line, stick to it. In addition to being uniform in shoes, we want our singers to uniformly have "happy" feet. Hurting feet do not attach themselves to joyful bodies making beautiful sounds. Dress shoes are very expensive and young singers' feet have such growth spurts that the shoes worn for fall concert may be painful to wear at the spring performances. Recommend economical shoe stores. The Salvation Army and Goodwill sell used shoes, if money is an issue.

Whenever the choir is in uniform, the full uniform should be worn at all times. The exception to this would be for gentlemen to offer their tux jackets to the girls in the event of cold weather. It tarnishes a choir's image when it is seen removing bow ties or un-tucking shirttails. Whether the choir is simply returning to a bus, going out to eat, or waiting for its next event in competition, it shows pride in one's group and school to remain properly attired at all times. The good (and great) choirs don't move about looking sloppy.

Organizing your uniform closet

The trick here is to put like-things together, labeled in a permanent way, keeping them both clean and in their right place so they can be used at a moment's notice. For each item (tux jacket, tux pants, gown, robe, etc.), sort what you have by size. Number each garment by size and garment number. (For example, 36L – 1, 36L – 2.) Hang like sizes together as you would find them on the rack in a retail store. If possible, acquire the plastic disks that label professional garment racks (or make them yourself out of heavy cardboard) to best identify them by sight. Within each size of each garment, hang from shortest to longest if any alterations have been done. Unfortunately, when permission to alter garments is given, all your size sevens or size fourteens are no longer the same fit for each girl. As you label each sized article of uniforms, make an index card (or log for computerization) for that item so when it is checked out, you know the date and name of singer who wore it. Never put a dirty uniform in your closet, even a "lightly soiled" garment.

Uniform fitting day ("Oh joy, oh rapture!")

The overall process in getting uniforms issued without bloodshed includes giving singers ample notice of dates and times, and securing adequate volunteers to set up, work, and clean up. In advance of fitting day(s), determine how many volunteer workers you will need to assist you. This is best done with a combination of choir officers and parent volunteers. If your choir wears robes, you've got it made in the shade as you can quickly fit singers in one room, handing out a stole (if used) to each singer as they leave. However, if you have tuxes and gowns, read on!

Secure two rooms (choir room plus one other) so ladies can report to one room and gentlemen can report to the other. Set up each room with an efficient traffic pattern. Cover all windows so privacy is assured. You might choose to fit on a first-come, first-served basis or have students sign up for the time period they would like to come. A volunteer sitting outside the door will take the damage deposit prior to a student being admitted to the fitting room. Students are admitted in small groups according to the space available for fittings. Fitting six to eight girls at one time can keep volunteers busy. Use one or two student volunteers to hand gowns out of the uniform closet and one or two students assisting girls in getting dresses back and forth to dressing areas. Do the same with tuxes for the boys. Be sure to explain how the waist of tux pants can be made more or less snug without alterations. An adult volunteer can be used to assist in identifying hemming length and pinning. When a student leaves, the next student should enter. After a student feels they have a garment that fit them, have the student "cleared" by the parent volunteer as being properly fit. Use more volunteers to hand out bow ties, cummerbunds, pearls or other accessories, if worn. At the end of the day, secure all uniforms until the next day.

Here are some "tricks of the trade" to keep in mind. Student volunteers should be fitted before any other singers. This insures that those serving the choir will have first shot at the widest array of garments, giving a strong incentive to volunteer. Provide an alternate fitting time for those school athletes and marching band members who will have practices during early fall fitting times. Uniform sizes may not match the size number a singer is accustomed to purchasing and wearing. This may be a manufacturing issue or just the style of the garment. Remind students that the size is only a number. Do keep uniform records private, however, so those numbers are not the subject of discussion, humor, or admiration. Do not let students bring book bags, laptops or other bulky items into the fitting rooms. You won't have the floor space to spare and, if you do, you can afford to serve more students at one time. Under no circumstances should students bring friends, carpool members, or parents into the fitting room. You don't need the additional traffic. Also, there aren't enough aspirin in the Western Hemisphere to prepare you for a student's mother who expects a three-session professional fitting for her child. Explain what "hem" means to all singers. Remind singers that uniforms are not custom-fit garments and will be "approximate" fits. Each style has its own quirks of fitting. You'll find yours soon enough.

For personal or religious reasons, some students may desire more coverage than standard uniforms may afford. Robes will likely solve any problem in this realm. In the case of gowns, directors have used specially made dickeys or large, loose over-collars so the neck and any part of the shoulder can be fully covered. Whatever adaptations need to be made to honor a student's beliefs should be made without question or hesitation. Students who are physically challenged in any way may need uniform modifications. These types of concerns and modification for individual students are very much appreciated.

It is probably wise to place all uniform deposits in the booster club's hands for deposit in their account. This grants you more flexibility in refunding cash upon uniform return and keeps the business office from needing to write individual checks. It is imperative that the booster club knows that this is not money available for any other use. Because checks can bounce, you may want to consider cash only for uniform deposits. As with any cash transaction, always issue a self-duplicating receipt for any monies received.

When students return a garment, it may or may not be clean. For this reason, it is recommended that students receive a clean garment and return a worn garment for you to clean. Deduct the dry-cleaning expense from their deposit and refund the difference. This is a saving for the student since the school can have its uniforms cleaned without sales tax. In addition, the group rates you can arrange are a fraction of the cleaning cost individual students can find as individual consumers. If a student grows enough during a school year to need a new uniform fitting, get the old uniform back and charge the student for two dry-cleanings at the end of the year. Note this on your uniform software for easy recall.

Returning uniforms

By far, the easiest way to do this is to have students bring a change of clothes to the final concert of the year. After the concert students can turn in their uniform and receive the balance of their deposit (minus dry cleaning charge) in cash. The downside of this method is that it can rob students of the afterglow of their last concert together, going out with family and friends afterward, because of long lines with a near simultaneous uniform turn-in. The plus side is that everyone is there anyway, and the return of uniforms can be done quickly. An alternative is to have uniform turn-in day on your calendar for the year and return deposits on that day alone. Late-returns receive no balance of deposit back (include this information in your choir handbook), which gives students a financial incentive to be timely in returning their uniforms. The negative in this method is that some students will always forget, dragging out the return process for a week or more, thus delaying all uniforms going to the dry cleaner at the same time.

Always have a student sign next to their name on a check-in roster verifying they received cash back from their deposit. Student should write their full name, not check off a name on a list. This is your proof that a refund was made should there be any question. You might consider letting a proxy turn in the uniform for any student with a conflict on turn-in day. This could be a friend or the singer's parent, but the proxy must sign their name next to the singer's name on your list as proof of monies received.

Dry cleaners

Always negotiate competitive group-rate dry cleaning for your uniforms. The volume of business you bring to a dry cleaner is substantial. Cleaners will prepare finished garments to your preferences regarding cleaning bags (or not), tissue paper in sleeves (takes up much more room on storage racks during the summer but holds shape nicely), etc. Be prepared to deliver the cleaning in large, carefully labeled, and inventoried plastic bags. Package each part of the uniform in separate bags, noting what is in the bag and how many, and label with your school name. (For example, twenty robes, ten tux jackets, one hundred twenty band bow ties, etc.). If you use lawn trash bags for this, buy the thicker ones so odors are contained and the bags don't break when moved. Also, do not store these garbage bags where they could be mistaken for refuse, not even overnight! A thorough night custodian could be helpful by throwing away ten bags of uniforms masquerading as garbage! Trust us, no matter how fervently the cries of freedom call your name, do not leave the garments imprisoned in garbage bags over the summer. We know a director who did this...just once. It only takes once.

Ideally, you will find a reputable cleaner that does excellent work, to which you can return year after year. Some cleaners will offer to pick up your uniforms without additional charge. Most dry cleaners do not have the storage space to keep two hundred or more garments, so plan to pick up the cleaned garments before you take off for the summer.

The conductor's attire

Dressing the part is an important part of your contribution on stage as well as presenting yourself professionally. Concerts are a fine time for that haircut you've been putting off. Shine those shoes. Present a polished, not slovenly, appearance. Toward this end, consider the following guidelines.

In most cases, gentlemen will wear a tuxedo. It should fit you well with enough room for the physicality of conducting a concert. If you do not perform frequently, make sure to try on your tux from time to time to insure that it still fits. For ultra-formal occasions (but only after six o'clock in the evening), you may opt to wear tails. Tails are not worn for daytime concerts, no matter what the formality. For informal concerts, a classic suit would be appropriate. The goal is to match the formality of your dress with the choir. If they were wearing robes, you would choose a robe or suit. If they were wearing long gowns and tuxes, you would wear a tux.

Concerts are a fine time for that haircut you've been putting off.

Ladies should avoid backless gowns, deeply slit skirts, revealing bodices, and short dresses. If you could wear the dress for a romantic evening out on the town, it's not the right dress for a concert. Audience focus should be on the choir, not the director. Dress conservatively. A formal gown is the most gracious on stage, and if your singers are wearing floor-length gowns, you are obliged to do the same. If not, a tea length dress would be acceptable for less formal concerts. Be aware that depending on the design of the concert venue, those standing on stage may reveal an additional six to ten inches of leg to the audience. "Basic black" is a good rule of thumb and affords your most professional look.

Little Known Facts of the Western World

The tiny pleats on cummerbunds always face up.
Their original purpose was to catch table crumbs dropped into a gentleman's lap as he dined.

Clothes make the man.
Naked people have little or no influence on society.
—Mark Twain

➤ Music Library Organization and Management

A place for everything and everything in its place...

There's no alternative. You've got to put all the music in order and you've got to do it now. If you've inherited a fine library, you may need to update or fine-tune its organization. If you have come into a clutter of photocopies, mismatched inner pages, and thirty-two copies of "Dandy Disco Dandies," you won't have time for hobbies for a while. As with everything else, your time is best spent on the offensive. Therefore, it's best to labor to get the music library in order and resolve to keep it that way. There are no short cuts. Grin and bear it. Your basic goals are to keep like things together, know what you have, and make it easy to get (and keep) your hands on materials when you need them.

Printed music

Purge and destroy any photocopies of music you may find. Using duplicated copies is illegal and copyright infringement is a serious crime that can result in substantial fines. Never file or process photocopied music. Take a single copy of each title in your library and three-hole punch it for a binder. Each copy should be stamped with your school's name and a music library storage number. (Stamps for this purpose can be made to order economically at most office supply stores.) Pencil in the number of copies your music library has of each title on the front of each octavo in the binder. Sort titles by voicing (treble, tenor-bass, mixed) and category (a cappella, accompanied, pop/novelty, holiday, sacred, secular) as your library warrants. Alphabetize by title in each category and place into binders. Label binders by voicing and category. In a sizeable library, you will need multiple binders per category.

Organize the storage of your music in folders or music storage boxes on shelves or in filing cabinets. Folders are cheaper (or free) and take up less space. Boxes are more easily labeled clearly on the outside but are bulky and expensive. Place folders or boxes in numerical order. Do not file alphabetically by title. This will cause a never-ending reorganization issue as you regularly move everything over a notch or shelf. Don't even think about it! Some directors color coded labels on folders and boxes for easier identification, such as pink (treble music), blue (tenor-bass), and yellow (mixed literature). This can coordinate with the colors of labels on your single copy binders.

Develop a master database of your library's content. Index cards went out with shag carpet and carbon paper. Buy some quality music library software at your professional convention or develop your own Excel spreadsheet. You will want the ability to sort by song title, library number, composer/arranger, voicing, quantity of copies owned, and category (sacred, musicals, etc.). If space and budget allow, organize sight-reading octavos and books in a similar fashion. In the library, have places for three kinds of folders or boxes: what your choir is currently using now, music to be filed, and music you have loaned out. When music is turned in (or returned from a loan), recount the number of copies and adjust the number you now have in the library both on your computer database and on the cover of the single copy filed in the binder.

Like a garden untended, weeds can choke out all blossoms of your hard work very quickly.

Be open to loaning music. Know that you may or may not get it all back or have it returned in a timely manner. Nevertheless, sharing is a professional courtesy and a way to stretch your music budget. Never loan out the folder or box from which the titles came. Keep them in your "loaned stack" in the library. Always keep a list of who borrowed a given piece along with its title, library number, how many copies you loaned, and the date borrowed. At some point toward the end of the year, you may have to put out a friendly reminder so loaned materials can be restored to your library prior to summer. Some directors use a two-part form on which this lending information can be placed, with one part staying and the other accompanying the music being loaned. See appendix 7b for a music loaned form.

A word of admonition: once your music library is organized, it won't stay organized unless you are vigilant to keep it that way. Like a garden untended, weeds can choke out all blossoms of your hard work very quickly. Keep up with it. It seems like there will be a better time to do regular maintenance on the library but, in truth, there is never a better time. By carefully supervising student and parent volunteers, you can maintain order and organization. Those who work in the library have a greatly expanded appreciation for the care of their music and folders.

Space is limited for music storage so you will be tempted to weed out titles that are dated or unlikely to ever be used. This is a complicated matter, for one person's junk is another's treasure, and the library must reflect the past diversity of directors as well as the present and future directors.

Consider that with retrospective themed concerts, you may actually need those sixties pop titles or older than decrepit novelty numbers. A key factor in whether you weed out music that seems unneeded is to know your district and school policies clearly. Many districts consider this school property that cannot be sold, given away, or destroyed.

If music is considered a consumable by your district and can be disposed of as you choose, discuss establishing a district music library with your central administration and choral colleagues. Titles rarely performed at your school could serve as a lending library for all schools' needs. This would utilize off-campus storage and give you more room to grow at your school. Make a list of available titles and offer them to your colleagues on a first-come, first-served basis. You could even bring the list to professional, regional, and district meetings as a way to let colleagues know what you have available. Copies of currently un-used octavos can also be used for make-up work materials. If you do weed a title out of your library, keep a posted list of the library number that is now no longer used and is available for your next purchase of new music. Fill in these empty numbers before you continue numerically.

Placing new music in folders can be accomplished in a number of ways. It can be passed out during rehearsal, section leaders may pass music out to their sections, folders could be filled prior to class, or students could pick up individual copies of music from a designated place. Music can be returned to the library by passing it in during rehearsal (note that absent singers or those who left their folder at home will add to the process by returning it late) or taken out of folders by a music librarian or other volunteers. Always ask singers to erase and mend their music prior to returning it to the library. If there are late returns, place them in your "to be filed" stack in the music library for filing when a volunteer is present.

When students first get a new piece of music they should write their name on the cover in pencil. This will identify it as their copy and will be erased (as well as any other markings except measure numbers) prior to music being passed in. Some directors prefer to use numbered copies of music that corre-, spond to the number of the singer's folder which provides increased accountability for lost or stolen music. This takes extra work in numbering the copies, filling in numbers for subsequent use for missing octavos, and this may or may not be worth the trouble. If you fine for lost or stolen music, make sure to price it by replacement cost, not original price.

Recordings

Recordings are a valuable part of any music library. Maintaining one can cause people to flock to you for examples of performances of certain pieces or by certain groups. To organize recordings, remove CDs from their plastic cases and place in an organizer pouch. Set up a computer catalogue of each title on each CD, including the title of the selection, composer, artist or performing group, CD number, and track number. Organize CD jackets in a similar fashion. Loan recordings using the same system you established for loaning printed music. You can organize videotapes, DVDs, and cassettes in much the same way.

One of the advantages of being disorderly is that one is constantly making exciting discoveries.
—A. A. Milne

8 How to Keep the Tail from Wagging the Dog

➤ Show, Pop, Jazz
   and Swing Choirs

➤ Chamber Singers
   and Madrigal Groups

➤ Show, Pop, Jazz and Swing Choirs

Putting On The Ritz...

Show, Pop, Jazz, and Swing Choirs are a popular topic for discussion in the choral directing community. Are they valid art forms, worthy of careful planning and curriculum? More like a nightmare from far beyond Elm Street? Did you silently think, "Do I have to?" at your job interview? Many choral musicians hold specialty groups at arm's length. Perhaps their own experience and education in these genres is limited. Perhaps they are afraid that the entire soprano section will start to sound like Ethyl Merman. In the meantime, students rush to join these groups instead of signing up for more Mozart. Choral directors wring their hands. Parents find money for head-to-toe sequins when they might not have had cash available for basic choir needs you consider more pressing. The fact is that these performance groups can be a very positive part of your choral department, serving many purposes and bringing a new dimension to your program.

Show, Pop, Jazz, and Swing Choirs involve more students in the choral program and provide arts opportunities reaching out to special interests and groups within the student body. Performing organizations that can present concerts (or "shows") to any number of schools, retirement centers, community meetings, and other venues add opportunities to expand your program, perhaps giving additional rationale to increased staffing. They provide higher visibility on campus and in the community as well as additional opportunities for gifted students to gain performing experience. How can all this be accomplished? The key is oh-so-simple: Do not let the tail wag the dog!

The main thrust of a traditional choral program is to guide and direct choirs in a wide range of choral works, usually representing the Renaissance through Contemporary periods. Singers usually stand on risers, in position, and might burst forth in minor choreography on a novelty number in alternating years. However, each of the above-mentioned styles of vocal performance represents its own valid art form and can richly contribute to your program. One does not have to conflict with the other. Each style celebrates a tradition or culture whose beauty will be appreciated by singers and audiences alike. The music of such greats as Irving Berlin, George Gershwin, and Stephen Sondheim is deserving of your time and effort.

So how do the "tail" and the "dog" factor into this equation? Well, let's begin by saying that the main part of your choral program will continue to be the "dog," traditional choirs; mixed, treble, or tenor-bass. Your "specialty groups" are the "tail," attached to the main part of things but not controlling the overall picture or direction you've established. Students cannot enroll in a pop or show-type group unless they are in one of your other choirs. The rationalization? Traditional choirs teach the musical skills needed to function effectively in a specialty group. Your traditional choirs will teach sight-reading, tone production, breath support, and vocal health. The specialty groups will apply this knowledge and experience to these new styles, adding new music vocabulary, notation symbols, vocal timbres and the like to their basic foundation.

Your best singers will be in your mixed choir (or an advanced girls' group) and in this way your advanced choir will not suffer by losing singers to the "fun" group. This requirement has stood the test of time in many schools and is a reasonable expectation if you'll remember the rationale given above regarding the "applications" reasoning. Students may sign up for a non-auditioned class, or choose to try out for your more selective groups according to their interest, abilities, training, time, and schedule. This does make it more difficult for top students to schedule show choir because they will need to commit two elective slots to choir (choir and show choir). This can prove to be prohibitive for students carrying a demanding academic load. If a choice has to be made, the student should choose to be a member of one of the main choral groups in your program. Many great students would love to sing in a school's pop group but just don't have the time, either in the traditional school day as a course, or for after school choreography sessions and performances.

In developing this component of your choral program, you will want to study these musical styles before embarking on this new venture. There are many books, workshops, web sites, and experts you will want to consult. There are some questions you'll need to answer as you develop your groups. You will want to become familiar with what is considered "appropriate" in vocal timbre for this style of music, teaching your students to sing healthily and correctly while respecting performance practice. If the tone quality for a specialty group is different from your traditional choir, how will you keep students enrolled in both from singing Bach with their "pop" tone?

Do you feel qualified to teach choreography? If not, who will, and what will the scheduling and financial implications be? You may wish to seek out someone who is a gifted dance teacher and also conversant with singing and dancing simultaneously. There is a fine art to marrying movement to singing. Some excellent choreographers can set movement to a piece of music but cannot "think" the dimension of text, breath, and the importance of quality singing throughout. If choreography is included on some or all numbers, remind singers that they are a choir that sings, not a dance group that hums along (or sings lightly) while they dance. Always expect fine choral work from your singers across the full range of musical styles. The addition of movement is a bonus, not a substitute, for quality singing. You

There is a fine art to marrying movement to singing.

will need to decide if the choreography will involve couples dancing or a unisex dance troupe style. Couples imply similar (or same) numbers of male and female singers, so the number of qualified gentlemen will limit the number of ladies you can admit to the group. If you use couples' choreography, what impact might this have on singers whose body shape might restrict movement? Must boy/girl heights be proportionate?

Auditions for these groups are another consideration. Will you hold traditional auditions first, to determine the most advanced students able to handle tight jazz harmonies or complex popular rhythms? If a student is not in your "top" choir, will they be able to handle the level of difficulty? How much will stage presence or general appearance effect a student's audition outcome? You might consider restricting auditions to those students entering their second year of high school or older. First year students have sufficient challenges, transitioning between middle and high schools, and will need time to study. This gives students something to look forward to in future years. It also prevents gifted young students from using up four years worth of elective credits in one or two years, preventing them from continuing in your program past their sophomore year.

Determine what you will include in the audition. Will it include singing in the style of music your group will present? Will it include a dance component? If so, will you have someone hold a dance class to teach and drill audition choreography? Strongly consider using an outside panel of judges for this audition. (Note: "show choir" is being used but also applies to pop groups, jazz singers, etc.) This protects you from appearing to choose the "teacher's pets," and gives the auditions more credibility. Certainly, you must retain a veto vote. At the end of deliberations, judges should destroy all notes taken and scores assigned and present you with a list of the group's members. If you have any question about the advisability of using an outside panel, talk to the sponsor of a cheerleading squad (or drill team) about the aftermath of posting audition results. Returning members should be required to re-audition for the following year. They should have acquired enough training and experience to present themselves head and shoulders above new recruits. This keeps everyone on his or her toes and gives new and old students the same chance to be judged equally. Always be honest with students. They need to know what you will expect of them vocally, physically and in extra rehearsals in addition to the projected type of music and audiences they might expect. Choose whether your group will compete and travel or not.

Decide how you will schedule these specialty groups. What period in the school day involves the least conflict for the most students? Can that period be built around the end of the day without conflicting with athletics? Could the group be scheduled at the lunch hour, or period that has an activity, study, or assembly time attached regularly? Either of these would afford the opportunity for during-school performances without missing additional class time. Including travel time to and from a venue, you can likely find groups for which to perform within an easy travel radius of your school. This opens up more possible candidates for membership, as performances would not always be outside the traditional school day.

Hold a weekend camp for your group to get a head start on group dynamics, bonding exercises, and extended rehearsals to master the basics of a good fifteen to twenty minute show. Check with your local YMCA to see if there are camp dorms or other facilities you might use free, or rent at low cost. Another option is a suite-type motel with a kitchen, assigning each section one meal to plan and prepare for the group. This is more fun than you can imagine and bonds students together while providing a little competition to present the most delicious (or the least burnt) meal of the weekend.

Will the group perform acoustically or through a sound system? If you plan to use a sound system, it must be of the highest quality to avoid vocal distortion. This is particularly true for singers who are dancing, requiring headset style amplification. What instrumentation will accompany the group, if any? Some jazz groups pride themselves on singing a cappella. Many groups sing with keyboard (piano or electric) alone, while others have a full "pit band" style accompaniment of instrumentalists who are also enrolled in the class as full members. What is your philosophy about using accompaniment tapes in lieu of live musicians? There are strong feelings about this either way. The answer likely leans toward live accompaniment, piano or full band, to retain the creativity and flexibility this affords singers. It also eliminates concerns about having tapes cued up properly and dead time between songs. Thematic musical bridges provide unparalleled flow between numbers as singers move from one song to the next. These can be constructed based on chord progressions or a melodic phrase. Begin a bridge as applause begins to die and play until students are in place for their next tune. Students should move in the pace and mood of the next piece.

You might consider having a student manager as a full member of the group to assist you with bookings, providing maps and directions for all drivers, or the bus driver. This might be a student who truly wanted to be in the group but wasn't selected to be a performing member. On your audition sheet, include a line that asks if the student (if not selected as a performing member of the group) would like to be considered for the position of manager. Select this student yourself.

Know what type of music you would like your group to perform. Will you try to include current music that is on the "charts?" If not, will students be disappointed? Initially, students may want to sing the newest number one song on Billboard's pop, rock, or R & B list. However, if you frame the question realistically, students may quickly accept old standards and "tried and proven" oldies for their shows. Choose only the highest quality literature for your specialty groups. There is an extensive repertoire of quality literature for all varieties of specialty choirs, but you may also find junk. There is no excuse for singing poor arrangements of great songs, or any arrangement of poor quality music. Challenge your students' musical abilities. Don't fall into having students sing in octaves on the melody to facilitate more complex choreography. Perform age-appropriate texts. Some contemporary music may offend community standards so it is important that you choose wholesome materials. This care should extend to appropriate dance movements. Though performed on television and stage, there have been certain dances that can and should be left out of your group's repertoire.

You may need to have a conversation with your students such as this: "You aren't a rock band. No matter how hard you try, you won't be able to sound like a group of men and women who are older than you are. I'm a pianist. No matter how hard I try, I can't sound like a guitar, bass, and drums." (If you plan to use instrumentalists, you might say "No matter how hard three students practice, they will not be able to play at the volume level of a rock group.") Isn't it better to be really good at what we can do rather than impersonate something we're not? Students respond to logic. Vocal arrangements of popular tunes are available for purchase but can your group perform them? These are questions to ask yourself and your students when you form your first group. One way of addressing "not sounding like the record" is to make your goal to sound exactly like the record by learning songs from repeatedly listening to the recording. Though students are not reading music, they are gaining skills unique and valuable to any musician when they hear the various layers of sound and identify what parts can be replicated. Singers will soon learn to listen for "their" part on the recording and develop a keen analytical ear.

Uniforms for show choirs can be costly. Do separate fund-raising to help offset student costs, if necessary. Outfits can be simple or more elaborate. How will dresses (if worn) be made? Will you purchase them from a vendor in the exhibit hall at your state's music educator convention? This is a great time to see what is new and attractive instead of looking at pictures in a catalog. Feel the fabric for roughness and or potential irritation for your dancers. See how it moves and what is required to launder them. Would you prefer to use a seamstress so your group's dresses will be unique and unlike any others? If so, be sure to employ a professional seamstress who is accustomed to constructing dance garments. A standard seamstress may be in the dark about how skirts should move, the benefits of two skirts, fishlike hems, weighted hems, circularly cut skirts, two-way versus four-way stretch lycra, etc. What shoes will you choose? For groups that dance, think about low-heeled beige character shoes to make the leg look more extended than the same shoes in black. For gentlemen, jazz shoes are heaven to dance in but wear out quickly if worn "on the street" for very long. Be a competitive shopper.

There are many things to consider when scheduling performances for your show choir. Know your audience as you choose from the literature your group has mastered. Most audiences will be well served by a perform-ance that is fifteen to twenty minutes long. Leave the audience wanting

---

Choose only the highest quality literature
for your specialty groups.

---

more. Remember that children or a room full of older folks may not enjoy literature that is appealing to a high school assembly. Develop a wide enough repertoire that you can handpick a show order according to the audience. Start and end a show with a strong, up-tempo tune. Song number two can be moderate tempo, with song number three a ballad. Song number four might be a novelty number, ending with song number five as another up-beat song for a good closer. This will form a tight show of appropriate length for most performances.

Have a student introduce the group, perhaps following your first number. Some groups have each dance couple step forward and introduce themselves by first name. Prior to your last number, this student should thank the audi-ence and always include the words "before our last number" somewhere in the statement. Avoid using big sound systems in nursing homes and other venues with a quieter atmosphere. Decide in advance what your philosophy (and invitation acceptance) will be on providing entertainment while the audience is eating a meal. Extraneous noise can be trying, and most groups do not want to be considered "background music." You will find that the louder you sing, the louder diners will talk, so we encourage you to schedule singers for performances either before, or after a meal.

When programming the show choir at local elementary schools, offer to perform mini-shows for most of the student lunch times if your group meets during lunch hour at your own school. Performances can include three songs each, lasting five to six minutes. This gives each lunch period enough talking time for youngsters to listen reasonably quietly. You can usually fit two such mini-shows into each twenty-minute time frame, alternating groups of pieces so that no student hears the same song twice.

If you are planning to have a pop group or an ensemble that performs with live instrumentation and sound equipment, know that this is an investment of money and further differentiates it as a unique part of your choir program. Sounds systems can be as simple as a few group microphones and speakers costing a few hundred dollars to a much more complex system including monitors, equalizer, amps, wireless headsets and other professional quality equipment costing several thousand dollars. Here are standard lists of sound equipment you will need to consider to purchase for such a group:

Sound equipment
- 2 Main PA Speakers
- 4 Monitor speakers
- Amps to power both systems
- Mixer board, 12-16-24-32-36 channels depending on how many singers and instruments in your group
- Professional quality equalizer (EQ)
- Microphones, one per singer preferably (handheld or headset)
- Microphone stands
- 100 ft. "Snake" (elaborate cable going to the mixer board)
- Equipment cases
- Sufficient cords for speakers and microphones
- Power distribution system

Live instrumentation
- Electric guitar and case
- Acoustic guitar and case
- Bass guitar and case
- Guitar amp

- Bass guitar amp
- 3 direct boxes (to amplify guitars)
- Synthesizer (one per player)
- Trap drum set
- Drum microphones
- Additional percussion instruments (wind chimes, claves, tambourine, rain stick, triangle)
- Sufficient cords

Quality equipment brand names:
(Most distributors give schools a considerable discount.)
- Yamaha
- JBL
- Peavey
- Crest (power amp)
- Soundcraft
- Mackie
- Whirlwind (snakes)
- Sure (microphones)
- Crown (amps)
- AKG (microphones)
- Sender (guitar amps)
- Gallen Kinger (bass amp)

Performances using this complexity of equipment may run as long as four hours each, including meeting at school, loading, travel time, unloading, set-up, warm-up, changing into performance attire, and performing, then reversing the order until students return back to school. This is a serious commitment of time for which there is no shortcut if you choose to use a complex sound system and full instrumentation.

If you choose to use sound equipment, it is important to know terminology, common troubleshooting techniques, and how to serve as your own sound engineer. Some years you may have a gifted student with experience in this area, but sometimes you will not. The more sound equipment you use, the more transportation and security you will need, and you will also need to plan set-up and strike each and every time the group performs. Equipment also carries with it routine maintenance costs and repairs as needed, and general upkeep. Using a large sound system is time consuming, a continuing financial burden, and can create a dependency on it in order for your group to perform.

Many top-notch show choirs perform acoustically, without microphones and sound equipment, in favor of smaller venues and a more personal touch. This affords groups the opportunity to get in and out of venues quickly and easily, and perform for smaller groups in tighter spaces. Often this style allows for performances during the class period itself, requiring fewer afternoons and evenings of its members (and director) and allowing greater participation by multi-talented students juggling heavy academic and extra-curricular loads. Students in acoustically based groups can easily perform once a week without monopolizing student time and your singers will enjoy leaving the building, even if only going down the street to the local library, school, or nursing facility. The same group could add a sound system for large shows, conventions, and other venues that require amplification to be heard clearly.

This is a distinct decision you will make on behalf of your specialty groups. There is no wrong choice. The teaching experience of the authors has included both styles of group, with one using substantial technology and the other preferring a largely acoustic performing style. Both styles have won festivals and the hearts of audiences.

You may wish to add props and staging boxes, risers, stools, or small ladders to present visual levels and variety. Remember that each item added to the performance will necessitate someone loading and unloading it, as well as additional space in vehicles to transport.

Jazz choirs

Jazz is one of America's own original art forms. A jazz choir can be a thrilling addition to your school's choral department if you will devote the time and attention needed to study this musical form and become familiar with its terminology, vocal timbre, and literature. There is a wealth of information about jazz choirs and you are encouraged to begin by listening to some of the jazz greats, both soloists and vocal groups. Recommended individual jazz singers:

- Ella Fitzgerald
- Billy Holiday
- Dinah Washington
- Bessie Smith
- Sarah Vaughan
- Nat King Cole

- Bobby McFerrin
- Nina Simone
- Norah Jones
- Mahalia Jackson
- Al Green

Vocal jazz groups:

- The Manhattan Transfer
- The Swingle Singers
- The Spirits of Rhythm
- The Pied Pipers
- The Dandridge Sisters
- The University of North Texas Jazz Singers directed by Paris Rutherford

Professional resources and information on jazz styling:

Friedwald, Will. *Jazz Singing: America's Great Voices from Bessie Smith to Bebop and Beyond*

Robinson, Russell. *Jazz Style and Improvisation For Choirs*

Stoloff, Bob. *Scat! Vocal Improvisation Techniques*

Walker, Cherilee W. *Pedagogical Practices in Vocal Jazz Improvisation*

Weir, Michele. *Jazz Singer's Handbook: The Artistry and Mastery of Singing Jazz*

Zegree, Stephen. *The Complete Guide To Teaching Vocal Jazz*

An intellectual snob is someone who can listen to the 'William Tell Overture' and not think of The Lone Ranger.
—Dan Rather

➤ Chamber Choirs and Madrigal Groups

Divide and conquer... into smaller, specialized vocal groups

Not unlike pop, jazz, and show choirs, vocal ensembles such as chamber choirs and madrigal groups are welcome additions to any choral program. They afford talented and musically dedicated students a musical outlet unique from their traditional choir class. Although it may be tempting to address more advanced groups such as these with extra time, money, and effort, a choir director must always realize these students are but one part of the choral department. The choir director should recognize and maintain a delicate balance between the school's select vocal ensemble and the larger parent group in which all its singers are members. Likewise such groups can and should be an outlet for superior choral literature at more advanced levels, stretching both director and singers. Many outstanding high school singers graduate with one or more years of performing in select choral ensembles in addition to choir.

Unlike groups that focus on contemporary music, these ensembles primarily perform literature that has withstood the test of time. Musical elements such as tone, blend, balance, intonation and phrasing are finely tuned in smaller musical settings. Consequently, participation in these musical organizations serves as an extension of the gifted student's music education.

Musical elements such as tone, blend, balance, intonation and phrasing are finely tuned in smaller musical settings.

Scheduling rehearsals for these groups often necessitates rehearsals before or after school. Participation in these "extra" groups may test the dedication and desire of the members and director. However, because of these and other sacrifices, the desire for musical excellence and pride connected to these groups make them more than worthwhile.

Attire is usually different from the standard choir uniform in order to add prestige and distinction to select ensembles. Allowing students to have input into these uniforms (with the director's guidance) gives students additional ownership in the group. Attire can range from simple and inexpensive to costly and elaborate but should be appropriate to the style of music performed.

Standing arrangements for these ensembles should be creative, ranging from semi-circles to mixed or scattered formations as appropriate to the literature performed.

Chamber choirs

Chamber Choirs are smaller ensembles that number between fifteen to thirty members and sing a wide variety of musical styles. There is a wealth of Renaissance literature available to such groups, from madrigals and chansons to motets and chorales. Chamber choirs may be conducted, or not, with reasonably equal effectiveness. Unaccompanied singing assists singers in becoming more aware of correct intonation, though chamber groups should also be equally open to varied accompaniments. A variety of musical genres are available and should be embraced by chamber choirs.

Ensemble as well as solo singing should be equally emphasized in chamber choir groups. Consequently, solo and ensemble festivals and contests are appropriate and worthwhile outlets for chamber singers. The development of effective individual and group stage presence may be an emphasis in such groups.

Chamber choirs are popular, versatile ensembles during holiday time. Smaller performance venues are ideal for caroling and intimate choral concerts. If no risers or sound equipment are utilized, chamber choirs are able to perform concerts in a variety of venues with a minimal need for setup time. Such opportunities are invaluable, allowing your chamber choir to serve as musical ambassadors on behalf of your choral department.

Madrigal groups

There are many similarities between chamber choirs and madrigal groups. One difference is that madrigal groups limit their repertoire to music of the Renaissance period. Madrigal ensembles primarily perform without a director's conducting, emphasizing student-generated tempi, nuance, and articulation. In some schools, Madrigal Dinners or Feasts become a focus of the performance season, often presented during the holiday season. (See "The Blessings of Added Extras" in chapter three.)

Costumes for a madrigal group distinguish its members from other chamber ensembles. These can be costly to purchase or rent, but patterns are available for costumes to be made by hand. Great care should be taken to insure that all outfits are of acceptable quality and as authentic as possible. Collecting a complete madrigal group wardrobe may take several years but will afford your singers a costume closet for future use. Costuming information is available through the Internet as well as theatrical and music performing resources.

Opera is when a guy gets stabbed in the back and, instead of bleeding, he sings.
—Ed Gardner

Get Set...

- ➤ **Choir Traditions**

- ➤ **Fun and Games**

- ➤ **Trips, Tours, Parties and Banquets**

➤ Choir Traditions

Creating memories for your choir's treasure chest...

Roots run deep through the lives of those with whom we have spent many hours, sharing lives and making music together; the roots run very deep indeed. Choir traditions are the unique events, honors, and moments singers share each year as the unifying bond between each other and choirs of the past, present and future. Do something students and parents find magical only one time, and it may suddenly become a new "tradition." Do this same thing two years in a row and you're in cement, with both feet. Knowing this, carefully consider anything you might create within your program. What may seem like a surge of brilliance early in your tenure may be a burden ten years later. Trust us, students may forget another name for G clef, but they will never forget a tradition they want to keep!

When transitioning to a different school, be slow to change existing traditions during your first year. Thereafter you will have time to modify old traditions gradually (or eliminate them quietly) over several years. Obviously, if you inherit traditions that include anything inappropriate or illegal, make changes from the beginning. Before announcing (or not observing) such traditions or changes, meet with your choir officers. Let them feel a part of the decision-making and explain how an old action has, or could have a negative impact on individuals or the group. Word may filter out to choir members in advance of your saying or doing anything, but if you've been adequately persuasive with your officers, the choir will come around to your thinking. If you simply chop off traditions of longstanding seemingly arbitrarily, you run the risk of alienating the choir and its supporters. When in doubt, discuss traditions or changes with your principal first.

Avoid any form of "initiation." Many districts have policies that prohibit initiations of any type, and we find that they can go from zero to disaster in under ten seconds. Students get carried away easily. Think through things very carefully and always stay in control of what your students do. You are ultimately responsible for anything associated with choir, and any problems or damages will come directly to you. The traditions your choir holds dear will be as unique as your choir program. We would like to share a few of our favorites.

Choir "angels" is a service project that brings students, faculty, and staff together before the beginning of the school year. The "angels" will be at the school on teacher workdays to help carry books to rooms, stamp books with teacher names, scrub tops of desks, help put up bulletin boards, run errands within the school, and generally serve as an extra pair of arms and legs for the teachers. (This help will be received with a measure of amazement, shortly followed by unbounded glee.) Advertise the angels to your faculty and staff with a flyer in each mailbox, a sign in the faculty lounges or mail-room, and an announcement at one of the first faculty meetings on the first day of in-building staff development. Tell teachers where the angels will report and what they will be wearing. (A nametag, hat, certain color of T-shirt will suffice.) Angels are assigned first come, first served, so teachers can haul one off to help them for as long as they are needed.

To prepare for this project schedule separate morning and afternoon hours, and ask choir officers to contact all members to remind them of the dates and times volunteers are needed at the school. Some teachers will contact you to "reserve" an angel. Feel free to honor this, or even put up a sign-up sheet in the teacher lounge to better estimate how much help will be needed, but we have found that every hard worker reporting to the school on behalf of the choir will be used! You can't have too many people. Extend the offer of help to counselors who may be filing, alphabetizing, or boxing up old records. The goodwill between the faculty, staff, and admin-istration of your school is more than equal to the organization and time involved in this project! You can feel good that older teachers aren't trying to carry stacks of books from the bookroom to their classroom. Teachers can use their time for higher-level tasks, leaving grunt work to student helpers. Students begin the year in a spirit of volunteerism, sowing seeds of positive energy before the year even starts, while having fun in the process.

A popular tradition that many choirs share is to end each concert with a signature song. Examples of songs that have been used in this way are "The Lord Bless You and Keep You" by Peter Lutkin, and Joyce Eilers' "Go Ye Now In Peace." Some choirs choose to sing their alma mater or school fight song in class on "football" Fridays. Choirs may even adopt a cheer, saying, or motto, sometimes printing it on choir T-shirts.

Invite your choir to begin a tradition of supporting other organizations in the school. Prior to various competitions and major events in other school groups, have the choir make signs wishing good luck and showing their support, posting them around your building. In this same way one choir can show support for other choirs involved in competitions or festi-vals. Another way to show support would be to make good luck bags for individual competitors for city, region, and state events. These might include little notes from members of all choirs in addition to candies, pencils, or other fun treats.

Traditions involving the seniors in your choir program can be very meaningful for everyone. These can be as simple as giving the seniors "privileges" such as boarding the bus first, getting the first choice of seats, or if there is more than one bus, the "senior" bus is always in front. With honor goes responsibility. Be sure that your senior students understand this, providing appropriate leadership and deportment. Seniors can be recognized at the final concert, and can write senior "wills" (I, Peggy, bequeath my choir folder to my little sis, Darla.) at the end of the year choir banquet. Perform with a choir of seniors for graduation or Baccalaureate if one of your choirs isn't already scheduled as an entire group, or let a choir of senior parents sing a song at your last concert of the year.

With honor goes responsibility.

You may decide to hold an annual "Senior Day" on the last day of classes seniors attend. Ask underclassmen to bring poems, handmade cards, balloons, flowers, or other remembrances in honor of senior students. Be sure that every senior gets something and no one is forgotten. Give each senior the opportunity to speak to the choir. Seniors will know this day is coming and will have prepared to speak, sing, or do whatever they wish. Or, they may opt not to say anything, passing to the next person. Seniors can offer words of wisdom, advice to underclassmen, thank the group, read a poem or passage which represents their feelings, or just say what choir has meant to them. Have several boxes of tissue in strategic locations in the room and end class with your choir's traditional closer for the last time. Keep an eye on the clock. You may need to consider the length of your class period and divide it up by the numbers of seniors you have in that particular choir. If you have few seniors, you can pad the period by singing old songs. If you have many seniors, you may need to give an informal time limit per student. This event gives underclassmen a moment to mourn the departure of senior members and celebrate their elevation to elder statesmanship. It can encourage members to continue to sing with you the following year (who might have been planning to drop choir) as they consider how much choir has meant to them and how they want to have this same time of positive reflection about their years of singing. It also provides a sense of closure to one year and acknowledges that the torch is passing to the next group of students.

Some choral departments sponsor a separate senior banquet on a weekend night prior to the departmental choir banquet. It may be held for choir seniors and directors only, for a more intimate celebration of their high school years together. This can take place in a country club or other special venue as funding permits. Tables can be formed into a square so the group can see all members from their seats. Seniors can reminisce about each year, beginning with their first audition. Each student around the table goes in turn (or may pass), adding their special memories to what has already been said. Comments should be restricted to positive (or humorous) choir memories. Students may only speak one at a time and once a year of memories has been concluded, there is no return to that year for additions. The turns around the table begin with singers' freshman year in choir, then sophomore year, and so on. The last round of comments should center on the future; what students want to do or accomplish in the future, plans for continuing education, hopes and dreams. To add to the mystique of the occasion, seniors promise to keep all details about senior banquet a complete secret so future seniors have no idea what to expect. Dress is "Sunday best."

A senior "soiree" can be held on the last night of a choir trip, including senior students and senior parent chaperones only, adding one or two underclassmen to serve finger foods and sparkling cider in plastic champagne goblets. Let any seniors who wish to speak to the group do so. Some of them will have been in school together for twelve years, so roots run deep. Let parents and chaperones of seniors speak to the group. Parents could read short passages, say a few words or even sing a song a cappella to the seniors as their "gift." Your assistant director can speak, ending with any special remarks you wish to make for your seniors assembled without the others present. Have boxes of tissue as needed.

Traditions involving your entire program might include a symbolic representation of past choir presidents displayed in the choir room, monthly theme parties (see appendix 9a-9e), sponsoring a named scholarship, and creating a Penny Plaque. This professionally engraved plaque can commemorate a top contest award, including a "choir of pennies," with a bright new penny representing each singer that sang on the risers that day, placed in riser formation. A unique choir tradition is the post-contest ganga. A ganga is a type of rural song originating in Croatia and Herzegovina characterized by one singer beginning a line of text with others then joining in a wailing style. It is a very passionate form of singing that has undergone many transformations and has been incorporated into contemporary Croatian music. Our variation involves simultaneously intoning a monosyllable in the loudest possible fashion, essentially a musical "scream." In a tight cluster, designate someone to begin the ganga and have this person bring the ganga to a conclusion with some form of appropriate movement. There is good reason why the ganga originated in remote areas. With this in mind, find one before commencing to wail! Gather students away from buildings, preferably in a field somewhere.

Traditions are the guideposts
driven deep in our subconscious minds.
The most powerful ones are those we can't even describe,
aren't even aware of.
—Ellen Goodman

➤ Fun and Games

A plethora of icebreakers, bonding exercises,
and other dandy treats…

Everyone has favorite games and tricks for helping students get to know one another, as well as games for sight-reading and music review. Some are simple and can be done quickly in class while others evolve into longer activities. We'd like to share a few we have used.

Match the Shoe

Ask singers to take off one shoe and put it on the floor in the middle of the room. When given the signal, singers should pick one shoe from the pile and walk around the room, looking for the person wearing the shoe they are carrying. When they find that person, they should give back the matching shoe while introducing themselves.

Showtime

Divide the choir into groups. Explain that there will be a live show with wonderful acting and singing, and that they are the performers. In advance, prepare a bag for each group containing the following:

- Several unusual objects that will serve as curious props.

- Some random pieces of clothing, wigs, glasses, hats, etc. to be used as costumes in addition to whatever the singers are already wearing.

- Index cards with the name of a profession/job on it (fireman, blind dentist, opera singer, plumber, etc.) that will serve as a key character in the skit, the category (comedy, soap opera, game show, reality TV, science fiction, etc.), and setting (at the local gym, wild west, at the mall, ballgame, etc.).

Never place a student in a position of uneasiness.

Have the same number of items in each bag but include one unique item. Give each group fifteen minutes to prepare a three to five minute scene. Each skit must use all items in the group's bag, contain at least one short original song, and involve all group members in some way. Pull the groups together as an audience and let them perform, one at a time. Creativity will reign supreme! Try to mix introverted students with more boisterous ones, "veterans" and "new recruits," giving each person a comfort zone. Never place a student in a position of uneasiness. Remember, this is supposed to be fun!

Produce a Commercial

Divide the choir into small groups of four to nine students and give them ten minutes to create a commercial advertisement for your choir or an upcoming event in the choral department.

The Dictionary Game

This game plays best with smaller groups to avoid becoming tedious. It also plays to the strengths of highly verbal students; so if student abilities are diverse, try playing with two on a team instead of individually. Provide each student with a sheet of paper and a pen. You will have as unabridged dictionary as your media center will loan out. In advance, find a word with a meaning no one in the group is likely to know. Funny sounding words can be the best. You cannot use proper names or any capitalized words and it's recommended that you avoid prefixes and word roots that will give the players too close an idea of what the real definition might be. Ask each student to write the word down followed by his or her original definition, designed to be as close to what the actual definition might be. As students finish their answers, they will pass you their sheets, face down. Read over them so you can become familiar with the handwriting and words so you can read it aloud in a believable way. When the last student has passed their sheet to you, take the pile of sheets and scramble the order, including the dictionary definition. Read each one aloud with all the dignity you can muster, as if it were the real definition. After reading all definitions, each student will say which definition they believe is the correct one, starting to your left and going around in a circle one by one. You will keep track (scratch paper) of how many votes each definition gets. No one may vote for his or her own definition. One point is earned for each person who chooses one of the student's fake definitions as the real one. One point is earned for each student who chooses the true definition as the correct one. You receive one point if you stump the entire group. After all players have made their guesses, read the correct definition aloud. Ask the group who wrote the other definitions that received votes so you can keep score. The player with the most points at the end of the game wins.

Who Am I?

Have an index card for each student on which you will neatly print the name of a famous person (actor, singer, historical figure, sports star, etc.). As singers enter the room, tape an index card to their back. Everyone else can see "who" that person is, leaving each individual to ask yes or no questions to learn more about their identity until they correctly guess "who they are." When they have declared the correct answer, the singer should sit down.

Charades

Try playing charades using only song titles. This can include everything from childhood songs, Christmas carols, folk tunes, pop/rock hits, and works learned in choir. The wider the pool of sources, the more fun it is.

Find Your Song's Other Half

Write the titles of common, easy to sing songs on index cards, putting each title on two cards. Shuffle the cards and hand them out. At your signal, all singers will begin singing their song. The object of the game is to find the person singing the same song that they are. With large groups this can be bedlam for a while, but enjoyable bedlam. When the partner singing the same song is located, they should sit together and get to know each other using some general questions you may want to provide before starting.

Encore

The board game has been around since the earth cooled but still fun if played in teams like a game show.

Fill In The Blanks

Prepare a sheet of descriptors which fit one or more of your students in the room such as plays varsity baseball, has lived in at least three states, speaks Russian, loves sushi, hates chocolate, etc. At your signal, students should walk around the room asking each other if they play varsity baseball, can recite a Shakespearean sonnet from memory, etc. until all blanks are filled in. This gives the group a chance to learn a little more about each other and enjoy getting to appreciate the diverse backgrounds and interests within the choir.

Name Your Section

During the first week of school, have each section of the choir form a separate circle in the room. Students should say their first name in turn while going around the circle. The object of the activity is for everyone in the section to learn everyone else's first name. After names are spoken the first time around the circle, sections should try chanting the names as a group as they go around the circle again remembering each name as it is chanted. Some groups will develop fun rhythms, motions, and other memory aids to remember all the names. When the groups are confident that they know all the names in their section, call on one student in each section to stand and name each singer in their section, going around the circle in order. When all four sections have done this, go on to other things. During the first week or two, you might revisit this activity but vary it by combining sections until the entire choir has formed one large circle and everyone can chant names individually. This is a good way to get to know one another by first name and gives each singer an individual identity within the group. (It will help you remember who's who as well!)

Name That Tune

Divide the choir into groups. Clues must all be names of songs.

30 Second Game

Sing several lines of sight-reading exercises in unison with the choir. Now the game begins. The director calls out the name of a student. That student will call another student's name, with the second student calling on a third student, the third calling on a fourth until thirty seconds has elapsed. A student may not call the name of the person who called on them or anyone who has previously been named; students must pay close attention. When "time" is called, the last person to have been named must sight-read the exercise. Each student has three seconds to say the next name or the game stops, leaving the person who erred to sing the sight-reading line. If a choir has more than one member with the same first name, one can call the first and last name or just the last name. If a student calls an incorrect name, the game stops and that student sings the sight-reading line. If the student on whom the game stops lacks the confidence to sight-read the exercise alone, allow them to pick someone to sing along or say, "I'll help you" and sing along with them yourself. When the choir has memorized the sight-reading, switch to new lines or another class activity. The game gains momentum if the director pares down the time to twenty seconds, then fifteen seconds, etc. until students are in a veritable frenzy. A fun variation involves challenging the choir to name each student going across each successive row of risers, naming all students in less than thirty seconds. If they succeed, the choir gets to pick any line of sight-reading for the director to sing. Be ready to pay up in choirs with fewer than sixty members. (The downside of this game's concept is that getting to sight-read is structured to be the "punishment" in the game, not an association we want students to make.)

Sight-reading Football

The choir is divided into two teams. Each team should number off so that no player takes a turn until all players on the team have taken a turn. Have a group of sight-reading examples handy. When the "ball" comes to a team, its next numbered player can choose to pass (sing all eight measures of the exercise correctly), or run the ball (sing four measures correctly). Design the game so that students always have a choice of an easier or harder sight-reading example. The harder example counts as a pass, while the easier example counts as a run. When students have a given exercise memorized, change to a new line or another activity. If the singer makes an error, it's a fumble and other team "gets" the ball, with its next numbered singer attempting to do the exercise. If a team member sings accurately, the team keeps the ball and takes another turn. After a touchdown, a team may read an extra line for the extra point. Men's choirs will happily sight-read their way into oblivion, playing this game. True aficionados purchase little magnetized football players of two colors and move them across the blackboard (which has been marked with yard lines, etc.) as each down is called and yardage moves the players down the field.

Jeopardy

Just like the game show of the same name, an excellent review can be constructed by a director who has the time to make sufficient answers to questions in various musical categories such as dynamic markings, musical symbols, choral composers, abbreviations, conducting patterns, solfege names, key signatures, lines and spaces of various clefs, etc. Making the board and clues takes a good bit of time, but if you laminate everything it will last for years and works extremely well as a test or exam review.

If you watch a game, it's fun. If you play at it, it's recreation.
If you work at it, it's golf.
—Bob Hope

➤ Trips, Tours, Parties, and Banquets

Are we there yet...?

Trips and tours

Students benefit from in-field learning opportunities during which they may receive professional critiques from choral specialists as well as observe the work done by choirs in other locales. Through such field trips, students gain a deeper understanding of the choral art that would be difficult, if not impossible, to capture in the standard classroom. Students see trips and tours in a different way: "We love choir trip! It's one of our favorite things of the year; leaving class, having fun with our friends, and doing neat stuff." They are a treasured part of the school year for choir students and can motivate singers to join your groups. Consider traveling with your students annually (or alternating years) as an extension of learning activities. "Trips" generally refer to traveling to the site of a festival or contest. "Tours" usually involve singing concerts at specified locations without adjudication.

If you should encounter a group whose middle name is "anarchy," do not take them farther than the hall water fountain.

Bear in mind that trips are a privilege, not a right, and students should understand that their work ethic and deportment through the year build confidence that they can responsibly travel and represent the school in a positive light. If you should encounter a group whose middle name is "anarchy," do not take them farther than the hall water fountain. However, most students will rise to your level of trust and expectations, both musically and personally, and you will enjoy taking them to a different city or state to sing.

Trips can be as simple as arranging for a bus and singing at a local amusement park's festival. They can be as complex as bus travel to another state, jetting to another part of the country, or even involve international competition and concert tours. Although Vienna sounds a lot more exciting than Minner Switch, it is truly the group's traveling together that excites students. Vienna could be as dull as an educational travelogue with a dull director. With a spirit of adventure, Minner Switch could be an exciting journey into a different way of life. Vienna could be all pollution and traffic for a group with nasty attitudes. Minner Switch could mean horseback riding and singing at an old church dating back to the Civil War days to kids who are ready to roll with the punches. The truth is that Vienna is a superb destination for a choir. We've both been there and done that, happily, and would do it again. Afford your students a musical opportunity that goes beyond the routine and remember, it doesn't have to break the bank to so do! Unique considerations for tours:

- Do you have contacts in several cities through which your choir might travel?
- Are these individuals with schools who would sponsor an assembly or other event for which your choir might sing while traveling?
- Are there local churches that might host a concert?
- Do you want to consider home stays (students staying in pairs with local students and their families for one night while they are in that town) for one or more nights in lieu of hotels?
- Can your choir be prepared to perform a full concert (versus three songs at a festival)?
- Unique considerations for festivals:
- What companies offer festivals in which cities on the dates your school calendar has open?
- What is the cost of entry fees for the choir or individual participation fees for each student in the choir?
- Does the festival sponsor an awards ceremony?
- Is a celebratory dinner, dance, or culminating activity included in your fee?
- Who might we expect as adjudicators for the festival?
- Are the judges active in choral music and sensitive to working with students in your choirs' age group?
- Are judges' comments written, taped, or is a mini-clinic provided onstage after your choir's performance?
- Are there guidelines for music selection or may you choose what the choir will sing without constraint?
- How many choirs generally attend this festival? What categories of awards are offered?

Travel considerations

Make certain that the cost of the trip does not prohibit any member from participation. It is your responsibility to provide fundraising opportunities to offset costs for your students. Ideally, choir trips would be fully funded through choir fund-raising.

Sponsoring an annual or alternating-year event can be a tradition that will build student confidence and serve as a powerful recruiting tool. The primary purpose of traveling with your group is to provide a musical opportunity for the choir in an appealing venue, so search for destinations that have sights of interest, historical significance, or general appeal. Always try to personalize a trip by including at least one activity and meal for which your destination is known. You have to take the choir to a hot dog stand in New York City and view the Statue of Liberty, taking in a Broadway show or concert at Carnegie Hall. In Philadelphia, it is mandatory to see the Liberty Bell and maybe commandeer your bus out into Amish country, grabbing a Philly cheese steak sandwich or eating in one of the well-known, quirky diners in the area. When possible, taking your students to at least one museum, several sites of historical interest, and experiencing local color and flair is an important component to any trip.

Traveling with a group is very different from traveling as an individual or family. Be prepared to work far in advance to organize your trip and mentally "walk through" all aspects. Check your school calendar prior to setting dates for the choir trip. Search for a weekend with little or no conflict for your choir members. These dates are best chosen the spring of the preceding year. Obtain permission to travel with your students from the appropriate levels of approval. This generally takes the form of a trip proposal to your principal that includes destination, how many students will be traveling, cost of the trip per student, how many chaperones you will be taking, the time and date of departure and return, how many class periods or school days will be missed by participating students, if a substitute teacher is required while you travel, and the source of funding for the trip. Your district will want to know that students are being afforded a year-long series of fund-raising opportunities so that no student has to pay for the trip out of his or her own pocket, and that no student is being left home for lack of ability to pay.

Arrange transportation as needed throughout the trip. Remember that buses with bathrooms are well worth the cost. If you are not traveling by bus, plan for transfers to and from the airport and between points of interest. Create a well-balanced itinerary, mixing work and play, and plan meals in advance. Know where you will have meals, price, and if discounts can be arranged through a prix fixe menu or group rate. Meals can represent great expense for students depending on your destination and length of time away from home. Give students enough time to plan for how much money they should bring (earn ahead of time) for meals. It will invariably cost double what students might guess. Your chaperones will need to join you in watching that no students are going without meals for lack of money or suffering from "souvenir-ism."

Chaperones

Identify the chaperones that will travel with your group. Some directors let the officers, carefully guided in discussion by the director, select those parents best suited to chaperone the trip. This deflects the ire of slighted mothers and fathers who weren't invited to come along. The director should be present and shape the discussion so students are led to make wise choices. The officers issue the formal invitations to serve as chaperones. Some people let the Booster Club choose trip chaperones. Directors have the least control over the outcome of choices with this system. Other directors prefer to choose the chaperones directly, based upon factors important to them. Consider your choices carefully, as they will have a dramatic impact on the ease and fun of travel, both for you and your students.

Chaperoning is a grueling job if done well.

Parents always seem more prepared to chaperone a trip than mop floors after a fund-raising dinner. You may want to consider adopting the "dance with the one what brought you" philosophy by choosing those parents whose volunteerism and hard work have contributed the most to the choir's success. Take personality, willingness to stand behind your policies and procedures equitably, and ability to be firm yet likable with students. Chaperoning is a grueling job if done well. Strive to have adults whose phys-icality, energy level, and positive personality can withstand active, eighteen-hour days. Some really terrific people may not be able to "keep up" with the group, much less stay on the front side of what is going on, and you may need to pass over these good people for this job.

Determine what financial contribution, if any, your chaperones will pay on behalf of the cost of their inclusion. Some directors take chaperones on trips gratis, distributing their costs and fees among the group. The thought here is that chaperones will be working non-stop, not going on the trip for their own enjoyment, so charging them to come would be expecting them to pay to work exhaustively. Other directors discount trip costs. Chaperones should be responsible for their own meal costs and incidental expenses. Including an administrator (or two) is your decision and invitation to make.

An administrator can help deter problems and handle any student "issues" that might arise.

Preparations and planning ahead

Choose those parents whose ability to work with you is established, those who are strong enough to keep students in obedient flocks and yet fun enough to enjoy the students without being overbearing. Be confident that all chaperones will support your rules equally for all students. Try to arrange for one chaperone for every six to eight students at minimum. If possible, include one chaperone who has a nursing or medical background, should the need arise. Make an effort to balance men and women as well as parents of older and younger singers. Chaperones should be energetic and able to function adequately with limited sleep.

Give thought to assign every traveling student a duty. The most arduous task is the work crew that loads and unloads buses. Consider giving first seat choice on the bus to these hard workers or some other reward for their extra sacrifice of time and effort.

There will be times in nearly all trips when it will be an advantage to split up into smaller groups in order to dine in multiple establishments or tour in a group of less than seventy. Plan for the choir to have trip "families." Allow students sign up in advance of the trip for the small group they want to be a part of when these times present themselves. Each "family" is shepherded by a chaperone whose word is law. Divide your choir by the number of chaperones going on the trip (excluding only yourself) and you will have the number of singers that can be included in one "family." Post a sheet of paper with numbered "openings" with the name of the chaperone clearly at the top. Have a separate sheet for each chaperone and post all at the same time. Once the numbered slots for a chaperone are taken, that family is "closed" and remaining students must sign up for another small group with openings. The benefit of doing this is that students have the opportunity to select the people they want to be with when the group as a whole breaks up into smaller units. Students also have the chance to sign up for the chaperone they know or like the best. At any time, you can divide up your traveling students by saying, "Please get into your families." This can be useful in crowded venues, for roll check, and the assurance that all students will always be accompanied by an adult chaperone.

Walkie-talkies and cell phones can keep multiple buses together like a charm. Make sure to make a master list of cell phone numbers for each chaperone prior to departure. Acquire all necessary medical release forms.

Keep them in a three-hole binder, alphabetized by last name. Should you need to use one, time is of the essence.

Remember that adult chaperones can also have unexpected health issues and suffer injury while on a choir trip. Give chaperones the option of giving you their own personal health history or pertinent medical information for use during the trip, sealed in an envelope if they prefer. Provide your own health information in the notebook, should an emergency warrant. Print and distribute the trip itinerary to students, parents, and appropriate school and district personnel. Provide addresses and phone numbers of hotels for parents as well as your cell phone number in case of emergency.

As you plan the trip consult the festival regulations and schedule. Create a bookkeeping system for payments and for tracking individual fund-raising by student. Maintain a schedule of deadlines for entries, confirmation of reservations at each point in the trip, and payment to sub-contracted companies. Arrange sightseeing tours, either pre-packaged or constructed on your own, planning for all entry fees and costs to be built into the overall cost of the trip. At every juncture, arrange for group discounts and student prices, and arrange concert venues, if touring. See appendix 9f and 9g for sample trip itineraries and ancillary materials.

Parent information

Provide parents with a short informative letter at the beginning of the year that includes the destination and cost of the trip, as well as planned fund-raising events that will directly benefit trip costs. As time for payments and fund-raising is close, prepare a one page synopsis of the planned activities for the trip including what entrance fees, meals, and tours are included (and which are not), mode of transportation, and number of chaperones. Hold a chaperones meeting at which you distribute working copies of the itinerary, clearly marked as such, for review. Be clear about your rules and regulations and make sure all parents are fully prepared to stand behind them, supporting you fully. This is a good time to trade cell phone numbers and discuss any special needs students may have on a need-to-know basis. Some directors share a photocopy of the medical release form with students' chaperones to alert them to any specific concerns that might arise. Chaperones may review the itinerary at this time, having a chance to speak to any concern or omission in the plans that might require discussion.

Directly before leaving on trip, hold a mandatory parent informational meeting. At this time, give each parent a copy of the final, detailed itinerary that will include times, specific places, names, and phone numbers. As you cover rules and regulations with parents, maintain a serious affect and be specific about your intent to enforce consequences of any student misbehavior. While you want to be positive in the meeting, this is no subject about which to be lighthearted. Be clear that you must act in the best interest of the choir, not necessarily the individual student, in the event of behavioral or noncompliance situations.

Choir parties

Social events and parties can serve as a bonding tool for your choirs if they are planned in a way that interests the majority of your choir members. Gatherings following a competition or parties to celebrate the culmination of a difficult project or rehearsal week can be effective motivators as well as give students the opportunity to relax and enjoy each other's company. Keep costs to a minimum so there is no financial burden to parent hosts or student

Encourage creativity within wholesome boundaries.

members. Strive for high percentage attendance, scheduling social activities on dates and times that do not conflict with other school events. Use your choir officers to plan parties, provide class announcements, updates, and perhaps a bulletin board display about the upcoming event. Encourage creativity within wholesome boundaries. Arrange for chaperones for any choir-sponsored event. Parents who chaperone will benefit from getting to know one another (and you) better as well as seeing the positive interaction between students fostered by choir. Be careful that a great idea doesn't become a monster of a tradition that is difficult to "top" from year to year.

Choir banquets

The culminating celebration of a choir year is a final concert *and* the banquet. These are treasured events that can be as simple or as formal as you like, as inexpensive or as costly as you wish. Gathering parents, students, and invited guests together to celebrate a year well sung is not to be missed!

Remember that banquets should be a special event, a time for dressing up and taking photos. Decide if parents will be included in banquet invitations. Will all parents be allowed to attend and purchase a ticket? Do you want to restrict the group to parents of seniors, chaperones and volunteers? Consider adopting a "no dates" policy for choir banquet. Necessarily the program will be choir-specific and a "date" will not be included in the memories, jokes, and references. This is a special night for the choir "family" and is usually best enjoyed if choir members and parents are invited. If no one brings a date, singers will dance with other singers or as a group and the focus will be on the group, not two people focused more on each other. ("No dates" policy is a major benefit for all the guys in your men's choir, some of whom have probably never danced with a girl before. Live it up, guys! There are always more girl choirs on campus than men's choirs.)

Arrange for the nicest venue your budget will afford. Consider having a theme for the banquet that will run through the program, table decorations, and colors. Announce awards during the banquet, asking all-district, all-region, and all-state singers to stand to be recognized. Invite officers to stand to be recognized and honor all booster club officers. Have all medal-winning soloists and ensemble members stand to be recognized, and announce any choir awards you may wish to give, voted on by students or selected by the director(s).

Consider having each grade vote for one or two singers as "most outstanding." Freshmen vote for the one or two most outstanding freshmen in choir, sophomores vote for the sophomores, etc. Seniors may vote for all grade levels. This is an outstanding way to recognize the rank-and-file members of your organizations who have contributed so much to the success of the choir year. Remind students that "most outstanding" should be their own definition of what is "outstanding" in choir. It may not be the prettiest voice, but the hardest worker. It might be a hard-working officer or a natural leader whose positive help has shaped the choir for the better. This voting system tends to promote fairness versus a popularity contest. Announce each grade, beginning with the most outstanding freshmen, and ask each individual (in alphabetical order) to come to the podium to receive their award. How many awards will you give for each grade? Use your own discretion. In all likelihood, this number will vary from year to year according to how strong your choir members were during that academic year. (See appendix 9h for a sample banquet award certificate.) Announce choir scholarship recipients. Honor your choir seniors in special ways, perhaps first choice of seating, memory books in the lobby for choir members to sign for each senior, etc. Announce choir officers for the following year.

Remember to include voice teachers and feeder school directors in your invitation list. Special guests such as administrators and colleagues are not charged for their tickets. You should either distribute this handful of tickets across the anticipated ticket sales for your group or fund these dinner tickets through another source. Bring all trophies and awards received during the school year to display. Consider hiring a DJ or band to play for a dance following the dinner and program. Choose a menu that will please the majority of your attendees and make provisions for those who may be vegetarian or vegan. The order of the evening may run somewhat like this:

1. Welcome

2. Dinner

3. The year-in-review (most entertainingly done by two or three students who write the script, detailing the activities and awards through the choir year, sprinkled with humor)

4. Humorous awards

5. Awards through the choir year (all-region, solo and ensemble, etc.)

6. Choir scholarship recipient

7. Most Outstanding Choir member awards

8. Director's remarks (if any) a song, humorous or tender remarks, or advice.

   See appendix 9i for sample director remarks.

9. Senior recognition (Call the name of each senior, having them come forward individually to receive a flower or small gift and a handshake or hug.)

10. Announcement of next year's officers

11. Multi-media show including pictures from all choirs and events, not just advanced or traveling choirs. You are encouraged to make this a power point presentation for tightest organization, synchronized with appropriate music. A great ending to the multi-media show is pictures of the seniors! Acquire a baby picture of each senior, immediately followed by a senior portrait or other favorite "serious" photo from this final year in high school. The crowd will love these, as they first see each baby picture and try to figure out which baby grew up to be which senior. This will pull at parents' heartstrings as they see their sons and daughters, one after the other, shown as they once were and now as adults. You might consider ending with a baby photo and current picture of yourself and your staff.

12. Closing song sung in one large circle around the room

13. The dance! Meet with the DJ in advance of the banquet to state your expectations regarding appropriate lyrics and music content for the evening. Remind the DJ that this dance will be for young people and their parents. Let your officers work on a play list to present to the DJ well in advance of the banquet date. Make sure they understand the need to self-censor their recommendations.

Allow choir members to submit titles of songs and groups they would like to have represented on the play list. From all submissions, ask officers to meet and come up with a play list they believe students will enjoy. Include a variety of student selections. Insure that all lyrics are school-appropriate. Students continue to revel in old standards thrown in such as "The Hokey Pokey" and "YMCA," no matter their generation. Those who don't know one or more of these will enjoy learning them. Throw in a swing number and watch as a couple of parents and student dancers in the crowd jump up and go to town!

> *Most of the time I don't have much fun.*
> *The rest of the time I don't have any fun at all.*
> —Woody Allen

10 All the Rest That's Fit to Print

➤ Topics Sometimes
Overlooked in MusEd101

➤ The Great Miscellany of It All

➤ Topics Sometimes Overlooked in MusEd101

The Didn't-Get-Mentionables...

There are hundreds of situations and topics that will come up during the course of a teaching career that will prompt you to wonder why no one ever told you "this" or "that." Let us offer some tips in a few of those areas.

Choir folders

Some directors will have the funding to permit singers to use individual folders and music. If your program is large or growing, and you have such funding, we offer some suggestions regarding folders. If not, adapt the following to best serve your needs.

Organize folder cabinets with numbered slots and assign numbered folders. If singers will be sharing folders, consider how you want to configure the sharing, pairing stronger singers with weaker singers, experienced members with newer members, adept and slower sight-readers, friends working together, and any number of other pairings. If more than one folder cabinet is needed, consider placement in several locations to facilitate traffic flow.

Consider using a separate folder color for each choir to facilitate identification and organization. Use black for your top group performing with

Singers and directors should view the folder as a textbook.

music for extended works or as individual singers in honor choirs. If possible, have the name of the school and choir embossed on the front of each folder as well as the folder number. Allow students to use one adhesive nametag (that you provide) to personalize their folder with name, section, etc. on the inside of the folder. The folders' outside cover should be unaltered, keeping a uniform folder appearance for potential use in concerts.

Singers and directors should view a folder as a textbook, with individual accountability for folders at all times. Folders must not be lost or left in undesignated places. Have periodic folder checks, assessing grades for items inside folders including marked music, sight-reading book, and any other materials you require. Avoid students' placing materials other than music (sight-reading exercises you compose, theory materials, etc.) in the pockets of the folder, as they stretch out the sized pockets. If you routinely have these types of materials and don't want them to just sit inside the folder (but not in the pockets), you may want to consider a larger, instrumental-type folder. However, this type of folder may not fit standard choir folder cabinets, so check your dimensions carefully prior to ordering.

Transportation issues and costs

Learn and adhere to school and district policy regarding approved modes of transportation to and from school and choir activities. Know if there are any restrictions regarding the use of district and chartered busses, and determine whether student or parent cars are allowed to transport singers to various venues. If so, what liability falls on the student or parent drivers and the choral director?

When permitted and appropriate, solicit parent transportation to maximize fund use. Be aware of driver and director legal liabilities in doing so. Never put yourself in the position of having to defend your transportation decisions by compromising student safety, cost, availability, schedule, or comfort. Legally, it is wise not to carry more passengers on a bus than the stated maximum occupancy, in cars, allow only as many passengers as there are seat belts.

Investigate and discuss transportation costs and budgeting prior to booking any bus or van, and know who, or what fund will pay for the transportation, and where and to whom the bill should be sent. Know if an invoice must be provided in advance of the transportation (district-use) or a purchase order secured for charter company use. Plan for any additional costs involved such as a gasoline surcharge, or hotel room provided for each driver on an overnight trip.

Accompanists

There is a huge difference between a proficient pianist and a gifted accompanist. Seek a fine accompanist, not necessarily the concerto contest winner. Always choose the finest accompanist available (and affordable) to you and your choir for the venue at hand. In choosing an accompanist, consider technical ability (can they physically "play the notes?"), experience as an accompanist (will they follow your direction easily or will you be left to follow their tempi and interpretation), availability for both rehearsal and performance dates, and dependability. Do they have the ability to perform under pressure? This is a real factor to consider with student accompanists and should be carefully weighed for contest or acute-stress concerts. Consider adaptability between piano and organ if the rehearsal pianist might double on the organ for a particular work or venue. Accompanists must be able to demonstrate professional and appropriate deportment around your students and parents. You are ultimately responsible for the behavior, dress, and language of anyone you bring in to accompany, teach lessons, clinic, or for any other purpose, so choose accordingly.

When possible, use student accompanists. This provides them an outstanding musical education while saving you money. However, in providing opportunities for student accompanists, be aware that a student may do best in rehearsals only, leaving the pressure of concerts and contests to a more seasoned performer. You don't want to be one to put a student in a situation beyond their readiness, which has the potential to impact future opportunities. As a professional, protect student performers, planning experiences that will be positive ones. It is perfectly acceptable to use one person as a rehearsal accompanist and another for concerts and contests. Protect the feelings of all persons concerned.

Be cautious before committing to use a parent, teacher, student, or friend as an accompanist until you can accurately assess their abilities and any potential complications that might surface in using them. Do not put yourself in an awkward situation with an accompanist that isn't comfortable with the demands of the music. On the other hand, you could be passing up a brilliant accompanist by assuming that a parent cannot play well. Do your homework!

Be respectful of your accompanist's time.

Provide ample time for accompanists to prepare the music. Never use the choir's time to rehearse the accompanist. If an accompanist's abilities are in question, arrange a private rehearsal with them prior to rehearsal with the choir. This will prevent an uncomfortable situation in front of the choir if the accompanist is unable to play a particular work at an acceptable level of performance. If you find that a particular person is not up to the task at hand, you face a sensitive decision, whether to continue to use them or to pay them in full, replacing them with another accompanist. It may be necessary for you to cut your losses and change accompanists at some point. However, no friendship or professional relationship should be broken over a three-minute piece. To honor a person's feelings, you may want to grin and bear it (and make other choices for future concerts). To avoid finding yourself in this situation, do your homework! Consider the source when accepting recommendations.

Establish a good working relationship with your accompanist. This eases potential rehearsal tensions and facilities an easy flow between you as you work. Be respectful of your accompanist's time. If you play for your own rehearsals and your accompanist is "ready for prime time," use them only as needed. (This will also save you money.) Be aware of the going rate for accompanists and pay accordingly. Please do not be cheap. Conversely, there is no need to overpay. Treat people fairly and professionally. Be prepared to present an envelope with payment enclosed at the conclusion of the concert or festival, after services are rendered. Provide any instrumentalists and your accompanist with all pertinent details, dates, times, concert attire, payment amount, and any other special requests or information that would be helpful.

Piano tuning

Learn what monies are available for tuning, maintenance, and repair of school pianos. This funding might come from your local building, a district line-item code, or from your fund-raising money. Some tuners do better work than others! Seek one who is good, flexible, affordable, and accessible. Schedule piano tunings for the academic year in advance. Get on your tuner's schedule with appropriate dates preceding significant concerts or after vacations when the absence of appropriate climate control may have wreaked more havoc with the tuning than usual. Pay tuners promptly and inquire about discounts for multiple pianos tuned at the same site. Most tuners will help you save money in this way.

Pianos can lose their tuning at varying rates according to the quality of the instrument, how long it has been between tunings, any moving of the instrument, and the environment in which the piano is used. Discuss tuner availability and costs for a "touch up" tuning, if needed. This is substantially less costly than a full tuning and may be free if close enough to the initial tuning. Whenever possible, do not move pianos. Each time they are moved even a few feet the tuning is compromised. If a piano must be moved, do so slowly, avoiding bumps. This will minimize the damage to the tuning.

Consider regular piano tuning as preventative maintenance, not a frill. If neglected, pianos can become nearly impossible to keep in tune, losing their value and usefulness. Effective piano tuning requires absolutely silence. There should be nothing scheduled in the choir room or its surrounding areas during a tuning. Avoid scheduling tunings during band rehearsals across the hall, as this will affect the tuner's ability to do good work. Allocate forty-five to sixty minutes per spinet or studio piano, more for grand pianos.

Community service

Along with public relations, find ways to involve your choir in school and community efforts such as food drives, choir angels (see Traditions, chapter nine) trash pick-up day, volunteer work with senior citizen groups, and performances for special needs audiences. These audiences might include retirement centers, children's hospitals, Ronald McDonald House, or any local charity. Contact groups that may have less access to free entertainment and programming and offer to serve. Consider making your choir available for funerals of students, employees, or administrators; this is a unique gift you can give which will comfort and support an individual family on behalf of a school or district and will be deeply appreciated and remembered.

You may inherit a program for which service is a foreign concept. This provides a great opportunity to introduce students to a world of new concepts, performances, events and priorities. As the tradition of service grows, it will flourish. It can begin as simply as scheduling a short program at a local nursing home. It can begin as easily as a canned food drive at a concert, asking audience members to each bring one can of food to benefit a local food pantry. (Strive to schedule this at a time of year other than November and December when food pantries receive the greatest number of donations. They have greater needs at almost all other times of the year.)

Remember that community service involvement will necessitate some unique lesson plans, particularly in preparing students to provide choral music performances for special needs audiences and events. The value of learning about appropriate dress, and things to say and do are of lasting benefit to choir members and do not appear in any syllabus in your building.

Special needs students

In a sense, every student has "special" needs that deserve your attention since each is a unique person and a complex sum of his or her parts, mental, physical, emotional, and spiritual. Our job as educators is to understand what special needs students are all about and then creatively work to include them in our choral programs.

Young people with physical, mental, or emotional differences deserve the same opportunity to sing and develop musical talent and interests as anyone else. The fact that a student needs adaptations to your classroom routine is simple enough to accommodate, especially when you see how appreciative these students are for the benefits of your extra effort. To address this topic adequately would take many books. We will not pretend to include, or know all the answers, but we can suggest some of the best questions to ask.

Learn. Ask questions. Work as a team with specialized professionals in your building and district to modify instruction and classroom routine or materials for the students involved. Welcome special students into your program without reservation. Be willing to be taught. Let students and parents know how glad you are for everyone singing in your choir, and that you are there to help. Your school special education department will identify special needs students to you as well as suggest individual modifications in your courses as appropriate for that student. The school nurse will be your resource for health conditions and diseases that you should know about. Your compassion and resolve to "go to the extra mile" will grow as your knowledge and understanding increase.

Some special needs students would benefit from being paired with a veteran choir "buddy." Use extreme sensitivity and discretion in teaming up students so that both students are willing and able to work together. Don't assume that a student who appears different needs any special assistance at all. Often, students will show no signs of needing some sort of special modification. It is a blessing to see students as singers, period, and not think differently about a student who carries a "label." Still, it is important for you to know your students and their special needs so you can be at your best for them. Challenge yourself to embrace diversity in all its forms and don't let the word "different" carry a negative connotation. "Different" is just that: different. "Different" may be as uncomplicated as providing a vegetarian or vegan meal option at banquets and restaurants. It may include awareness of planned student absences from school (and choir rehearsals) for religious observations that are not aligned with major school district holidays.

Over the years, you will have the opportunity to work with many types of personalities, temperaments, and voices. You will also encounter any number of differently "abled" students whose challenges you will learn. The list that follows is not intended to overwhelm you. You may have a handful of special education or special needs students each year, so there is time to do homework on various acronyms and disabilities. This list is designed to introduce you to some of the terms you may encounter so they will not be completely new to you.

Asperger's Syndrome, "At risk," Attention Deficit Disorder (ADD), Attention Deficit & Hyperactivity Disorder (ADHD), Autism, Behavioral Disorders, Cerebral Palsy, Chemical Dependency/Addiction, Down syndrome, Dyslexia, Eating Disorders, Emotionally Disturbed (ED), Epilepsy, Fragile X Syndrome, Hearing Impairments, Hyperlexia, Learning Disabilities, Limited English Proficiency (LEP) and/or English As a Second Language (ESL), Mental Retardation, Multiple Disabilities, Orthopedic

Impairment, Phenylketonuria, Speech or language impairment, Section 504, Spina Bifida, Tourette's Syndrome, Turner's Syndrome, Visual Impairment (or blindness), and William's Syndrome.

You will also likely teach students who routinely take medications and observe special health regimens for a variety of reasons. These health issues will present some items for your to-do list prior to performances and field trips to insure that each student can participate. You will want to learn what considerations should be given to modify the usual routine to make students dealing with these health challenges feel safe, understood, and confident. These health issues might include Asthma, Depression, Diabetes, Heart Conditions, Hemophilia, Leukemia, and Sickle Cell Anemia.

Small obstacles can cause limited participation or comfort for students in wheelchairs. Try seeing the world from their perspective. Doorways can be oddly angled in halls, making turns difficult if not impossible. Hold doors open widely. Do not place furniture close to the entrance to your room to provide maximum accessibility. "Handicapped" bathrooms do not necessarily mean facilities for wheelchairs. They may meet legal requirements by offering a wider stall but lack grab bars and other modifications on which a wheelchair-bound individual count. Personal needs may require a parent or nurse to assist a student. Communicate with parents before field trips, tours, or trips to festivals to determine what arrangements are best for their son or daughter. It is possible to charter buses that have wheelchair lifts, though they have fewer total seats. Some students and parents may prefer to follow a choir bus in their own vehicle. Communicate and plan!

A curb or a step or two is a huge hurdle. "Scope out the territory" on behalf of students, to be certain that all singers can negotiate hotels and venues. When possible, do this in person or ask for help in verifying all information relating to special considerations. A last choice would be for a team of strong singers to lift a wheelchair-bound student while seated in his or her chair. This can be dangerous for the student's health and mobility equipment and is discouraged. It is better to plan ahead. Preserve the dignity and privacy of students at all times. Using a chair may carry a perceived stigma of exclusion because being included means some extra effort for others. It is understandable that people in wheelchairs fear barriers. Be proactive in championing the inclusion of singers in wheelchairs.

Special consideration and planning are also warranted for students with a history of fainting as well as those who have recently suffered injuries or serious illnesses. Students who need the assistance of braces, crutches, or walkers can be provided appropriate riser positions to meet their physical needs. Plan to put singers with extra need for stable footing on the floor level of the stage whenever possible. Students who would prefer to sit can easily be accommodated by the placement of a chair in front of the section of risers representing their voice part.

Braille sight-reading books, choral works, and music textbooks can be provided on behalf of a blind student at your request. This is a lengthy, costly process and should be reserved for materials that will have lasting use. Your district specialist should have the contact information you will need to learn more about this. In most states, this service is provided free of charge. Bear in mind that reading music in Braille is completely different than reading words or books in Braille. It requires extensive training and practice on the part of a visually impaired student, so ask first before securing specialized materials. For more information, you can also contact your state health department.

English as a second language (ESL), and limited English proficiency (LEP) students are a wonderful group of singers to include in your choirs! Students who are newer to English benefit significantly from participation in choir, repeatedly chanting or singing texts and reinforcing pronunciation skills. The same diction help the general choir requires will doubly benefit the student who seeks to learn a new language. Do not stress over your inability to speak all languages represented in your choirs. If you have a working knowledge of other languages, use them occasionally to help your non-English speakers.

Let your counselors know that ESL and LEP students are welcome in your choirs if they are interested in singing. Pair these students with a helpful partner, perhaps even one who speaks the same language. Multilingual choir members will instinctively assist those who need help understanding verbal instructions and information. Know that there are free web sites dedicated to translating written passages into various world languages, such as www.freetranslation.com. Additionally, many school districts have specialists who can assist you in translating your handbook and basic information for use by students and their parents.

Legal issues

Teacher, conductor, artist, musician, counselor, preacher, mentor... and you need to be a lawyer, too? Sadly, our choir halls are not immune from the sting of legal entanglement. Good people with good intentions do get into legal problems occasionally. The best we can do is to be aware, informed, and obvious about our actions and intent. We can also be INSURED.

Your state's music educators association may offer professional liability insurance. It should cover legal advice and, if necessary, counsel if you get into a school-related legal dispute. BUY IT! If you cannot buy coverage through your MEA, you may need to turn to a local teachers union for insurance. This is more expensive because you will first need to become a member of the union and then buy the supplemental insurance policy. If you're on a limited budget, and what teacher isn't, cut corners somewhere else. Always pay the extra money and carry full coverage against potential litigation. Remember that while you may be innocent of any charges brought against you, it will be expensive to retain legal assistance and that bill will far exceed a teacher's income. Read your policy carefully and know what it covers. Check details like coverage on field trips and choir trips, coverage on your personal vehicle if used to carry students on school or district business, and coverage for coaching sessions or other uses of your home.

Work diligently to earn the trust of your administration, faculty, students, and parents. Once earned, maintain that trust. It takes years to build a reputation and a moment's careless misjudgment to destroy. Remember that perceptions are reality. Don't put yourself in the position to having to defend

---

It takes years to build a reputation and a moment's careless misjudgment to destroy.

---

or explain your personal life. It would be less than truthful to say that as long as you're not doing anything illegal, your job will not be affected by your life outside the workplace. You have chosen a profession that requires extreme discretion in lifestyle choices and general deportment. Whether it is fair or not to be held to a higher standard becomes a moot point, accept it and keep your private life exactly that. Those who reside in the same community in which they teach will be more carefully scrutinized. Use common sense. Some areas tend to get legally murky more easily than others, including the use of chartered busses, allegations of misconduct, and classroom issues.

When using chartered buses know the minimum dollar amount your district requires for insurance. Find out if the company you use out sources for buses and drivers during busy seasons, and what safeguards the charter company uses to hire drivers. The company should be able to provide information about personal and professional driving records, drug testing, history of alcohol abuse, and criminal history check. They should have address and reference verifications and information about emotional stability and suitability around young people. Know your personal liability, if any, if there is a mechanical defect, driver error, inappropriate behavior, injury, or death resulting from a student riding on one of your buses.

In the event of allegations of misconduct, a teacher's word versus the accusation of a student is a serious situation. Our best defense is an effective offense. We must conduct ourselves in such a way that our actions and intent are clearly seen as wholesome, appropriate, and professional. Our lives must be transparent so that no question arises regarding anything we may have said or done. Err on the side of caution. The reality of working in a litigious society forces us to maintain an invisible wall of protection around our vocabulary, comments to students, appearances of familiarity or inappropriate behavior, etc. in all that we say and do. Even if we have worked in a community for decades, it only takes one poor choice or bad judgment, however innocuous it may have actually been, for us to land in a world of trouble that saps our time, money, and resolve.

Be circumspect about vocabulary, eliminating any obscene, discrimina-tory, or racist references in your teaching, jokes, informal conversation, and e-mails. Establish and maintain appropriate professional distance between yourself and your students in regard to physical contact and personal rela-tionships outside class. Perceptions of younger teachers are particularly important in this area as the ages of teacher and student are similar or may even overlap. Remember that the relationship is a professional one, teacher to student, and not subject to an alternate age-appropriateness argument. If you're a hugger, continue to hug but be aware that while this approach to teaching can be warm and caring, it also carries extra risks. If you hug one child, make sure you hug many so your attentions are not exclusive to one student or group. Lawyers will tell you not to lay a finger on anyone at any time. This is your best legal advice, to be sure. However, a gentle hand on a shoulder or a pat on the back can carry healing and beneficial contact. Be careful, and if in doubt, don't. Carefully consider whether you will use your residence as a gathering place for students, venue for parties, or to coach singers for upcoming contests on Saturdays. If you use your personal vehicle, you are personally liable in the event of injury or death to a student riding with you.

Keep your use of alcohol, if any, a private matter. Never, ever serve liquor to any student for any reason, even as a prank or when offered a giant stein of beer on choir tour in Bavaria. Eliminate t-shirts and other items carrying logos or advertisements for any brand or type of alcohol from your wardrobe. Be judicious regarding prescription drug use if side effects might be visible to students, i.e. the perception of being "under the influence."

Illegal drugs: just say no. Note that it is illegal to give students an aspirin or other over the counter medication in many districts. Learn the policy and heed it.

You are liable for all events and behavior in your class. Leaving your class unattended, even briefly, is an invitation to disaster. Always lock your classroom door when you leave the room. Whatever happens inside your room is your responsibility, whether you're in there or not. Key points here are potential theft of equipment and inappropriate activities by students who might wander into your room and find safe haven for their fancies. You are responsible for the whereabouts and use of your keys.

Budgets

In most cases, choir budgets will fall into several categories. It is the responsibility of the choral director to maintain each budget and know the policies, procedures, and guidelines for each. Accounts available to you may include activity funds, capital outlay, Booster club fund and local building and school district funds.

The activity or "choir" fund is usually earned through choir sponsored fund-raising activities, honorariums from concerts, and donations. You will note that this is legally school money; if you have earmarked student fund-raising accounts on an individual basis, students are not allowed to access "their" money. Generally, the choir activity fund is lumped in with all other activity funds from the school into one large account: band, football, student council, debate, drama, etc. Be aware that your principal has the legal right to use this money to benefit the school as needed. A good principal will rarely spend money from an organization's activity account but you should be aware that he or she has that right. On the other hand, there may come a time when you could use a few extra dollars in an emergency and your principal may have "extra" in one of the sub-accounts that can be loaned or given to your organization.

The use of the school activity fund necessitates the choral director's adherence to all school and district policies through the school's business manager. Plan ahead if a school or district check must be cut. This fund usually carries over from year to year. It is wise to keep a certain amount in your fund over the summer to provide for departmental financial needs until the next year's fund-raising projects generate new income. Be aware that there may also be a maximum amount of dollars that may be held over from one year to another since schools (and their organizations) hold non-profit status with the IRS.

Capital outlay is also known as "major purchase" or "special equipment money" and is designed to pay for those expensive items needed on a one-time basis. The local building or the district fine arts office most often governs these funds. Investigate the procedures and deadlines for applying for capital equipment with purchases such as risers, folder equipment, sound shells, etc. It is likely that you will have to make application for funding for any proposed purchase. Know the deadlines as well as all details about your proposed purchase: model number, brand, current price, vendor(s), and the like. Applications for this funding may be highly competitive so be prepared to turn requests in early, documenting the need for what you request. Be fair. Someone else may need what he or she is requesting more than you need what you are requesting. Hopefully, funding availability will provide for everybody's needs but be prepared to take turns receiving a nod for these dollars. If a request for capital outlay equipment can be shared or used by multiple groups within a school, the likelihood of approval is increased. If the band, orchestra, and choir all sign off on a request for a new sound shell, there is a greater chance that money will be allocated, as more students will benefit from the dollars spent. Differentiate between wants and needs and portray each accurately and honestly.

Never be the cosigner on any booster club bank account!

The booster club fund may be your most easily accessed fund but is also the one that requires the most personal accountability. Just as a quick phone call to the booster club treasurer may get you a near-immediate check for an emergency expenditure for the choir, an equally speedy receipt and ample documentation should be provided (with a copy saved in your file) and retained. More directors have lost jobs over misuse of booster club funds than any other account, probably because initial documentation is the least formal and strenuous. Be vigilant in documenting all expenditures from your booster club account and provide for regular self-audits. Never be the co-signer on any booster club bank account! A two-signature check is your best protection against misuse of funds by an enthusiastic parent who feels that a gross of velvet paintings of "Singing Dogs Playing Poker" would make the perfect banquet gift for choir volunteers. Do not ask to use booster club funds for your own benefit or purposes which would have been unapproved by other funding sources.

Though the school has no control over how booster club monies are spent, they certainly have jurisdiction over the accountability and validity of the fund itself. Booster club monies should be spent to benefit the choir department as a whole, perhaps including items not covered by other sources, such as scholarships, choir trips, choir social activities, and accompanists. The booster club should have guidelines in place to address the purpose for the booster club's funds and an internal structure of checks and balances to insure that there is no question about how these dollars have been spent. In a worst-case scenario, a booster club can be disbanded and a director fired or jailed for wrongful use of these funds.

Local building and school district funds are commonly referred to as "budget" money. There may be one source for this money or a certain amount in the local school account while other sums are assigned on a district level through your fine arts office. Generally, the building principal divides a large amount of money among various organizations for their use. Your fine arts director may also be doing the same. This money is "announced" after the entire school district budget is determined and approved by vote of the school board, often after a particular academic year has already begun. Because of this timing, it is wise to spend spring funds for beginning of school needs to assure availability of funds and the timely receipt of materials needed. Purposes for these allocated monies may include your choirs' music, folders, office supplies, contest entry fees, transportation, piano tunings, etc. Be aware that there will be a spring cutoff date, sometimes as early as mid-March, by which all such funds must be spent. After this deadline, funds are lost to your use, so spend what you need accordingly.

There are tricks of the trade to provide ways to purchase a certain amount of music over the summer while charging it against your fall budget. This is often termed "hold for P.O." (purchase order). Obviously, you must be prudent to spend only that which is necessary to start up school, as your budget, if any, is yet to be determined and you're charging against an unknown, unauthorized account until approved by the board. You do not want to be left responsible for paying these not yet funded summer bills, so learn from others in your district about working billing dates, budgetary approval and cutoff dates, and music vendor options in your particular location. Note that some districts have a list of "preferred" vendors and do not authorize billing to vendors not on the approved list. You could be personally responsible for this category of purchasing as well. Know the policies and procedures in your district.

Regardless of which budget(s) you use or to which you have access, keep accurate records and documentation. Spend wisely, as if these funds were coming from your own personal bank account. Be a good steward of public funds. Just because you have money in an account doesn't mean you have to spend it. On the other hand, Confucius say, "Wise man spend annual budget so it not be cut in the next year."

Nothing's hard, if you know how.
—John R. Volk

➤ The Great Miscellany of It All

A veritable cornucopia of wisdom…

On professional growth….

- You cannot teach what you do not know. Be a lifelong student of choral music, the arts, and life. Travel. Study. Attend workshops and take classes. Read. Listen to both live concerts and recordings. Live in a constant state of personal and professional growth!

- Be willing to learn a new style with which you may previously have been uncomfortable. You'll learn by doing and may find that you're mighty good at something new. Even if you're not the best, your singers will benefit from your efforts.

- Be open to trying new things. Every year, try a song in a different language. Today's publishers offer a rich variety of culturally diverse music. Delve right in. Try a piece from a historical period that has been less comfortable for you in the past. When you are willing to grow and take risks, you open the door to rewards and rejuvenation of mind and spirit. Don't be old and stodgy when you're twenty-five… or thirty-five… live life, each and every day. Stay alive!

The good guys always wear white hats….

- Respect must be earned. It is not issued along with your faculty ID.

- Make all choirs your priority, not just the "top" group. Don't slight the entry level and intermediate students when sharing the best of your planning, teaching, and focus.

- Give your school counselors an exemplary printout that clearly shows which student should be placed in which choir. (Appendix 10a)

- It is essential to consider the feelings and sensitivities of all racial, ethnic, religious, and other groups. The history of the world is marked with many words, verbal slurs, and topics that are neither wholesome nor appropriate. With so much good music from which to choose, there is no reason to pursue literature that will be hurtful. This goes beyond the scope of your choir and singers' families and into the community and country at large. We must be committed to respect for the world's diversity. Ignorance of the history of words and their context cannot be an excuse for treading on the pride of others.

- Never underestimate the impact of your personal energy on your choirs in regard to motivation and achievement.
- When in doubt, smile.
- Praise your choir and its individual members. Practice "random acts of communication" in which you call or write parents of students to note how hard they are trying, how much they accomplished in a particular choir activity, etc. Leave a thank you note on the message center several times a week for various students who are giving you their best effort, or who have done something to help the group or each other. Take note of those things and say something nice. "Positives" grow on each other so start the snowball rolling. See appendix 10b for a sample "note of appreciation" to use with students.

Staying Out Of Trouble....

- If your school keys are lost, you may be liable for the expense of re-keying your room and any doors for which you had a key on the missing ring. This is an arts educator's worst nightmare due to the number of keys and locations to which we are given access. The worst-case scenario is losing an "inside master" or "outside master," in which case you may be responsible for re-keying the entire school.
- Do not accept keys from unauthorized sources. Know what your keys open when they are issued to you. If you are given a master key, be professional in using it for necessary and approved uses only. Letting yourself into a neighbor's room to borrow a book you neglected to ask for during traditional school hours is not an approved use.
- NEVER give a student your school keys. You may end up doing this at some point, (many of us have) but if you do, get the keys back immediately after a specific use. Keep master keys on a separate ring that never leaves your possession. NEVER hand a student a master key unless death and destruction are imminent and maybe think twice, even then.
- Word your PA announcements succinctly but cleverly for optimum ear-appeal.
- If you receive an emergency phone call your choir president or other student director should be prepared to act in your stead. As you leave the phone to join the rehearsal, step in and continue the student leader's work seamlessly. This develops student leadership, respect between choir members, uses time effectively, manages class behavior if you're tied up for a while, and gives you ease that life will

go on if you have to visit the powder room in a real fix one day. (Caution: a class left unattended is an invitation to disaster.)

- Develop leadership in choir officers from the inside out. Leadership can be developed and fine-tuned by example and with training. See appendix 10c for qualities of leadership definitions.
- Learn the history of Title IX and why most school registrars list women's choir as "Treble Choir" and men's group as "Tenor-Bass Choir" on scheduling paperwork and in course descriptions. These terms generate many questions when a student wants to know what "Treble III" means when she was chosen to sing in the "Normandy Hills Women's Chorale." If legal labeling keeps course names in compliance with the intent of the law, answer the question and move on.
- Insure that movie ratings are appropriate for your students' age level before showing any videos outside school, as with chartered buses on long trips. Have a parent or two on each bus approve any video brought by students for viewing.
- Keep parents in the information loop. Publish a regular newsletter and post it on your choir website for insurance that it gets home. See appendix 10d for a sample newsletter.

Keeping the choir on its toes...

- To limit the noise level when students want to show support for one another in class, adopt the tradition of offering a single clap by the group, known as an "applaw."
- Bribery works.
- Make contests out of routine sight-reading drills or tests. Reward the section with the highest average.
- Offer incentives for singing a passage or section of a piece.
- Reward the choir for good attendance.
- If the basses beat the tenors on a written test, offer to sing any sight-reading line in the book.
- Suggest that if the choir's GPA for the next grading period is above a ninety percent you'll treat for ice cream.
- Rewards can be leaving first for lunch, ending class by telling a few good jokes, or other no cost perk.
- Vary how you say, "be quiet" so singer's ears don't tune you out, such as: please be quiet, hush, *subito!* (immediately in Italian), *silencio!* (silence in Spanish), *salmate!* (calm yourself down in Spanish), talk as

loud as you wish as long as we can't hear it, does your mother know you're talking, con sordino! (with mute in Italian), two ears, one mouth: talk less, listen more, tacet, and could we all please listen at the same time?

• Sometime, just for fun, save ten minutes at the end of class and ask the choir to be seated in place. To be excused from the risers, individual students will have to raise their hands and, when selected, tell the choir one clean joke. Only a certain number of students will be accommodated in these ten minutes, but the whole group will have a good laugh and choir spirit will soar.

• Shortcuts to standing and sitting instructions: position one: standing on the risers in proper singing position, position two: seated, in proper singing position, position three: slouch! "Position one, please," works so much better than, "Choir, let's get on the blahblahblah…"

Another way to teach it…

• Suspensions: Car one is driving down the street in its lane, minding its own business when car two begins to pull into car one's lane, headed for impact as it continues directly at car one. Car one sees the impending crash and moves away from car two. They are now facing in the same direction, parallel to each other, as car two continues toward car one but car one turns to the lane away from car two's lane. Car two realizes what has happened and straightens out its tires, taking its new lane. Car one is relieved and also straightens out its tires. The two cars continue to drive down the road safely, each in its own lane. This can be charted out on the board, using singer's names in lieu of car numbers. Add some narrative drama and the explanation will become all the more memorable. Once everyone has had a good laugh it is easy to explain preparation, suspension, and resolution, by comparing it to the two cars. The preparation and resolution are generally consonant. The suspension itself is dissonant. This is easily compared to the peaceful drive in one's own lane as opposed to the calamity of seeing a car pulling into yours.

• Music history: Share the historical highlights in the world during the time each composer and poet created a work. There are some wonderful side-by-side chronologies in flowchart and column designs that show what was happening in literature, architecture, music, the visual arts, and world events throughout history. Help your singers see how it all fits together as they relate their musical education to their other classes.

- Ask students to evaluate their own work in choir. You may use these reflections in the grading process if you choose, but either way students will become more aware of what they are doing by considering their own effort, attention, and behavior during rehearsals. See appendix 10e for a sample student self-assessment form

- Ask students to imagine that they have noses all around their waists, asking them to breathe through these noses in order to feel diaphragmatic breathing.

- When the choir only needs a little bit of the soprano I high note in a chord, suggest the following: "A chord is like an ice cream sundae. How would it be if your sundae had a tablespoon of ice cream, a tablespoon of topping, and fifty-two cherries on top? Most of the weight and good stuff is in the main part of the sundae. The cherry on top has to be light to sit on top of the whipped cream and is really more for decoration than flavor." This nearly always works and you can pick your high, light sopranos without offending others with darker voices. Someone will always argue that they like sundaes with fifty-two cherries on top. Accept it and go on.

- Ask lower voices to crescendo the most and upper voices to crescendo the least.

- "Keep your corners in," is another way to tell students not to spread their vowels. Ask students to touch the sides of their mouths to feel their lips wanting to spread horizontally in a smile. "Smile with your eyes, not your mouth when you sing."

- Type "vibrating vocal cords" into your favorite search engine and find public domain visual representations of vocal cords in motion while speaking and singing. Actually seeing what is happening to their vocal cords when students cough, sing, clear their throats, or speak is worth a thousand words! This can help boys understand their changing voices, and warn students about vocal abuse and damage by seeing vocal cords with nodes attempt to work.

Musical Tidbits...

- When students have trouble understanding the phrasing of a passage, ask them to speak the text aloud. Ask different singers to speak the text dramatically, even a bit exaggerated, to get the right inflection.

- Are your students fully conversant in major and minor? Use warm-ups based on ancient Greek modes. Sing on solfege, using hand signs, and try these exercises. Play C chord. Students hum tonic as you play the chord, opening into the word "Ionian." They then sing up and down the scale, getting back to the tonic, when they sing the word "Ionian" again. Play d minor chord. Students hum "d" as their new tonic and open into the word "Dorian," singing up and down the scale until they get back to "d" and repeat the word "Dorian" sung on that pitch. Continue through the seventh pitch of the scale, going up and down Locrian, and then call it a day and go on to something else. They will remember the names, hear new intervallic patterns, and you will provide variety to your rehearsal. This can also be done a cappella if you want to challenge the choir to tune ascending and descending scales with precision.

- Students may want to underline stressed syllables or circle important words that need motion and energy in their vocal part.

- Dealing with slouchers? Ask students to stand with pride or like champions. Ask students to put an extra inch of "tallness" between their waist and rib cage.

- Do your students have trouble holding dotted notes for their full length? Try having them pulse the sub-beats (eighth notes within the dotted quarter note, quarter notes within a dotted half note, etc.) creating a surge of sound on each. This helps account for all parts of the note, the original value and the value the dot adds.

- "Dots always want to grow." Dotted notes need to build through the note's value, going past the dotted part of the note's length unto it peaks in excitement at the next structurally important pitch. Another way of saying this is that "dots must spin."

- Sometimes sustained pitches want to sag. "Keep them alive" or use the word "percolating" to describe the continued "life" of the note.

- Fight the singers' misconception that "softer" also means "slower." Likewise, a crescendo is not automatically accompanied by an implied accelerando.

- Compare an inappropriately abrupt crescendo or decrescendo to the sound of planes landing, a non-preferred sound to say the least. Have the choir crescendo (or decrescendo) steadily while you count to a particular number and back down again. Start with a count of seven, beginning at pianissimo and crescendo to fortissimo, then decrescendo back down to a pianissimo again to another count of seven. Students will get very good at this and you can expand their control by increasing the number to which you count. Skillful singers will learn to steadily measure out their voices to a count of fifteen, which will serve most songs they will encounter. Use this same technique to teach a niente to the choir by counting until there is silence.

- If students need more variety in intervallic sight-reading but are singing harmonically at that point in the year, have them switch parts. This drills new intervals in all voice parts, each of which has typical skips for that vocal line which occur regularly but may not occur often in other sections.

- Vowels promote the beauty and melodious parts of choral music. Consonants bring rhythmic crispness and energy.

- Teach your students correct terminology and symbols so they can mark their music accurately and uniformly.

- Compare projection and breath focus to shooting an arrow at a far away target.

- Are you working with reluctant singers unable to grasp diaphragmatic breathing? Have the choir lay on their backs around the room to feel the involuntary "correct" singing breathing. (Caution: if you hear snoring, you've let this go on too long.) Have students place their hands at and just below their waistlines and have them try to blow out birthday cake candles located on the room's ceiling by puffing them out with great force. This gives students a chance to feel their own musculature work in the breath process. When students stand again, have them work to replicate the same feeling. Note: Students who just don't "get it" about shoulders raising and lowering when they breathe can "get it" lying down. As they involuntarily breathe diaphragmatically, ask them to place their hands on their own shoulders to feel if they are going up and down. Most class members will see how silly this notion is and laugh. If you want to revisit this concept, ask students to get into "singing positions."

- "Breathe in the cool air, feeling it come into your body. Breathe out your warm air as you sing."

- At some point in the year, have students sing without vibrato.

- Turn out the lights in the room and ask students to sing a piece of music without visual distractions. They will stay together without a conductor, using their ears to work together. Doing this brings goose bump moments to most choirs. The conductor isn't seen, there are no distractions, and the music alone becomes the focus of all senses. Experiment with this.

• If you are having trouble trying to make a point about a particular vocal line, ask another section sing the first section's part the way you are asking it to be performed. Most of the time, they can do it immediately and successfully and the original group of singers is shamed into improvement. At worst, a good laugh is had by all.

• Arrange your choir in a giant circle, or sectional circles. Have them walk to the tempo and style of the music while singing, to energize it. Challenge them to keep the motion in their singing even when standing in place.

More teaching tips...

• Are you unsure if parts are secure? Walk away from the piano. Without keyboard help, you'll be forced to hear things as they are.

• Do not fear walking around the room as you teach, approaching different sections at various times whether you're addressing them specifically or not. This brings vitality and variety to your rehearsal.

• When approaching a higher pitch by skip, think "higher than the pitch" and come down to it. Don't reach up for it.

• Utilize free websites as a way of directing students to additional help, skill reinforcement, and learning games. You might try the following websites: www.ossmann.com/bigears, www.philtuga.com, www.melodymemorygame.com, and www.artsalive.ca.

• After teaching polyphony and preparing a complex Renaissance work, take the choir to a cathedral whose echoes will mirror those of old European cathedrals. Hearing why the pitches had to line up in certain ways to work with (instead of against) the architecture of the day will drive home the lesson more than all the historical orations you might offer in explanation.

• Center the vibrato in the middle of the pitch, not on either side of it.

• For an ethereal sound in your soprano section, try adding a couple of tenors who may or may not have a strong upper range but who can "pop" into their high falsetto. The androgynous, plaintive timbre can be haunting on a passage like John Rutter's "Open Thou Mine Eyes." The tie-ins to teaching about the British cathedral tone, and the history of boys singing soprano as an outgrowth of church practice is enriching to the curriculum and brings the music alive.

- There is an exactly right split second that is correct for every attack and each release. Any other split second is wrong. How can you test the rhythmic precision of attacks and cutoffs in a song of slower tempo? Set a metronome at the tempo of the song you are working on. Ask singers to clap at the beginning of each new pitch. (Tap the fingers of one hand sharply against the palm of the other for a short, crisp sound.) Students should mouth the words but not sing. Ask students to listen to hear if they are slightly ahead, or behind others with the same rhythms. Another technique is to ask students to sing each pitch on a crisp, percussive syllable (like a precision "too" or "pah") instead of text. Regardless of the written duration of a pitch, each new pitch will be sung as the shortest, most staccato note. The rest of its value will be a rest. See how students align with others on their part. Wrongly placed attacks will stick out like sore thumbs. These two techniques are also valuable for teaching counter rhythms in polyphonic music, illuminating rhythmic interest and variety, and energizing sustained pitches.

- No two notes are the same. Drama is either building or diminishing. The melody is either rising or falling. Tension is tightening or relaxing. If one applies this to performance, singing becomes extremely challenging and rewarding as one constantly has ask, "Does the next beat go toward or against? Does the next note complete an existing thought or begin a new phrase?"

A positive attitude may not solve all your problems,
but it will annoy enough people to make it worth the effort.
—Herm Albright

11 Vaulting Into the Big Leagues

➤ VIPS of the Profession

➤ "You Are Cordially Invited…"

➤ International Travel

➤ VIPs of the Profession

Welcome to the realm of the pedestal...

At some point in your career you may consider elevating the profile of your choir, and yourself as a choral director by venturing into loftier turf. This may mean becoming more involved in professional organizations and seeking elected office. You may dream of judging festivals or being a clinician. On behalf of your choir, you may choose to pursue music educators' convention performances, international concert tours, and festivals. These are all worthy goals that will encourage continued growth and development.

Leadership positions in professional organizations

Whether you aspire to help your profession locally or dream of seeing your photo on the cover of a professional magazine as a newly elected leader, there are countless ways to invest your time and expertise in the choral profession. For every person you see working at a convention or festival, there are at least ten others who have done many small things to contribute to the success of the whole.

Word spreads quickly when a director shows excellent organizational skills, dependability, professionalism

Word spreads quickly when a director shows excellent organizational skills, dependability, professionalism, and a strong work ethic. If you want to become more involved, the way to start is by volunteering to help. Do not assume that "everything is taken care of" or that "only those people do those jobs, they certainly wouldn't need anybody like me to help." The opposite is true. There is always a great deal to be done and most tasks can be effectively undertaken by anyone in the profession who is willing to work hard. Make these responses your mantra: "Sure! Why not? I'd be glad to help. I'd love to. May I help? You look like you could use a hand with that...Let me help you carry...Be happy to help! Absolutely! When do you need me? Is there anything else I can do?"

Some specific ways to become more involved

- Volunteer to work at convention registration. There is always a need for more volunteers and there is no better place to meet new colleagues and improve your professional visibility.

- Serve on committees to set up and strike risers and other equipment.
- Work with convention "ways and means" committees, or "hospitality."
- Volunteer to host or organize solo and ensemble contests, festivals, All-City and All-Region choirs and other large events.
- Volunteer to serve as a mentor to new teachers in the profession.
- Remember that there is no job too small for you to do, whether you're a rank and file member of an organization or its president. Always be ready to lend a helping hand where needed.

As you prove yourself in smaller tasks and limited positions, you may be considered for higher-level jobs and nomination for elected office. Leadership openings in MEA and CDA organizations offer proven leaders and organizers a place to invest time and energy over several years. As your career builds in scope and complexity you may find yourself with fewer hours of spare time to call your own. However, remember that it is the busiest people who accomplish the majority of great things. By working smart and being organized, you can be like the circus performer who spins one plate at the top of a long pole, adding additional plates while keeping all spinning concurrently. Ask for help and learn to delegate duties. Remember that "somebody" has to do these jobs, and it is both an honor and professional obligation to so do.

Becoming an adjudicator

After several years of successful teaching, you may be asked to serve as a judge for a choir festival or other event. This is a position of tremendous responsibility, not to be taken lightly, just as you would want judges at the festivals you attend to take their positions seriously. In order to be an effective judge you must be fair and impartial, know the age group you will be judging and the standards of performance and/ sight-reading expected of this level of singers. Be diplomatic in both spoken and written word. Do not write or say anything that will cause hurt feelings or personal offense. There are many ways to convey a message; your job is to find the clearest way to document what you heard, both strengths and weaknesses alike, in a positive manner. Provide comments that will help both the director and choir grow from this festival experience. Focus on choral basics and polish, writing remarks that will both praise a choir's achievements and challenge it to even higher goals.

Maintain a consistent standard throughout the festival. Your grading scale should not be "curved" because of the name of a well-known director. On the other hand, don't be a "giant killer," by being a know-it-all with unrealistic expectations that are impossible to meet, even by the most successful choirs and directors. Assign ratings with care. Make sure that your written comments match the overall rating earned by a choir. If all comments written are complimentary and only one or two minor flaws are mentioned, you will not have sustained "the burden of proof" if you assigned a lower rating to a group. Be compassionate yet realize that a festival isn't a game show giveaway. A multi-judge panel adjudicates most festivals. The composite rating will reflect several points of view and listener expectations.

Be so professional, equitable, and diplomatic that
you make no personal enemies or lose friendships as
a result of serving as an adjudicator.

Seek to affiliate with state or local associations so your name can be included on lists of recommended judges. Be so professional, equitable, and diplomatic that you make no personal enemies or lose friendships as a result of serving as an adjudicator. Focus on fairness and a fixed standard of excellence so the act of judging is never personal.

Serving as a clinician

Colleagues will begin considering you as a potential clinician when you have established a proven level of work and are respected in your field. You must be able to produce excellent results with your own choir before others will be confident that you can do so with theirs. When you are invited to clinic a choir dress professionally but comfortably. You want to look and feel as good at noon as you did at the beginning of the day and this is hard work! Know your time frame precisely, including how many songs you will work on and how long you will have with the choir. Know the proximity of the festival or concert in relation to the date of your clinic so you can realistically tackle those aspects of the performance that can be effectively remedied or polished in the time remaining. Do not frustrate the choir by focusing on areas that cannot be changed or for which there is insufficient time to make meaningful improvement.

Remember that you are working with someone else's students. You will not have a personal relationship established over a period of time with the singers. As a result, you will not necessarily share the same musical vocabulary or reference points to which you might point with your own choir. "Inside jokes" and sarcasm may fall flat with strangers when you are accustomed to your own students' familiarity with your sense of humor and style.

Strive to quickly establish a positive rapport with the choir. Maintain an effective pace while expecting a strong sense of self-discipline and work ethic on the risers. (You can always lighten up, much like the first week of school, but it is difficult to "rein in" a stampeding mob.) Your job is to analyze strengths and weaknesses and make a meaningful contribution to the choir's performance in your work, not to win a popularity contest. Be genuine. Students can spot a fake a mile away. Always be yourself and work in the style with which you are most comfortable.

Serving as a guest conductor

An invitation to serve as a conductor of an All-City, All-District, All-Region, or All-State Choir is an opportunity to be savored. It carries with it the message that you have established your career and maintained outstanding achievement over a sustained number of years. All-Region invitations may come to you based on performances of your own choirs, both the quality of choral work and the energy and personality you brought to the performance. Guest conductors must be able to motivate, pace rehearsals in a compact sequence of hours, and create cohesive, musical performances with singers unaccustomed to working and performing together. People may learn your name from your own mentors and past choral directors with whom you have worked. Still others may have visited one of your rehearsals or obtained your name through word-of-mouth about what you are doing in your home school.

If you are honored with an invitation to serve as a guest conductor, stay humble. It's a wonderful thing to know how to do things; it's offensive to be a know-it-all. Check your schedule carefully to insure that the dates and times you would be serving are clear of conflict. Consider travel time and preparation of music in your planning. It is important to be prepared and dependable. Respond promptly to the person who contacted you. If the invitation is extended over the phone, say that you will call back within a day so you can clear your calendar for the dates and times involved. Remember to call back, whether accepting or declining.

Review the list of past conductors for the group with whom you will be working. Seek information on past preparation level of students, the number of students expected to sing with the group, and what the proposed schedule of rehearsals will be. Dress comfortably but professionally and arrive with a carefully constructed "game plan" of what you expect to accomplish in each section of rehearsal time. Allow sufficient time for rehearsing with any soloists, instrumentalists, and working on stage in preparation for the concert. Arrive early to all stated report times. Arrange all transportation so you will never run the risk of being late.

> *No matter how rich you become, how famous or powerful,*
> *when you die the size of your funeral will still pretty much*
> *depend on the weather.*
> —Michael Pritchard

➤ "You Are Cordially Invited..."

Performing at our profession's music conventions...gulp!

If you lack nerves of steel, this may not be for you. (If you do have nerves of steel, be assured that the nervous tick you may develop in singing for a music educators' convention will go away in time.) The bad news is that you will find yourself performing before most of the adjudicators for whom you have ever sung (and will sing in the future), all at the same concert. Trained specialists in your field, each instinctively critiquing every aspect of your choir's performance, will occupy the seats in the audience. Participation restrictions based on students' academic standing may cause you to lose key singers, travel expenses can be formidable additions to your budget, and the selection of literature will drive you close to madness. Given a clear vision of these realities, who in their right mind would choose to subject themselves and their students to such a rigorous pummeling of body and nerves? Why do it?

The good news is that when you press beyond nightmarish fears you will never find a more appreciative and respectful audience, understanding every nuance in what you do musically. Listeners will appreciate the dedication, work, planning, and resolve to present such a concert. If your concert is wonderful, you will be well received and your choral program (and personal reputation before your colleagues) will be enhanced.

First, you must carefully consider the timing of your application to perform. Recordings are usually submitted in the spring, to be considered for performance the following school year. Depending on the rules for the specific convention for which you would like to perform, your submission will likely be required to include selections from several previous years to show consistency of your work. It is imperative that you realistically consider the best time to submit a recording for consideration according to whom you will have in your choir during the performance year to come. It may be that you have had several exceptional years in a row and can compile a submission tape that is extraordinary. You do yourself (and your students) a profound disservice by believing that being selected is the core honor in this situation. In fact, it is successfully performing an exemplary concert the next year that should be your total focus when submitting your choir. Look carefully at your roster of returning students. How many are upperclassmen, bringing maturity of sound and musical understanding to a potential performance? How many students are graduating at the end of the submission year? Will this substantially change the learning curve and sound quality in the coming year? Are there any sections that appear "lean" for the following fall? Is the fate of your tenor section dependant on prayer, fasting, and worry beads?

The time to submit an application (from a musical standpoint) is when you are heading into a "dynasty year" of voices, experience, and work ethic that can withstand the rigors of high-level mastery of thirty minutes of choral performance. You will also need to have completed several years of high quality performances if your recorded submission is to be found at the top of the selection committee's list. Your choir must have the emotional maturity to sustain festival preparation focus for the better part of an entire school year. Instead of concentrating their efforts on three songs to perform, singers will be mastering six or seven songs for a standard length convention concert. Your time will necessarily be slanted toward the convention choir for large portions of the year, with additional rehearsals and clinics scheduled. Singers must be prepared to devote extra individual and group rehearsal time for the cause. Talent will only take the choir so far. Self-discipline and a strong work ethic is key to convention success.

You will want to make every effort to submit a recording when personal circumstances allow. This additional undertaking will require a great deal of your time and emotional energy. It is likely that you'll be away from home more than usual. It may not be the ideal time to adopt a new puppy or list your home "for sale by owner." If your wife is pregnant with twins or you are a caregiver for an aging or ailing family member, the timing may not be best for you, so factor reality into your decisions. Life does, at least occasionally, have other important facets besides our work.

The ovation that may result from a strong state MEA, regional or national ACDA performance is an experience that may be a high point of a singer's career in high school. However, that ovation has its price in the investment of extra time in what can be many months of grueling stress as you prepare the students for what is to come. If the performance goes well, your school's choral program will vault from little league success to major league ballpark status. From a student's perspective, is it worth the extra work and pressure? That is something only you can answer, knowing your students well and their readiness to undertake a project that will make or break the choir's reputation, and yours. Both authors of this book have performed multiple times for professional conventions and know the clear benefits for your school, its choral program, and for you as the director. We encourage you to consider submitting a recording when the timing is right.

Before you submit a recording for consideration, assess the level of support you will have from students, parents, local building administrators, and your fine arts office.

Prepare a "what-if" budget and know what funding resources you might have to pay for additional music, clinicians, transportation, and lodging for the choir.

Once you've decided to submit an application for the coming year make a quality recording of your choir. This will involve a compilation of several recordings made at recent festivals in several preceding years. Follow the rules carefully regarding inclusion of any identifying announcer or other speaking on the recording. Most committees select choirs anonymously, identifying and discussing each without knowing the name of directors or schools. Neatly complete all written applications and provide any signed documents from your principal as required.

Know what your choir does best.

Be honest. Do not bend the rules. To be invited to sing at convention without having the required continuity of strong years at your school is a recipe for disaster. It is better not to sing than to be invited and do poorly. Read the rules carefully about how many years must be reflected in your submission and abide by them. The rules are there to protect you and your choir's best interests! Insure that all selections included in your submission demonstrate a high caliber performance. The selection committee will listen to short portions of one or more songs from your recording. Always start the submission with one of your strongest pieces. Grab the selection committee's ears from the first note!

If you are chosen to perform celebrate with wild abandon, notify all appropriate personnel, and get a good night's sleep. (It may be your last good night of sleep for some time to come.) Spend the ensuing months working on programming. As always, effective literature selection represents a key component to your performance's success. Consult colleagues who have "been there/done that."

Seek literature that will hold up under months of meticulous preparation yet can be mastered by your choir. Consider looking for new and fresh literature rather than repeating the same songs other choirs have done recently for the same audience. Search your local university's music library for lesser-known works. Become best friends with your local music retailer and delve into their browsers. Ask friends for names of songs they would recommend.

Ask colleagues what selection they think would be perfect for your choir. The literature must fit your strengths and the strengths of your choir. This concert is not the best occasion for trying something widely different from what you've done successfully in the past. Consult colleagues who have "been there/done that."

Know what your choir does best. When possible, choose literature that will be interesting, challenging, and even likeable for your singers. Consider what your audience will want to hear. Remember how you have felt as an audience member at convention concerts. What styles or historical periods were overly represented in programming? What did you long to hear that wasn't performed? Consider commissioning an original choral work to be premiered in this concert, and weigh the possibilities of using a theme, including plenty of variety. Have we mentioned that you should consult colleagues who have "been there/done that?" Truly, you need to consult experienced colleagues. Don't be too proud to ask for advice and help.

As you plan the trip to convention observe all deadlines for submitting photos, accompanying copy, bios, and other written materials and present neat, organized materials in a timely fashion. Provide high quality printed programs for this special occasion. Organize all funding and fund-raising. When possible, plan to be free of money issues the month preceding your concert so your focus can be musical rather than financial.

The timing of your program must be exact to convention specifications. If you are given a twenty-five minute time slot, it is essential that your program (including getting on and off the risers and applause) does not exceed twenty-five minutes. Conventions are tightly scheduled and any short delay or extension of your allotted time will be the convention chair-person's worst nightmare. Know your hall and consider its acoustics, for better or worse, when selecting your program. Include a list of acknowledgments in your printed program. No choir dazzles a convention audience without a goodly list of feeder school directors, administrators, voice teachers, and clinicians that have all contributed to the day's success.

Select clinicians carefully and have several come to work with your choir at various stages of preparation. Clinicians' critiques and rehearsals with your choir provide a new set of ears and ideas. They also give you the opportunity to sit and really focus on listening to your choir. You will likely find yourself making copious notes on your music of things you hear that might be improved or changed simply because you're not conducting and can concentrate on full-time listening. Plan a pre-convention concert so parents and local supporters may hear the "finished product."

After the concert is over, celebrate with your students at a special dinner or fun event. Find a venue at which singers may release months of pent-up tension and enjoy the afterglow of a concert well-sung. Send thank you notes to the convention chair, equipment chair, and all individuals who helped your students obtain and enjoy this fine opportunity. Acknowledge your students for their hard work and dedication and enjoy the new spotlight that will shine more brightly on your choir and its work. Plan to submit again, when the timing is right. Keep things in perspective. Your professional life will change after a music educators' convention performance. However lauded you may be as the next great choral shining "star" of the western world, be a good winner. Humility wears well over the years. Continue to work hard and strive for excellence in all you do, creating new goals to replace ones fulfilled. Remember, you're only as good as your last concert. Resting on your laurels should be postponed until twenty years after retirement.

Nurture others and encourage them to submit recordings when appropriate. Be a supportive audience member for future convention concerts. Once you have performed at convention, you will take on an entirely new appreciation for the people who stand before choirs in those vast convention hall ballrooms and other venues. The courage to stand before such an auspicious audience is, in itself, worthy of applause.

Courage is resistance to fear,
master of fear – not the absence of fear.
—Mark Twain

➤ International Travel

*In any language, international travel
with your choir is an incredible thrill...*

There is no doubt that it is thrilling to share the world's great cities and centers of cultural history with your students. Performing in the finest concert halls and cathedrals is an opportunity impossible to exaggerate. You will want to memorize chapter nine, "Trips, Tours, and Festivals" in at least three languages and then start packing! Appendix 11 includes information pertaining to international travel. As you ponder the possibility of taking your choir abroad, there are some things to consider.

When planning for the trip students will need to secure passports and individual visas as necessary. It is important to note that your singers may hold citizenship in countries other than your own. Check! The country from which a passport is issued may require additional documentation. If your student body is diverse, your choir may be traveling on passports from four or five countries and each will have its own challenges. Be sure you know the citizenship of all singers planning to travel so you can learn about special requirements, additional time required for processing documents, and travel restrictions for these students.

Consider world events when choosing destinations. While lightning can strike in your own backyard, it is still wise to bear in mind any areas that are current "hot beds" of political or social unrest. Traveling is complex enough without factoring in recent upheavals in potential festival or concert sites.

Seek as much input into your itinerary as possible, depending on your own travel history and comfort level in planning. Include as many points of historic and cultural interest as possible without exhausting your students and include visits to musically significant cities and places throughout history. Plan for scenic routes when travel time permits. Plan for all costs. International travel can be done more or less affordably, depending on your expectations for hotels and various amenities. Strive to obtain the most competitive airfares available. Consider dealing directly with the group sales office of your preferred airline carrier for optimum leverage in pricing.

Prepare your students carefully, both musically and personally, for the countries they will visit. A fine director once devised a "five minute a day" lesson on topics including units of currency, common words and phrases (if traveling to a non-English speaking area), and type of government. There were as many topics as there were students in the choir. Each student researched a topic and was assigned a date to present a five-minute lesson at the beginning of rehearsal. Mini-lessons included specific historical sites, units of currency, general history of the region, composers who lived or worked in the area, popular cuisine, and unique customs.

Consider the number of seconds of echo in churches, cathedrals, and concert halls when programming. This is particular true when selecting contemporary literature. Refrain from singing songs in the language of the country to which you will be traveling unless you are prepared for audience laughter. Remember that foreign audiences appreciate a healthy dose of music from the visiting choir's home country. Include folk songs, spirituals, and other works by American composers. Plan a pre-trip send-off concert for parents and friends.

Once you have traveled, the voyage never ends,
but is played out over and over again in the quietest chambers,
that the mind can never break off from the journey.
—Pat Conroy

Epilogue

The choral director's job is neither simple nor financially lucrative. The hours are long and demanding, taxing body, mind, and spirit. So why do it? Moreover, why keep doing it? Why do we devote our lives to this profession?

We choose to teach choral music because it is a deeply meaningful and important profession, one in which we may invest our lives in the lives of young people through song. We choose to teach and create transcendent beauty through music in a world that already exceeds its quota of ordinary and ugly. We choose to be choral directors because music is a healing force in our world, a bridge that connects people, and a language of beauty that transforms lives. We choose to do something important and lasting with our time. What could possibly be more wonderful? (Okay, maybe being a choral director and winning the lottery…)

Lucky are we, the music makers, who help shape young lives through the art of song. Too many people live in a world of conveyor belts and computer monitors, separated into tiny cubicles. We, on the other hand, have the opportunity to greet each day as new and unique. We work in a world with symphonic overtones and live in Technicolor, rather than merely existing in black and white. Unlike some of your friends, you will never have a boring day. Never! We enjoy countless smiles, laughs, and hugs on a daily basis. It just doesn't get any better than that!

We offer you a few last rules for the road:

Maintain a healthy balance in your life:
work, play, faith, family, and friends.

Always be yourself.

Never underestimate the value of a sense of humor.

Whatever the situation, always but always wear comfortable shoes!

Pursue the "road less traveled" as poet Robert Frost described. The journey is unsurpassed, the rewards are more than worth the ride, and, in the end, remember that some of the best scenery will be along the road; even along the smallest paths and most of the detours, and not reserved solely for your final destination.

Hail, friends of music!
In her praise we gather to do her honor in fellowship together.
Music's fair muse each human heart rejoices.
We join our voices here in praise of song.
—Wm. P. Bentz

CD Appendix

The following documents can be found on the CD that accompanies *Beyond Singing*. All appendix documents may be photocopied and used for educational purposes.

Chapter 1

    1a Sample choir calendar, Tutty High School

    1b Sample choir calendar, South Bay High School

    1c Choir handbook, South Bay High School

    1d Choir handbook, Bryce Canyon High School

    1e Choir handbook, Mary Messer High School

Chapter 2

    2a Formal lesson plan

    2b Informal lesson plan

    2c Standing chart

    2d Riser graphic

    2e Discipline management "groaner" jokes

    2f Lesson plan for substitute teacher

    2g Worksheet, *My Fair Lady*

    2h Worksheet, *Oklahoma*

    2i Worksheet, *The Sound of Music*

    2j Worksheet, Amadeus

    2k Worksheet, concert evaluation

    2l Worksheet, student choir evaluation

Chapter 3

    3a School testing calendar

    3b Program insert

    3c Winter concert program, South Bay High School

    3d Winter concert program, E.M. Brown High School

    3e Joint fall concert program, Irish High School and Pennington Academy

    3f Joint fall concert program, Cape Coast High School and Manaus Preparatory

Chapter 10

Chapter 11

About the Authors

Stan McGill began his professional choral teaching career in 1975 as the choral director in Camdenton, MO. He moved to Texas in 1979 and at the printing of this book is beginning his 33rd year of choral teaching. Mr. McGill has had extensive leadership service with ACDA, having served as site chair for four SWACDA conventions and as the SWACDA division President in 2002-2004. He is serving as program chair for the 50th Anniversary National ACDA Convention in 2009. His articles have appeared in the Common Times, Choral Journal, Southwestern Musician and Texas Sings. He is a published arranger with Shawnee Press and is a co-author of "90 Days to Sightreading Success", a sight-reading methods book with AMC Publications and "18 Lessons to Sightreading Success" published by Hal Leonard Corporation. Mr. McGill is a Past Vocal Chair and Past President of the Texas Music Educators Association. He is active as an adjudicator, speaker, director and clinician throughout the United States and has directed All-State choirs in Oklahoma, Arkansas, New Mexico, South Carolina and Connecticut.

South Garland High School (Texas) choirs under Mr. McGill's direction performed for nine TMEA and ACDA Conventions in the 23-year tenure he served as the head director. They twice toured Germany and Austria, performed in Carnegie Hall in 1993 and 1998, toured Hawaii, and have numerous outstanding choir honors in festivals nationwide and internationally, including Bournemouth, England's 1999 Music Makers Festival. His South Garland A Cappella Choir performed with The King Singers and the Kiev Boys Choir, and participated in nationally televised performances with Garth Brooks, Randy Travis, and Jessica Simpson. Mr. McGill became the head choral director at Highland Park High School in Dallas, Texas in 2005.

Born on Long Island, **Elizabeth Volk** grew up as a performer in school band, orchestra, and choir in New York, New Jersey, and Texas. She attended Southern Methodist University and graduated in three years with a Bachelor of Music (piano) at the age of twenty. While at SMU, she studied under Jane Marshall and Dr. Lloyd Pfautsch, returning to SMU for her Master of Music Education while continuing to teach full-time. She directed the choirs at Edward H. Cary Junior High School for seven years, during which time the award-winning choral program grew to include more than a third of the student body of 680 students. Ms. Volk taught at Thomas Jefferson High School for twelve years, where her choirs were highly acclaimed and consistently singled out in competition. Under her direction, the TJHS Concert Choir performed with The Kings Singers and toured Germany and Austria, also being named a winner at the 18th International Youth and Music Festival in Vienna. The Concert Choir performed for TMEA as well as the national convention of Urban School Superintendents, the National Association of Secondary School Principals, and a Presidential Prayer Breakfast for President and Mrs. Ronald Reagan. The T.J. show choir received the Outstanding Performer award at the Texas State solo and ensemble contest..

During her eleven-year tenure at Newman Smith High School, Ms. Volk's choirs continued to be consistent top award winners at contests and festivals throughout the nation. Under her direction, the Newman Smith Vocal Ensemble performed at TMEA and her A Cappella Choir sang in concert with the Kings Singers.

A published writer and composer, Ms. Volk is a member of TMEA, TCDA, TMAA, and ACDA, serving in numerous offices at city and regional levels as well as on the Board of Directors of TCDA. She was selected to membership in Pi Kappa Lambda, Alpha Lambda Delta, and Mu Phi Epsilon and awarded the PTA Lifetime Membership award and multiple Teacher of the Year honors. Ms. Volk is active as an adjudicator, speaker, honor choir conductor and clinician, choral composer and arranger, vocal coach, and accompanist.